90% attendance across term

DYNAMIC class lectures connect content to *real world* applications

A critical consumer of **INFORMATION**
Ready to Tackle the World

create an *intimate* class environment in the **LARGEST** course on campus

4.54 out of 5

highly trained TAs facilitate **PBL** tutorials with *campus-leading* evaluations

40,000+

GRADUATES since 2007

MAC IntroPsych
Personalized Learning Through Discovery

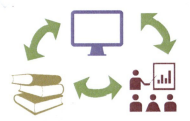
Blended Learning
provides students with the *best* of online & face-to-face learning

225

OFFICE HOURS (in class or online) per term give you *personal* attention when you **NEED IT**

4.65 out of 5
highly rated web modules provide students with **INTERACTIVE**

on demand access to course materials

TERM 2

MAC IntroPsych

Psychology 1XX3/1NN3/1FF3
Official Course Handbook 2022

Official Course Handbook 2022

Your one-stop course companion website.
Includes:

- Important links
- Academic advice
- Departmental information
- And more!

NOTICE:
These learning materials are to be used as a guide to assist you with understanding the module material – they are not a replacement to viewing the online modules, attending your tutorials and lectures, or taking your own notes. Your grade will be determined by your full participation in all aspects of this course.

If you find any errors or omissions within this document, please feel free to email us (intropsych@mcmaster.ca) and we will be sure to have the issue rectified for the next release of this handbook.

You may not reproduce or distribute any portion of this document

This handbook was made possible by the tireless efforts of our handbook team, consisting of:
Dr. Joe Kim: Course Instructor
Dr. Michelle Cadieux: Course Coordinator & Instructor
Veesta Mavandadi: Special Contributor
Arianna Davids and Zachary Chiodi: Head TAs
The Science Media Team

© Department of Psychology, Neuroscience & Behaviour
1280 Main Street West • Psychology Building
Hamilton, Ontario L8S 4K1
Phone 905.525.9140 x 24428
Email: intropsych@mcmaster.ca
Web: http://www.macintropsych.com

Contents

- Official Course Handbook 2022 3
- Quick Start Guide 6
  - Before your First Class 6
  - During the Semester 6
  - How to Use this Handbook 6
- Psychology 1XX3/1NN3 Course Outline – Winter 2022 9
  - Course Description 9
  - Class Activities 9
  - Materials & Fees 9
  - Virtual Course Delivery 10
- Course Overview and Assessment 10
  - Evaluation 11
    - Tutorial Participation (10%) 11
    - Avenue Quizzes (30%) 11
    - Lecture iclicker Bonus Points 12
    - Avenue QuizTerm (7%) 13
    - Final Exam (53%) 13
    - Multiple-Choice Questions – PeerWise 14
    - Research Participation Option – Sona 15
- Web Modules 17
- Additional Resources and Regulations 18
- Study Guide for Psychology 1XX3/1NN3/1FF3 20
  - How to Use Google Scholar 21
  - Taking Notes 21
  - Writing Tests 21
  - Multiple Choice Questions and Flashcards 22
- Campus Resources 26
- Academic Advising in PNB 27
- A Note from Dr. Joe Kim 28
- Development 1 & 2 30
  - Development 1 – Outline 31
  - Development 1 – Courseware Exercise 34
  - Development 1 – Review Questions 35
  - Development 2 – Outline 36
  - Development 2 – Courseware Exercises 42
  - Development 2 – Review Questions 43
  - Development 1 & 2 – Test Question 44
  - Development 1 & 2 – Bottleneck Concepts 45
- Evolution 1 & 2 60
  - Evolution 1 – Outline 61
  - Evolution 1 – Courseware Exercise 65
  - Evolution 1 – Review Questions 66
  - Evolution 2 – Outline 67
  - Evolution 2 – Courseware Exercise 73
  - Evolution 2 – Review Questions 74
  - Evolution 1 & 2 – Test Question 75
  - Evolution 1 & 2 – Bottleneck Concepts 76
- Neuroscience 1 86
  - Neuroscience 1 – Outline 87
  - Neuroscience 1 – Courseware Exercise 94
  - Neuroscience 1 – Review Questions 95
  - Neuroscience 1 – Test Question 96
  - Neuroscience 1 – Bottleneck Concepts 97
- Neuroscience 2 106
  - Neuroscience 2 – Outline 107

- Neuroscience 2 – Courseware Exercise 114
- Neuroscience 2 – Review Questions 115
- Neuroscience 2 – Test Question 116
- Neuroscience 2 – Bottleneck Concepts 117

Vision 1 & 2 130
- Vision 1 – Outline 131
- Vision 2 – Outline 135
- Vision 1 & 2 – Courseware Exercise 140
- Vision 1 & 2 – Review Questions 141
- Vision 1 & 2 – Test Question 142
- Vision 1 & 2 – Bottleneck Concepts 143

Colour Perception 156
- Colour Perception – Outline 157
- Colour Perception – Courseware Exercise 164
- Colour Perception – Review Questions 165
- Colour Perception – Test Question 166
- Colour Perception – Bottleneck Concepts 168

Form Perception 1 & 2 176
- Form Perception 1 – Outline 177
- Form Perception 1 – Courseware Exercise 183
- Form Perception 1 – Review Questions 184
- Form Perception 2 – Outline 186
- Form Perception 2 – Courseware Exercise 194
- Form Perception 2 – Review Questions 195
- Form Perception 1 & 2 – Test Question 196
- Form Perception 1 & 2 – Bottleneck Concepts 197

Audition 208
- Audition – Outline 209
- Audition – Courseware Exercise 217
- Audition – Review Questions 218
- Audition – Test Question 219
- Audition – Bottleneck Concepts 220

Hunger and the Chemical Senses 232
- Hunger and the Chemical Senses – Outline 233
- Hunger and the Chemical Senses – Courseware Exercise 240
- Hunger and the Chemical Senses – Review Questions 241
- Hunger and the Chemical Senses – Test Question 242
- Hunger and the Chemical Senses – Bottleneck Concepts 243

Psychological Disorders 1 & 2 250
- Psychological Disorders 1 – Outline 251
- Psychological Disorders 1 – Courseware Exercise 257
- Psychological Disorders 1 – Review Questions 258
- Psychological Disorders 2 – Outline 260
- Psychological Disorders 2 – Courseware Exercise 265
- Psychological Disorders 2 – Review Questions 266
- Psychological Disorders 1 & 2 – Test Question 268
- Psychological Disorders 1 & 2 – Bottleneck Concepts 269

Psychological Treatments 276
- Psychological Treatments – Outline 277
- Psychological Treatments – Courseware Exercise 283
- Psychological Treatments – Review Questions 284
- Psychological Treatments – Test Question 285
- Psychological Treatments – Bottleneck Concepts 286

ANSWER KEY 294
Glossary of Terms 301
Conclusion to Psychology: 1XX3 – Foundations of Psychology, Neuroscience & Behaviour 322

Quick Start Guide

Are you in Psych 1FF3? An updated syllabus is available on Avenue.

Before your First Class

1. Read the **ENTIRE** course outline.
2. Write the important dates in your calendar.
3. Make a checklist of the course features and check out each one!

During the Semester

1. Watch the weekly web modules **BEFORE** your lecture and tutorial. Take <u>effective</u> notes using the outline and slides provided in this handbook as a guide.
2. Use a separate notebook for additional notes and write down any questions you have or concepts that were not clear. Bring these questions to your tutorial to get help from your TA.
3. For weekly web modules, look up unfamiliar words in the glossary and review them to build a solid foundation. As with most university courses, the psychology knowledge base you are expected to understand is cumulative and small gaps in understanding can become large gaps over time.
4. Complete the assigned readings (textbook/journal articles) to gain context, background, and additional examples to consolidate your knowledge.
5. Join or start a study group with tutorial members or other peers on Avenue.
6. Complete the weekly activities and questions in this handbook. These can be a great starting point for your study group.
7. After completing each week's Pre-Quiz and Quiz, be sure to review the feedback on your results to see where you went wrong and right. Feedback for the Pre-Quizzes is available immediately, and feedback for the Quizzes is released on Tuesday mornings.

How to Use this Handbook

What Is Your Handbook?

Your handbook is the official courseware compiled by the Introductory Psychology instructional team and is designed to facilitate your academic experience in Psych 1XX3/1NN3/1FF3. This handbook is continually revised to ensure that students have effective study aids and up-to-date information for the course. Your handbook is not a textbook. It does not contain mandatory readings that are required for you to pass the course. However, it does have a wealth of resources to help you reach your academic goals in Psych 1XX3/1NN3/1FF3.

How To Use Your Handbook Effectively with the Rest of the Course Components

1. Read the week's intro and preview the key slides.

2. Watch the web module before reading the textbook, using the key slides as a guide to taking notes.

3. Carefully answer the checkpoint questions in the web module (note: these are basic level questions to make sure you are paying attention). If you get these wrong, you should review the preceding unit.

4. Complete activities, questions, and exercises in the handbook to apply and test your knowledge. Don't forget to make use of the flashcards!

5. Check out the challenging question (with a full explanation) from a previous Avenue Quiz in the handbook, which tests understanding rather than ability to memorize. Often, first-year students fall into the pattern of studying to gain a superficial factual knowledge, rather than a complex understanding, of the concept. If evaluations then simply asked you to regurgitate everything you had memorized, you would do fine. However, if you study like this, you're studying for the wrong type of test! The challenging questions demonstrate how you will be tested in this course. A hallmark of superior understanding is the ability to transfer knowledge to new contexts (Marsh). In these questions, you can't simply regurgitate terms you memorized. You really need to understand and apply your knowledge/what you've learned. The best way to do this is to test yourself. Force yourself to explain concepts in your own words, and better yet, try teaching them to a peer and drawing on personal examples to make your point. When you're ready, take the Pre-Quiz for the week. The questions on it are of a similar style and difficulty as the actual Quiz on Friday. It doesn't count, but it will give you a good idea of the level of challenge you should expect from the Quiz. It's graded immediately, and provides detailed explanatory feedback on your chosen option. Many students do not take advantage of the Pre-Quiz. Don't be one of these students!

6. Read the textbook to give you additional context and details to fill in the framework provided by the web modules. Complete the practice exercises at the end of each section in the handbook to consolidate your knowledge.

Handbook Sections

Taking Notes: The inclusion of important graphics is meant to facilitate your learning so that you do not have to recopy all of the information from the web modules. In addition, ample space has been provided beside each key slide for you to take notes in your own words. Furthermore, the skeleton notes are ordered sequentially, providing some additional structure to your note-taking. Copying down the script from the web modules word for word is not an effective way of studying. Instead, watch the web modules once, reflect on the material you've just viewed, and then go back to re-watch the modules while taking notes on the concepts you're struggling with.

Activities and Practice Questions: Completing the activities and practice questions at the end of each topic and checking your answers against the answer key at the end of the handbook is an effective way to learn and assess your understanding of important concepts. We encourage you to review the answers in the back of the handbook after finishing the questions to see if you're on the right track. Even if you have selected the correct answer, make sure to read through the explanations provided to ensure that your logic is accurate and to have trickier concepts explained again using different words.

Bottleneck Concepts: This section compares and contrasts concepts and terminology that students often get confused. One of the pairs is given a full explanation. You should practice by completing the others yourself!

Concept Maps: The concept maps are designed to help students see the "big picture". You can use concept maps as a quick pre-quiz review or to check if you have accurately understood all of the connections between the different elements in the module. As you begin studying for your final exam, you may also wish to use your concept maps to check if you have forgotten a key concept in the course.

Sample Quiz Question Explained: Make sure you answer the question yourself and write this answer down before reading the explanation provided. This way you can accurately assess whether or not you know the material before doing your pre-quiz or Avenue quiz. Additionally, if you've selected an incorrect answer, you may be able to identify why you did not choose the correct answer and how to avoid making the same mistake on future quizzes using the feedback provided. By critically evaluating your approach and performance on multiple-choice questions, you will find it easier to reach your desired level of performance on our quizzes and in the course. This may also be very helpful for your tests in other courses.

Glossary: Use the glossary as a quick reference for the key terms without having to re-watch modules to obtain definitions. The glossary clearly defines the key terms and even provides you with new examples. You can test your knowledge of these terms by covering the definitions, writing down your answers to a specific term, and then checking to see if you are correct. Conversely, you could cover the terms, read the definition, and see if you can accurately match the definition with its corresponding term.

Flash Cards: All glossary terms have also been made into cue cards that you can cut out to help you learn all of the important vocabulary. Remember to fill in the blank example section for each card. Coming up with your own example is the best way to learn new terms.

Psychology 1XX3/1NN3 Course Outline – Winter 2022

Course Staff	Location	Office Hours
Dr. Joe Kim Primary Instructor	PC/106 or Online	Posted weekly on Avenue
Dr. Michelle Cadieux Course Coordinator & Instructor	PC/110 or Online	Posted weekly on Avenue
Arianna Davids & Zachary Chiodi Head TAs		
TA Lobby hours	PC Lobby or Online	Tuesday - Thursday 11:00am - 1:00pm

All correspondence regarding this course should be sent to: *intropsych@mcmaster.ca* using your McMaster email and **NOT** your Avenue account. If you have additional questions regarding course material you have several options:

- Join the active discussions on Avenue. If you have questions about course content, the discussion boards are the best place to post it!
- Drop in on the TA office hours posted on Avenue.
- Ask Dr. Cadieux or Dr. Kim during Office hours. Hours and Bookings link posted on Avenue.

You may also call the MacIntroPsych office at ext. 24428. Please note that **phone messages will not be returned.** If you have a request, please book time during office hours or send an email to intropsych@mcmaster.ca. Note that during busy periods, it may take up to 48 hours to return your email. Please be patient!

Course Description

In this course, we will focus on the biological mechanisms informing Psychology, Neuroscience and Behaviour. In the first half of the course, our research framework will examine several levels of analysis (Development, Evolution, and Neuroscience). In the second half of the course, we will apply these analyses to Sensory Systems and Critical Behaviours.

In combination with Psych 1X03/1N03/1F03, students will emerge with the appropriate context, terminology, and skills to specifically support exploration of further courses in Psychology, Neuroscience and Behaviour. However, these are skills that will also transfer well to any discipline you pursue!

Class Activities

Each week you will be assigned a content unit. Each unit will have 1 or 2 web modules and an assigned reading. You will also be responsible for completing an Avenue quiz associate with each topic. This course has synchronous lecture and tutorial components.

Materials & Fees

1. **Custom E-text:** Discover Psychology: MacIntroPsych Essential Readings for 1XX3/1NN3/1FF3 - 2022. Purchase through the bookstore. Join code: 323463
2. **Custom Courseware:** MacIntroPsych Official Course Handbook 2022 1XX3/1NN3/1FF3. Purchase through the bookstore.
3. **iclicker:** Subscription to iclicker Reef polling. We use iclickers in lectures for bonus points.

Virtual Course Delivery

The course is planned for all components to be delivered in person. However, given the changing covid restrictions this may need to be modified and some components of the course may be delivered virtually. To follow and participate in virtual classes it is expected that you have reliable access to the following:
- A computer that meets performance requirements: found here https://uts.mcmaster.ca/technology-resources-for-mcmaster-students/#lab-content-device-recommendations
- An internet connection that is fast enough to stream video.
- Computer accessories that enable class participation, such as a microphone, speakers and webcam when needed.

If you think that you will not be able to meet these requirements, please contact uts@mcmaster.ca as soon as you can. If you use assistive technology or believe that our platforms might be a barrier to participating, please contact Student Accessibility Services (sas.mcmaster.ca - sas@mcmaster.ca) for support.

Course Overview and Assessment

The general schedule for this course content is given below. Any changes to this structure will be announced on Avenue. It is your responsibility to keep up to date with any schedule changes.

Week of	Web Module	Chapter Reading	Notes
Jan 10	Development 1 & 2	1	Quiz 1
Jan 17	Evolution 1 & 2	2	Quiz 2
Jan 24	Neuroscience 1	3	Quiz 3
Jan 31	Neuroscience 2	4	Quiz 4
Feb 7	Vision 1 & 2	5	Quiz 5
Feb 14	Review Week		QuizTerm
Feb. 21	**READING WEEK**		**NO CLASSES**
Feb 28	Colour Perception	6	Quiz 6
Mar 7	Form Perception 1 & 2	7	Quiz 7
Mar 14	Audition	8	Quiz 8
Mar 21	Hunger and the Chemical Senses	Journal Article	Quiz 9
Mar 28	Psychological Disorders 1 & 2	9	Quiz 10
April 4	Psychological Treatments	10	Quiz 11
April 11			No lecture or tutorial

Avenue Quizzes open each week on Friday at 6am and close promptly on Saturday at 6am.

Evaluation

Your final grade in Psychology 1XX3 will be determined by the following measures:

Tutorial Participation	10%
Avenue Quizzes	30%
QuizTerm	7%
Final Examination	53%
PeerWise Multiple Choice Questions (optional)	3% reweight of final exam
Sona Research participation (optional)	5% - 8% reweight of final exam

Tutorial Participation (10%)

Weekly tutorials are an important part of the course and contribute to 10% of your final grade. Your TA will expect **active** participation to create a dynamic learning environment. If you have specific issues with this process, you must speak to the course coordinator as soon as possible.

Your TA will assign you a grade out of 10 every three tutorials based on your participation in one tutorial (5 points) and your attendance in the other two (2.5 points each). To encourage participation during all tutorials, you will not be aware of which tutorial you are being marked for participation. You will be assessed on the elements of participation using the rubric below.

Element	Description
Knowledge	Demonstrates knowledge of course material
Insightfulness	Demonstrates insightful and critical thinking
Community	Demonstrates positive and constructive interactions with peers

Participation	Points	Description
Excellent	5	Consistently exemplifies all three elements of participation
Good	4	Consistently exemplifies two elements of participation
Satisfactory	3	Occasionally exemplifies some elements of participation
Poor	2	Rarely exemplifies elements of participation
Inadequate	1	Attends tutorial but does not participate
Absent	0	Does not attend tutorial

Your TA will also post a content-related question onto your tutorial's Avenue discussion board. Students who choose to answer all three discussion board posts within a marking period will receive a bonus mark (*i.e.* a mark of 8/10 would become 9/10).

Avenue Quizzes (30%)

There are 11 weekly online Avenue Quizzes during the semester which will cover material from the web modules, in-person lectures, and assigned readings. For example, Quiz 1 will contain material covered from the Development 1 and 2 web modules and in-person lecture, as well as Chapter 1 from the textbook. Each Quiz is "open book" and you may collaborate with your peers but you may NOT post questions online. Avenue Quizzes are an opportunity to assess and consolidate your knowledge of the week's content in preparation for the Final Exam where you will be working independently and without access to supporting resources.

The weekly quizzes are not cumulative. Each Avenue Quiz will consist of 10 multiple-choice questions. Avenue Quizzes will be made available online every Friday at 6AM and will promptly close on Saturday at 6AM. You will have 20 minutes to complete each quiz once you open it. After closing on Saturday, the Quiz will be reviewed and grades will be released on the following Tuesday.

Quiz questions are designed to go beyond mere recall and challenge you to apply and demonstrate your comprehension. In other words, simply memorizing terms will not lead to a favourable grade. To help you prepare and assess your studying, you will have a **Pre-Quiz** each week (released on Monday) that will be graded immediately and will provide you with feedback on why your chosen option was correct/incorrect. You can review the completed Pre-Quiz under the Quizzes tab on Avenue. The Pre-Quiz serves as an excellent learning tool as it contains questions of the same style and difficulty as your actual Friday Quiz, but does not officially count for grades. Note that the Pre-Quiz **MUST** be completed to gain access to the weekly Avenue Quiz.

Internet Problems
Internet issues can happen. We always recommend that you complete your quizzes in a location where a reliable Internet connection is guaranteed. While we do not accommodate for individual Internet issues, we can grade your quiz manually if you take screen shots. Please make sure that all photos have your name and timer in the shot.

Quiz Review
Quiz scores are released on Avenue Tuesday mornings. They can be found in the Grades section under the Assessments tab. Feedback on your quizzes is available once the grades are released. To see the feedback, go to the quiz page and scroll down to the bottom. You will see all of your past quizzes. A feedback option becomes visible next to the quiz when the grades are released. After each question you can also expand the feedback to get a more detailed reason why your answer was right or wrong. Students have one week after the quiz grades have been released to bring up any concerns related to a specific question. Please email a screenshot of the question to intropsych@mcmaster.ca. Don't forget to provide a detailed explanation of your concern.

Lecture iclicker Bonus Points

During your weekly lectures you will be given the opportunity to earn iclicker bonus points. Each week, you will have a short quiz during class. Each question will be worth a maximum of 2 points. You will receive 1 bonus point for answering the question individually and 1 additional point for answering correctly following collaboration.

All lecture bonus quizzes require an i<clicker remote or a subscription to Reef. Reef allows you to participate in iclicker polls online using your smartphone or computer. These can be purchased at the Campus Store. You can only earn iclicker bonus points in your registered lecture section. At the end of the term, your total number of points will earn you the following rewards:

Points	Reward
20 and above	Drop lowest participation grade
30 and above	Drop lowest participation grade + lowest quiz grade
40 and above	Drop lowest participation grade + 2 lowest quiz grades

Register your iclicker
To register your iclicker, please go to https://www.iclicker.com
You will need to create an account if this is your first time using iclicker. You MUST use your MacID in the student ID section during your registration. This is what you use to log in to Avenue/Mosaic. It is also the first part of your McMaster email address. Do NOT use your student number for this section.

Once you have created an account, you will need to add the course. You can search using Psych 1XX3 (or 1NN3 if you are a Conestoga student). **You need to select the correct core section for your course.**

If you are using the reef polling, you will also need to add your reef subscription to your profile. This can be done by clicking the menu button in the top left corner and selecting subscriptions. You will then see the option to enter the access code you purchased from the bookstore.

iclicker Trouble Shooting

iclicker points are updated weekly on Avenue. Only points that appear on Avenue are counted. If your points are not appearing on Avenue you have most likely made an error somewhere. The three most common mistakes are:

1) You have entered your student number in your iclicker profile. You need to enter your MacID (NOT your student number). Your MacID is your login for Avenue/Mosaic. To update this information, log in to the iclicker website and click the menu button in the top left and select Profile. Once this is corrected, your points will appear on Avenue during the next weekly refresh.

2) You are attending a lecture section that you are not registered in. You can only earn points in the lecture section you are registered in on Mosaic.

3) You are using a physical remote, but you have not added the remote ID to your iclicker profile. To update this information, log in to the iclicker website and click the menu button in the top left and select Profile. Once this is corrected, your points will appear on Avenue during the next weekly refresh.

If all of the above appears to be in order and you did not receive your points. Please take a screenshot of your iclicker profile and email it to intropsych@mcmaster.ca (using your McMaster email address). Please also include your lecture core section.

Avenue QuizTerm (7%)

The QuizTerm will take the form of a longer Avenue Quiz. It will be 30 multiple choice questions and you will be given 60 minutes to complete it. The QuizTerm will open on Friday February 18th at 6am and will close on Saturday February 19th at 6am. This is a cumulative assessment. It will contain information from Development, Evolution, Neuroscience 1, Neuroscience 2, and Vision. It will cover material presented in the web modules, in-person lecture, and assigned readings.

Final Exam (53%)

A cumulative Final Exam will be written in April as scheduled by the Registrar's Office. If you choose to complete both the optional multiple choice question writing and 4 credits of research participation option (see below), the weight of your final examination will be reduced from 53% to 42%. The Final Exam covers material presented in web modules, lectures, tutorials, and assigned readings from the entire term.

Multiple-Choice Questions – PeerWise

You have the option to reduce the weight of your Final Exam by 3% by creating and answering multiple-choice questions on PeerWise (https://peerwise.cs.auckland.ac.nz/at/?mcmaster_ca). There are two deadlines for this assignment, and you must meet both to earn the bonus. You must write 10 multiple choice questions and answer 10 questions created by your peers before the QuizTerm. You must also write and answer 10 more questions between the QuizTerm and the Final Exam.

Before QuizTerm	Between QuizTerm and Final Exam
Write 10 Questions Answer 10 Questions	Write 10 Questions Answer 10 Questions

This is an all-or-none assignment. You will not receive partial points if you complete or answer less than the required number of questions or if you complete them after the deadlines. The deadline for the first half of the assignment is the **start** of the QuizTerm at 6am on Friday February 18th. The second deadline is the start of the final exam.

Creating multiple-choice questions is a great way to study for the weekly quizzes and for the final exam. Writing questions requires you to reflect on what you learned in the course and explaining each option in the feedback section helps you to fully understand the concept. Writing plausible distractors is also trickier than you might think. You need to consider all the potential misconceptions and interpretations of a concept. Answering other students' questions may help you identify areas of weakness in your knowledge or view a topic from a perspective you hadn't thought about before. We recommend completing questions every week as a way to help study for the quizzes, instead of waiting to do it last minute before the deadline.

To participate on PeerWise you must first create an account. You can do this by clicking the registration button in the bottom left corner of the website. You will need 2 things to complete your registration: The course ID and your identifier. **The course ID is: 24202 and your identifier is your MacID (NOT your student number).** Your MacID is your login for Avenue and Mosaic. It is also the first part of your McMaster email address.

Writing Questions
Once you have logged in, under the "Your Questions" section click on "View Questions" and you should be directed to a new page. When writing multiple-choice questions you will need to provide the question text as well as 4 options for each question. Make sure your question is very clear and not likely to be ambiguous. Use professional language and avoid slang or spelling mistakes. You will also be asked to provide "tags" for your question. Please use this to indicate the relevant web module(s).

You will also need to provide an explanation for your question. This is one of the criteria for how your question is rated by your fellow students. For this section you should create a list and provide an explanation corresponding to each of the options. Indicate why each answer is right or wrong. This is the same as your weekly quizzes where you receive specific feedback on your answer and not just why one answer is correct.

Answering Questions
Once you have answered a question, you will be given feedback on the response you selected, and you will be shown an explanation of the answer. You will also be able to see how other students answered. You will then be given an opportunity to select the difficulty level you think best matches the question and to give the question a rating, which you should think about very carefully.

When rating a question, you should be judging two things:
- Whether you think the question is of a high enough quality that it could appear on an Avenue quiz.
- Whether you think the explanation provided with the question is sufficient so that if someone answered

the question incorrectly the explanation would help them to understand what they have done wrong.

Other things to keep in mind:
- You should not rate questions differently based on their difficulty – an easy question can be just as useful as a hard question. Everyone is at different levels of understanding.
- Be fair with your ratings – you should justify a poor rating with a comment to the author of the question, or by agreement with a previously written comment.
- Make sure any comments you provide are constructive – you are rating questions written by your peers so provide the kind of feedback that you would find useful and encouraging yourself.
- To encourage everyone to participate equally, all activity on PeerWise is anonymous (however your instructor is able to track contributions).

Research Participation Option – Sona

You have the option to reduce the weight of your Final Exam from 53% to 48% by completing and attaining **two credits** of research participation with the Department of Psychology, Neuroscience, and Behaviour. If you complete **three credits** you will reduce the weight of your final exam by 6.5%, making your exam worth 46.5%. If you complete **four credits** your exam will be worth 45% (8% reduction). In addition to providing you with extra credit, the research participation option allows you to take part in some of the exciting research at McMaster, and to observe how psychologists conduct their studies.

Please remember that your Sona participation is voluntary and that you can withdraw at any time. If you do not wish to participate as a research subject for any reason, you may still earn your research participation credit by *observing* experiments. If you would like to observe studies instead of participating, please email the course coordinator at intropsych@mcmaster.ca or visit during office hours. If you would like to sign up as a participant, please follow the instructions below.

The system that the department uses to track research participation is called Sona, which can be accessed at **mcmaster.sona-systems.com**. To access Sona for the first time, select the "Request Account" option on the right of your screen and enter your name, student number, and McMaster email address. You will also be asked to pick your courses. Please select Psych 1XX3 from the list. After a short delay, you will receive an email from Sona with a username and temporary password that you can use to access the website. You should change your password to something more memorable by selecting "My Profile". Make sure your student number is entered correctly! **Note: You must activate your McMaster ID before you can create a Sona account. To activate your ID, please go to** www.mcmaster.ca/uts/macid

Completing Your Research Participation Credit

When you log in to Sona for the first time, you will be asked to fill out a short survey. This information is used to filter out any experiments for which you are not eligible. To register for an experiment, select "Study Sign-Up" from the main Sona page. You will be presented with a list of currently available experiments, with a short description given about each. Before selecting an experiment, be sure to read the description carefully, making special note of any specific criteria for participation (for example, some experiments only allow females to participate, while others may require participants who speak a second language). When you have found an experiment that you would like to participate in, select "View Time Slots for this Study" to view available timeslots, then select "Sign-Up" to register for a time that fits your schedule. You will receive a confirmation email with the details of your selection. Be sure to write down the study number, experimenter name, location, and telephone extension from this email. For many online studies, you do not select a specific time to participate, but are instead provided with a participation deadline. You will be given a website link and must complete the study before the deadline.

In-Person studies: After completion of the study you should be given a debriefing sheet explaining what the study was all about. Shortly after completing an experiment, you should notice that your Sona account has been credited by the experimenter.

Online studies: We recommend you take a screenshot of the final completion screen as proof of your participation. You do not need to send this to anyone, it's just good to have in case something goes wrong with your credit. Credits for online studies are generally uploaded sometime after the study deadline so it may take a while for the credit to show up on Sona. Researchers are aware of our internal class deadlines and will be prompted to upload their credits earlier if their participation deadline is after the final exam.

Additional Notes
- You must complete two credits on Sona, and no less, if you wish to earn the 5% exam reweight.
- If you fail to show up for two experiments, you will lose your option to complete the research participation credit. If you know in advance that you will be unable to attend a scheduled experiment, please contact the experimenter as soon as possible. You can access their email by clicking on the envelope next to their name on the study information page.
- All credits must be completed by the day of the final exam (end of day).

Web Modules

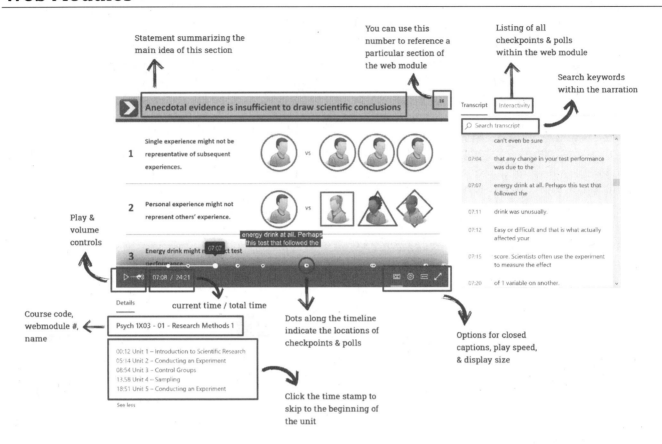

Navigation: You can pause, skip, and review each web module whenever you want. Tip: You can use the spacebar to quickly toggle between pause/play.

Play options: You can turn on closed captions or change the play speed.

Search: Stream allows you to search the transcript to easily find what you are looking for. In addition, if you check out the supplementary materials posted on avenue, you can find a downloadable transcript.

Checkpoints: Throughout the modules you will find checkpoint questions designed to assess your understanding.

Timestamps: The beginning of each unit has been timestamped and posted to allow you to quickly navigate to a specific section.

Additional Resources and Regulations

Requests for Relief for Missed Academic Term Work
McMaster Student Absence Form (MSAF): In the event of an absence for medical or other reasons, students should review and follow the Academic Regulation in the Undergraduate Calendar "Requests for Relief for Missed Academic Term Work". Once you have submitted the MSAF, please contact intropsych@mcmaster.ca.

Academic Accommodation of Students with Disabilities
Students with disabilities who require academic accommodation must contact Student Accessibility Services (SAS) at 905-525-9140 ext. 28652 or sas@mcmaster.ca to make arrangements with a Program Coordinator. For further information, consult McMaster University's Academic Accommodation of Students with Disabilities policy.

Academic Accommodation for Religious, Indigenous Or Spiritual Observances (Riso)
Students requiring academic accommodation based on religious, indigenous or spiritual observances should follow the procedures set out in the RISO policy. Students should submit their request to their Faculty Office **normally within 10 working days** of the beginning of term in which they anticipate a need for accommodation or to the Registrar's Office prior to their examinations. Students should contact their instructors as soon as possible to make alternative arrangements for classes, assignments, and tests.

Courses with An On-Line Element
Some courses may use on-line elements (e.g. e-mail, Avenue to Learn (A2L), LearnLink, web pages, capa, Moodle, ThinkingCap, etc.). Students should be aware that, when they access the electronic components of a course using these elements, private information such as first and last names, user names for the McMaster e-mail accounts, and program affiliation may become apparent to all other students in the same course. The available information is dependent on the technology used. Continuation in a course that uses on-line elements will be deemed consent to this disclosure. If you have any questions or concerns about such disclosure, please discuss this with the course instructor.

Online Proctoring
We will not be using proctoring software during this course.

Academic Integrity
You are expected to exhibit honesty and use ethical behaviour in all aspects of the learning process. Academic credentials you earn are rooted in principles of honesty and academic integrity.

It is your responsibility to understand what constitutes academic dishonesty.

Academic dishonesty is to knowingly act or fail to act in a way that results or could result in unearned academic credit or advantage. This behaviour can result in serious consequences, e.g. the grade of zero on an assignment, loss of credit with a notation on the transcript (notation reads: "Grade of F assigned for academic dishonesty"), and/or suspension or expulsion from the university. For information on the various types of academic dishonesty please refer to the Academic Integrity Policy, located at https://secretariat.mcmaster.ca/university-policies-procedures- guidelines/

The following illustrates only three forms of academic dishonesty:
- plagiarism, e.g. the submission of work that is not one's own or for which other credit has been obtained.
- improper collaboration in group work.
- copying or using unauthorized aids in tests and examinations.

Authenticity / Plagiarism Detection

Some courses may use a web-based service (Turnitin.com) to reveal authenticity and ownership of student submitted work. For courses using such software, students will be expected to submit their work electronically either directly to Turnitin.com or via an online learning platform (e.g. A2L, etc.) using plagiarism detection (a service supported by Turnitin.com) so it can be checked for academic dishonesty.

Students who do not wish their work to be submitted through the plagiarism detection software must inform the Instructor before the assignment is due. No penalty will be assigned to a student who does not submit work to the plagiarism detection software. **All submitted work is subject to normal verification that standards of academic integrity have been upheld** (e.g., on-line search, other software, etc.). For more details about McMaster's use of Turnitin.com please go to the McMaster Office of Academic Integrity's webpage.

Conduct Expectations

As a McMaster student, you have the right to experience, and the responsibility to demonstrate, respectful and dignified interactions within all our living, learning and working communities. These expectations are described in the Code of Student Rights & Responsibilities (the "Code"). All students share the responsibility of maintaining a positive environment for the academic and personal growth of all McMaster community members, **whether in person or online**.

It is essential that students be mindful of their interactions online, as the Code remains in effect in virtual learning environments. The Code applies to any interactions that adversely affect, disrupt, or interfere with reasonable participation in University activities. Student disruptions or behaviours that interfere with university functions on online platforms (e.g. use of Avenue 2 Learn, WebEx or Zoom for delivery), will be taken very seriously and will be investigated. Outcomes may include restriction or removal of the involved students' access to these platforms.

Copyright and Recording

Students are advised that lectures, demonstrations, performances, and any other course material provided by an instructor include copyright protected works. The Copyright Act and copyright law protect every original literary, dramatic, musical and artistic work, **including lectures** by University instructors.

The recording of lectures, tutorials, or other methods of instruction may occur during a course. Recording may be done by either the instructor for the purpose of authorized distribution, or by a student for the purpose of personal study. Students should be aware that their voice and/or image may be recorded by others during the class. Please speak with the instructor if this is a concern for you.

Extreme Circumstances

The University reserves the right to change the dates and deadlines for any or all courses in extreme circumstances (e.g., severe weather, labour disruptions, etc.). Changes will be communicated through regular McMaster communication channels, such as McMaster Daily News, A2L and/or McMaster email.

Study Guide for Psychology 1XX3/1NN3/1FF3

Welcome to PSYCH 1XX3: Foundations of Psychology, Neuroscience & Behaviour, one of two IntroPsych courses offered at McMaster University (PSYCH 1X03 is offered in Term 1). Your IntroPsych course follows in the tradition of McMaster University's long-standing reputation of excellence in innovative teaching and learning. In this course, you will experience a unique blended learning model that combines online learning technology with traditional face-to-face instruction. On your way to the weekly Quizzes and Final Exam, there are several resources available to help you master the curriculum:

Course Handbook: Your course handbook contains valuable information regarding course structure, outlines, and guides for web modules and tutorials.

Course Textbook: Your course textbook can be purchased at the McMaster Campus Store. It contains required readings with testable material for the course.

MacIntroPsych.com: There are many supplementary resources that have been specially developed to complement the handbook at MacIntroPsych.com including important links, information about course events, university services, and tips for academic success. You can also access our PNB talks, which are a series of short presentations created by our TAs.

Avenue to Learn: Your primary course content will be delivered through the Avenue learning management system located at **http://avenue.mcmaster.ca**. Avenue allows you access to weekly web modules, course announcements, discussion forums, and grade records. To access Avenue, use your MacID and password. Below are some of the features of Avenue.

Web Modules: The most unique feature of MacIntroPsych is the way you receive your primary course content—it's all online! You can access the web modules from the library, your room, or anywhere you have an internet connection. The interactive web modules feature audio, video animations, and vivid graphics. Check out the many advanced features that allow you to interact with the content according to your personal learning preferences. Use the navigation tools and integrated search function to move about the module. You can test your knowledge with checkpoints, participate in class polls, and learn more about faculty related research. Be sure to view the assigned web modules **before** you attend your weekly lecture and tutorial to stay on schedule, get points on the bonus quizzes, and actively participate.

Discussion Boards: More extended topic discussions are available on the Avenue Discussion Board. Join an existing discussion or start a new thread. Our discussion boards are consistently the most active in comparison to any other course on campus, so jump right in with your opinion!

Tutorials: You will join a small tutorial section (capped at 26 students) led by a Teaching Assistant (TA) who is enrolled in or has completed PSYCH 3TT3: Applied Educational Psychology, a course designed specifically to help TAs lead effective tutorials and guide you through MacIntroPsych. Each year, our TAs receive top ratings from students across campus so don't be shy to ask questions. If you think your TA is especially amazing, consider nominating them for the Kathy Steele Award, which honours the top TA of the year. Your TA will guide discussions, lead activities and demonstrations, and answer any questions you might have. Tutorials are updated each year by feedback from students and TAs.

Lobby Hours: Have a question? Still confused about a specific concept? Need some one-on-one time? Drop by during our office hours to speak with your TA. The times are posted on Avenue. If you have administrative questions please visit Dr. Michelle Cadieux, the course coordinator, or send her an email. Her office hours are updated on Avenue weekly.

How to Use Google Scholar

Google Scholar is a great tool to find peer-reviewed journal articles (a few of which will be assigned as your weekly reading). It is quick and simple. Below, we have outlined a few tips to make it even simpler.

How do I get there?
Easy! Type in http://scholar.google.ca, or just type "scholar" into Google.

I can't seem to access any articles, what do I do?
Most journals require you to purchase an article before you can access it. Luckily, McMaster has purchased these articles for us! All you have to do is click on "scholar preferences" at the top right of the window. Where it says "Library Links" enter "McMaster" then scroll to the bottom and save preferences. Simple!

I am trying to find articles about a general topic, what do I do?
Use the search box to search articles by their journal, author(s), title, or topic. Another search option is to click on "advanced scholar search" beside the search box. This will allow you to search for specific journals, authors, and titles. You can even search for articles about a particular topic published within a particular time frame and published in a particular journal. Play around with it and get used to this tool. It will come in handy not just this semester, but for much of your university career.

Taking Notes

Students often wonder (and worry) about how extensive their notes should be. This handbook provides outlines with key points and slides reproduced from the web modules to guide your own note taking. There really is no substitute for doing this yourself to learn the material. If, however, you can refer to your notes and answer the practice questions that follow the handbook outlines, you should find yourself in good shape for the weekly quizzes and the exam to come.

Writing Tests

With practice questions in this handbook, iclicker bonus point questions, Pre-Quizzes and Quizzes, you might be wondering "why are there so many tests?!". The simple answer is that testing has been shown to be the most effective way to learn information in the long term.

Retrieval-Enhanced Learning
Many students likely view testing as a negative necessity of their courses and would prefer to have as few tests as possible. Thinking about testing this way is due to years of experiencing tests as a high-stakes assessment of learning. This is unfortunate given the fact that testing improves learning. Over the past hundred years, research on the characteristics of human learning and memory has demonstrated that practice testing enhances learning and retention of information (e.g., Dunlosky et al., 2013; Roediger & Karpicke, 2006a). Practice testing can take many forms. It can refer to practicing your recall of information by using flashcards, completing practice problems or questions in a textbook, or completing low-stakes tests as part of a course requirement. This principle was the primary motivation for redesigning the MacIntroPsych course to have weekly, low stakes quizzes.

An excellent example of the power of testing memory comes from a study by Roediger and Karpicke (2006b), wherein undergraduate students were presented with short, educationally relevant texts for initial study. Following initial study, students either studied the material again or took a practice test. A final test was taken after a short retention interval (5 minutes) or long retention interval (2 days). After a short retention interval, restudying produced better recall than testing (81% vs. 75%). However, with the long retention interval, testing produced significantly better recall than restudying (68% vs. 54%). Thus, after two days, performance declined 27% for students who restudied the material, but only 7% for students who practiced recall.

Interestingly, providing students with the correct answer feedback after a test enhances the positive effect of testing. With feedback, learners are able to correct errors, and maintain their correct responses. Moreover, taking a test and reviewing feedback can enhance future study sessions. Research shows that when a student takes a test before restudying material, they learn **more** from the restudying session than if they restudy without taking a test beforehand (e.g., Karpicke, 2009). This is called test-potentiated learning.

Why does testing improve retention of information and how can I use it?
Explanations for the positive effects of testing focus on how the act of retrieval affects memory. Specifically, it is suggested that retrieving information leads to an elaboration of memory traces and the creation of additional retrieval paths. Together these changes to memory systems make it more likely that the information will be successfully retrieved again in the future. This suggests that testing is not just an assessment tool, but also an effective learning tool.

As a student in this course you can take advantage of retrieval enhanced learning each week in preparation for your weekly Quiz. This begins with studying web module content early in the week (e.g., Sunday or Monday). You can then engage in retrieval practice as a form of review after your initial study session. At this point you should be ready to complete the Pre-quiz and review the feedback (by Wednesday or Thursday). This gives you the opportunity to take advantage of test-potentiated learning when you review content again before completing your Quiz on Friday. This suggested schedule of studying, and incorporation of retrieval practice will help you learn and retain the course content. Engaging in this process each week enhances your long-term memory for course content and therefore advances your preparations for the final exam!

Suggested further reading:
1. Dunlosky, et al., (2013). *Psychological Science in the Public Interest, 14*(1), 4-58.
2. Karpicke, J. D. (2009). *Journal of Experimental Psychology: General, 138*, 469–486.
3. Roediger, H. L., & Karpicke, J. D. (2006a). *Psychological Science, 17*, 249–255.
4. Roediger, H. L., & Karpicke, J. D. (2006b). *Perspectives on Psychological Science, 1*, 181–210.

Multiple Choice Questions and Flashcards

Test questions can challenge you to demonstrate your mastery of course content through 3 levels of increasing difficulty:

1. To *remember* psychological terms, concepts, theories, and methods.
2. To *understand* information that has been remembered.
3. To *apply* understood information to novel situations (this is called *transfer* and demonstrates true mastery of learned material).

Let's take a look at an example of a psychological concept you will learn:

Confounding Variable: An extraneous variable whose presence affects the variables being studied so that the results do not reflect the actual relationship between the variables.

Here is a simple question that challenges your ability to *remember* the term:

1. Which of the following best describes a confounding variable?
   a. A dependent variable whose absence affects the variables being studied so that the results do reflect the actual relationship between variables.
   b. An independent variable whose absence affects the variables being studied so that the results do not reflect the actual relationship between variables.

    c. An extraneous variable whose presence affects the variables being studied so that the results do reflect the actual relationship between variables.
    d. An extraneous variable whose presence affects the variables being studied so that the results do not reflect the actual relationship between variables.

The correct answer is D, and knowing this requires the ability to *remember* (or look up) a word-for-word definition of confounding variable taken directly from the course material

2. If a confounding variable is unnoticed, it can lead a researcher to:
    a. Make a more accurate connection between an independent and dependent variable.
    b. Make a more accurate connection between two independent variables.
    c. Make an erroneous association between an independent and dependent variable.
    d. Make an erroneous association between several confounding variables.

The correct answer is C, and knowing this requires the ability to *understand* information that has been accurately remembered, because you must be able to recognize a definition of confounding variable that is composed of different words than the original definition.

3. A researcher gives the same IQ test questions to a group of children and discovers that arm length is positively correlated with number of correct responses. He concludes that longer arms lead to increased intelligence. What confounding variable may account for this finding to weaken this conclusion?
    a. Some children may have been purposely answering test questions incorrectly.
    b. Arm length increases with age, so this study may demonstrate that older children outperform younger children.
    c. IQ is a hypothetical construct that may not accurately reflect intelligence.
    d. IQ test questions may lack validity and reliability.

The correct answer is B, and knowing this requires the ability to *apply* understood information in a novel situation.

Using flashcards effectively can be a solid method for efficiently building your knowledge to prepare for the three types of test questions. On the back of each flashcard is a ready-prepared definition for the term to help you *remember*. When studying, you should try to rework this definition into your own words to help you *understand*. Finally, create an original example that illustrates the term to help you learn to *apply*.

To provide some additional help for effective use of the flashcards, we have included an additional set of cards on the following page. These flashcards will require you to go deeper with the concepts thus increasing your understanding and retention.

Bonus tip: One of the most robust findings in research on the science of learning is the distributed practice effect, which shows the benefits of spreading out study sessions over time. Let's say Thomas and Kristal both spend 4 hours studying the same material for a test. Thomas distributes his practice by studying 1 hour a day for 4 days and Kristal crams all 4 of her study hours in one long study marathon the night before the test. Even with time-on-task equated, Thomas will show significantly improved long-term benefits.

Describe a movie/television scene that depicts this concept MAC IntroPsych	**Pick two cards and make a connection between the concepts** MAC IntroPsych
Describe this concept without using any of the key words written on the flashcard MAC IntroPsych	**Draw this concept** MAC IntroPsych
How would you explain this concept to a child? MAC IntroPsych	**What is the opposite of this concept?** MAC IntroPsych
What situation in your life has depicted this concept? MAC IntroPsych	**Create a concept map with all of the cards from a module** MAC IntroPsych

Campus Resources

The following are some of the resources available to McMaster University students. Read over each description and familiarize yourself with what is available!

Student Accessibility Services
Student Accessibility Services offers various supports for students with disabilities. They work with full-time, part-time, and prospective students. SAS assists with academic and disability-related needs, including learning strategies, note-taking, assistive technologies, test & exam administration, accommodations for courses, groups, and events.
Website: http://sas.mcmaster.ca/
Phone: 905-525-9140 ext. 28652
Teletypewriter (TTY): 905-528-4307
Email: sas@mcmaster.ca
Office: McMaster University Student Centre (MUSC) - Basement, Room B107

Student Wellness Centre
The Student Wellness Centre offers medical & health services, personal counselling, and mental health services.
Medical & Health: The Student Wellness Centre provides a wide range of health services for students and will act as their personal health care provider throughout their studies at McMaster. Appointment bookings should be made ahead of time.
Personal Counselling & Mental Health: At some point, almost everyone experiences major concerns that may interfere with their success, happiness, and satisfaction at university. Common concerns are relationships, mood disorders, learning disabilities, body image, anxiety, and depression. The Student Wellness Centre provides experienced counsellors for bookings and emergency appointments.
Website: http://wellness.mcmaster.ca/
Phone: 905-525-9140 ext. 27700
Email: wellness@mcmaster.ca
Office: PGCLL 210/201

Emergency First Response Team (EFRT)
The McMaster Students Union Emergency First Response Team (EFRT) is a group of approximately 30 student volunteers who provide emergency medical services to the McMaster Campus, with an average response time of 2-3 minutes. All responders are certified Emergency Medical Responders, with more senior members being trained in International Trauma Life Support (ITLS), and Advanced Medical Life Support (AMLS). The EFRT is available 24/7 throughout the academic year except Thanksgiving, Easter, the Holiday Break, and both Reading Weeks.
Website: https://www.msumcmaster.ca/services-directory/7-emergency-first-response-team-efrt
Phone: "88" from any campus phone or 905-522-4135 on any cell phone

The MacPherson Institute for Leadership, Innovation and Excellence in Teaching
This institute is designed to enable success in teaching and learning. Their activities include both general and discipline-specific approaches to the promotion of successful learning in all its forms and contexts.
Website: mi.mcmaster.ca
Phone: 905-525-9140 ext. 24540
Office: Mills Library L504

Academic Advising in PNB

Ann Hollingshead is the academic advisor for anyone in the PNB department at McMaster. She has a lot of knowledge about upper-year courses and can help you make the best decisions about what courses to take. Ann is available Monday – Friday 9:00am-5:00pm for drop-in help or by appointment.

Email: hollings@mcmaster.ca
Phone: 905-525-9140 ext. 23005
Office: PC 109

Note: For academic advising for other departments, visit your faculty's website (Social Science, Science, Engineering, etc.) for more information.

A Note from Dr. Joe Kim

We have many talented and passionate members of the Instructional Staff and Development Team that work hard to bring you an outstanding course experience. MacIntroPsych was honoured with the 2010 President's Award for Excellence in Course and Resource Design. Our unique IntroPsych Program has been the topic of academic study and received widespread media attention in the Toronto Star, Globe and Mail, CHCH News, and Maclean's (not to mention Mac's own Daily News). Importantly, the continual development of the MacIntroPsych Blended Learning Environment model is supported by ongoing research. As the Director of the Education & Cognition Laboratory (EdCog Lab), I am actively interested in teaching, learning, and technology from both an academic and a practical perspective. For more information, visit https://edcog.ca or follow my twitter feed: @ProfJoeKim

University can sometimes seem like an impersonal and strange place, especially for Level 1 students who are dealing with many adjustments. I hope that in exploring the course resources, you will not forget that there is a real live faculty member responsible for the MacIntroPsych Program—me! I have regular office hours (posted weekly on Avenue) set aside solely to give me a chance to meet and talk with you. If you have a question, comment, complaint, concern, or just want to see and chat with a live faculty member, do come. Many students are reluctant to talk to a faculty member outside of class. Don't give in to the feeling! I have had many great conversations with students that have started off with a supposedly "silly" question.

As a Teaching Professor, my primary responsibilities are teaching and interacting with students; even my area of research interest concerns pedagogy—the formal study of teaching and learning. My goal is to help you understand and appreciate some of the really interesting and important things that we know (or think we know) about human thought and behaviour. In most fields—and as you will see, certainly in psychology—the simplest questions are often the most important and difficult to answer.

One last piece of advice—get involved in the course! MacIntroPsych is a fascinating world waiting to be explored by you! Keep up with the web modules, actively participate in tutorials, join the discussion forums, and watch the PNB talks on MacIntroPsych.com. It really will make all the difference. Following each web module, I would also encourage you to participate in the feedback surveys. Many of the most popular interactive features were suggested by students just like you. I really do read every single comment and they have contributed enormously to minor and major changes made to all aspects of the course, and this includes the very course handbook you hold in your hands.

On behalf of all the wonderful people that work hard on the frontlines and behind the scenes, best of luck and have a great year!

Dr. Joe Kim

Development 1 & 2

"Man acquires at birth, through heredity, a biological constitution which we must consider fixed and unalterable... In addition, during his lifetime, he acquires a cultural constitution which he adopts from society through communication and through many other types of influences. It is this cultural constitution which, with the passage of time, is subject to change and which determines to a very large extent the relationship between the individual and society."
- Albert Einstein

NASA Twin Study May Help Us Reach Mars
Imagine huddling around your television and watching in awe as the first astronaut takes their first steps on Mars. This historic moment is only possible if astronauts can survive the 8-month space journey to the planet. To ensure the astronauts' survival, we must explore the effects of extended space flight on the human body. NASA recently conducted a twin study to explore how a prolonged celestial environment may affect humans on a physiological, molecular, behavioural and genetic level. By using identical twin astronauts, Scott and Mark Kelly, NASA is exploring how a 340-day orbital spaceflight compares to 340 days on land by running continuous tests on two genetically identical bodies. This is the longest amount of time an American astronaut has ever spent in continuous space flight. While the study is still in progress, NASA's research may reveal answers to how space flight influences cognitive function, gene expression, organ function and more. Dr. Susan Bailey from Colorado State University hypothesizes that Scott Kelly (the space bound astronaut) may show evidence of telomere shortening which may be associated with early aging and death, which was in fact what was found! Not only can this research help NASA send astronauts to Mars in our lifetime, but it can shed light on our human biology. This unique twin study may also help tease out the age-old debate of nature versus nature: can two individuals with nearly identical genetics change as a result of being in different environments? Stay tuned to nasa.gov/twins-study to find out.

Dunn, A., & Abadie, L. (2014, March 7). NASA launches new research, seeks the subtle in parallel ways. *NASA: Human Research*. Retrieved from http://www.nasa.gov/content/nasa-launches-new-research-seeks-the-subtle-in-parallel-ways-u

Bailey, S., & George, K. (2015, January 13). Differential effects on telomeres and telomerase in twin astronauts associated with space flight. *NASA: Human Research*. Retrieved from http://www.nasa.gov/sites/default/files/files/telomeres.pdf

Weekly Checklist:
- ☐ **Web modules to watch: Development 1 & 2**
- ☐ **Readings: Chapter 1**
- ☐ **Pre-Quiz & Quiz 1**

Upper Year Courses:
If you enjoyed the content of this week's module, consider taking the following upper year courses:
- Psych 2AA3: Child Development
- Psych 3GG3: Essentials of Developmental Psychology

Development 1 – Outline

Unit 1: Introduction to Psychology 1XX3

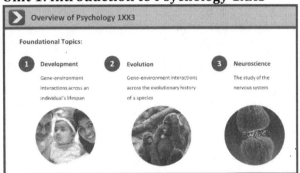

Unit 2: Introduction to Development 1XX3

Maturation and learning interact.

Interactionist Perspective: _____

_____
_____
_____
_____
_____
_____
_____

In Psych 1XX3, you will explore the biological basis of thought and behaviour in relation to development, evolution and neuroscience.

_____
_____
_____
_____
_____
_____
_____
_____
_____

Development is the study of how individuals change and remain the same between conception and death.

_____
_____

Maturation: _____
_____
_____
_____

Learning: _____
_____
_____
_____
_____
_____
_____
_____
_____
_____
_____
_____
_____
_____

Unit 3: Studying Development

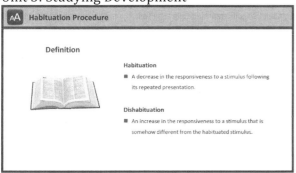

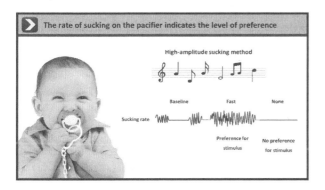

Competence-performance distinction:
_____
_____
_____
_____

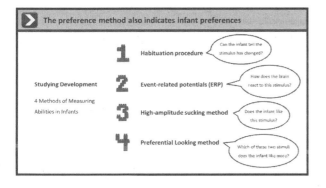

There are four ways to measure the dramatic changes that occur throughout infancy.
_____
_____

1) Habituation procedure: _____
_____
_____

Dishabituation: _____
_____
_____

2) Event-related potential: _____
_____

3) High-amplitude sucking method: _____
_____

4) Preference method: _____
_____

What do infants prefer? _____
_____
_____
_____

Each of the four techniques asks a different question
_____
_____
_____
_____
_____
_____
_____
_____
_____

Unit 4: Introduction to Developmental Research Methods

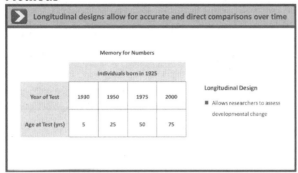

Ideal for assessing individual development, longitudinal designs repeatedly measure the same individual at various ages.

_____
_____
_____
_____

Advantages: _____
_____
_____
_____
_____

Disadvantages: _____
_____

Selective attrition: _____
_____
_____
_____

Practice effects: _____
_____
_____
_____

Ideal for uncovering age differences, cross-sectional designs compare individuals from many age groups at one time point.

_____

Advantages: _____
_____
_____

Disadvantages: _____
_____
_____
_____

Consider combining both research designs!

Development 1 – Courseware Exercise

1. Imagine that you are a developmental psychologist, seeking to understand whether 2-month old babies have developed the visual sensitivity to perceive slight changes in a visual pattern. What are two challenges that you may run across due to the age of your participants?

2. Explain how you would carry out your experiment in order to account for these challenges, mentioning specifically how your methodology overcomes each problem.

3. How would you modify your study if you were using 10-month old babies with strong motor coordination?

4. Would you use this same methodology on adult participants? Why or why not?

5. You are interested in how visual abilities change over time and decide to compare the performance of the 2-month old babies with the performance of 10-month old infants. What experimental design did you use when testing these two age groups?

6. Describe another way that you could test changing visual abilities and how would you modify your experimental design to do so?

Development 1 – Review Questions

1. Which is NOT an examples of how maturation affects learning:

   a) A one-year old toddler is unable to distinguish between certain phonemes that a 6-month old infant can distinguish between easily.

   b) Upon moving to a new country, a parent finds it more difficult to learn a language than their young child.

   c) A child develops longer fingers after playing the piano for many years.

   d) A 6-year-old child has difficulty understanding the world from other perspectives.

2. A researcher is interested in determining the age at which infants can discriminate between colours. What is the best method to determine this?
   a) Habituation
   b) Event-related potentials
   c) High-amplitude sucking
   d) Preference method

3. Which of the following research questions would be best examined with the use of the preference method?
   a) A researcher is interested whether infants show a preference for sweetened milk.
   b) A researcher is curious whether preferences for certain facial features develop as a result of exposure to one's culture or if it can be shown with infants.
   c) A researcher wants to determine whether infants prefer looking at patterns or solid images.
   d) A researcher is examining whether infants process two images differentially.

4. Recently, a large group of immigrants arrived in Canada from Russia. A study is being conducted to examine how these immigrants are adapting to living in Canada. In order to examine this question, what type of study should the researchers conduct?
   a) Longitudinal
   b) Cross-sectional
   c) Both
   d) Neither is appropriate

Explain your reasoning for your answer in number 4:

_____
_____
_____
_____
_____

Development 2 – Outline

Unit 1: Introduction to Hereditary Transmission

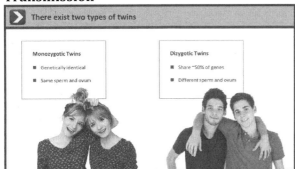

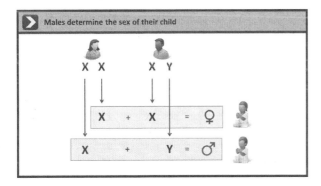

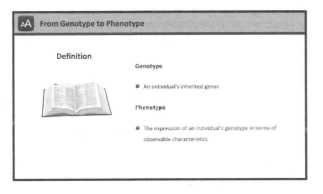

Genetic information and environmental stimuli interact to shape who we become.

Zygote: _____

Chromosomes: _____
_____
_____
_____
_____

Monozygotic twins: _____

Dizygotic twins: _____

The male provides the genetic information that determines the sex of an infant.
_____
_____

Autosomes: _____
_____

Sex chromosomes (M/F difference): _____
_____
_____
_____

There are four main ways by which genetic information is expressed as a phenotype.

Genotype: _____

Phenotype: _____
_____
_____
_____
_____
_____
_____

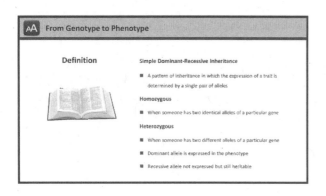

1) Dominant Recessive Inheritance

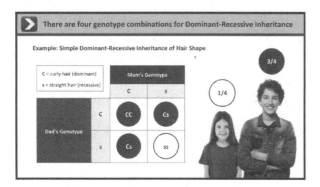

Creating a table can help you determine which phenotype will be expressed

2) Polygenic inheritance

3) Codominance

4) Sex-linked Inheritance

Unit 2: Introduction to the Interactionist Perspective

Our genes and our environment interact to influence our development.

Behaviourist (Nurture) View:
_____
_____
_____

Genetic (Nature) View:
_____
_____

Nature *vs.* Nurture?
_____
_____
_____
_____
_____

The canalization principle dictates that all individuals are restricted to a similar phenotype despite variations in the environment.

_____
_____
_____
_____
_____
_____
_____
_____

Babbling:
_____
_____
_____
_____
_____
_____
_____
_____
_____
_____

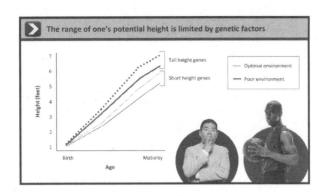

The range of reaction principle dictates that our genotype restricts us to a range of possible phenotypes whose expression is dependent on environmental conditions.

Height example:

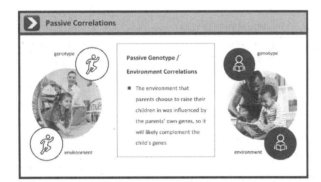

There are three ways that your genes can influence the types of environments sought out.

1) Passive correlations:

2) Evocative correlations:

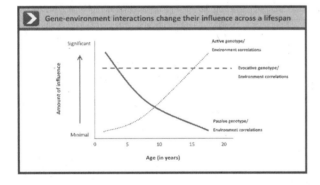

3) Active correlations:

Across the lifespan?

Twin studies allow us to probe the relative contribution of genes and the environment.

39

Unit 3: Introduction to Critical Periods

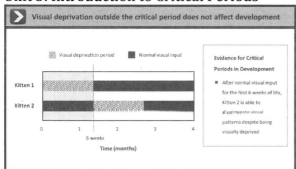

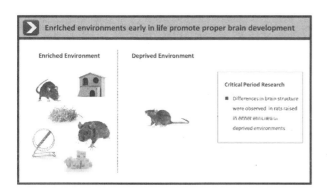

A critical period is a specific time window when certain experiences are required for normal development.

Visual deprivation in kittens:

Critical period in visual development?

Leap in thinking?

Laboratory research often compares group extremes; therefore, inferences must be made with caution.

Implications (3):

Problems with critical period evidence:

Brain circuitry remains malleable throughout the lifespan.

_____
_____
_____
_____
_____
_____
_____
_____
_____

There are two types of brain growth:

_____
_____
_____

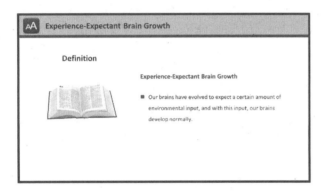

1) Experience-expectant brain growth: ____
_____
_____
_____

2) Experience-dependent brain growth: ____
_____
_____
_____
_____

Since our brains are much more malleable than once thought, critical periods are now referred to as sensitive periods.

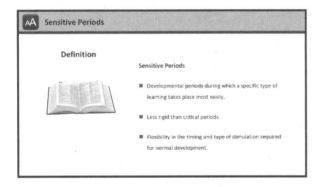

_____
_____
_____
_____
_____
_____
_____
_____
_____
_____

Development 2 – Courseware Exercises

The following graph illustrates the results of a theoretical experiment measuring a characteristic in children that is expressed either with a high quality or low quality set of genes. High and low quality genes, respectively, promote or suppress the characteristic from baseline. Each participant is categorized based on the quality of his or her genes and their respective environments. A test was administered to determine the level of gene expression (presence of the characteristic) that was displayed (as demonstrated on the y-axis).

1. Describe the results of the experiment. How do genes and the environment seem to interact for this particular experiment? Does the environment equally influence the expression of both types of genes?

_____
_____
_____
_____
_____

2. Which principle is key to this experimental design?

3. Compare and contrast the range of reaction principle and the canalization principle.

Range of Reaction Principle	Shared	Canalization Principle

Development 2 – Review Questions

1. Monozygotic twins have _____ genotype(s) and _____ phenotype(s).

    a) The same, the same
    b) The same, different
    c) Different, the same
    d) Different, different

2. Let's consider that there are three alleles that determine an individual's phenotype for a specific trait, denoted as A, B, and C. If an individual's genotype is AB then their phenotype will be A, if their genotype is BC then their phenotype will be C, if their phenotype is AC then their phenotype will be A. What pattern of genetic expression in being demonstrated?

    a) Dominant-recessive inheritance
    b) Polygenetic inheritance
    c) Co-dominance
    d) Sex-linked inheritance

3. Lucy has developed into a very intelligent girl, just like her parents. As she gets older she enjoys spending a lot of time reading in libraries. Which correlation best explains this phenomenon?

    a) Passive correlations
    b) Evocative correlations
    c) Active correlations

4. Which of the following is NOT true of a critical period?

    a) A critical period refers to a limited time during which an ability may develop.
    b) A critical period defines the period of time when special programs enhance infant development
    c) A critical period is supported by findings from animal studies
    d) A critical period has been implicated in the areas of visual development.

5. Which TWO of the following are examples of experience-dependent brain growth?

    a) One species of geese will imprint on another individual after birth, assuming that individual is their mother, and will then follow this individual around as they mature.
    b) A human child grows up hearing German and eventually learns to speak German.
    c) Once an infant learns to crawl, they are then able to learn to walk.
    d) A person grows up playing chess and learns to be an excellent chess player.

Development 1 & 2 – Test Question

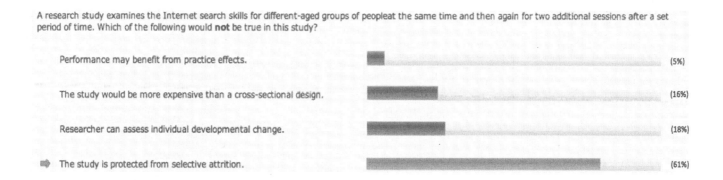

This is an actual question from the Development quiz that many students struggled with. Fortunately, we are going to go through this question together to identify what sort of errors students were making and how to avoid them in the future. To do so, we will look at each answer option individually and identify why it is correct or incorrect.

This question demonstrates what is known as a cross-sequential design, which is a combination of both longitudinal and cross-sectional designs. Remember to keep in mind that the question is looking for the UNTRUE option as we examine each option in turn.

A. We can rule out this option if we consider that practice effects **are** a limitation of longitudinal designs. Because the study is looking at Internet search skills at 3 different times, participants could be getting better at this task simply because they have been practicing their search skills as a part of the study.
B. Option B can also be ruled out by remembering that longitudinal studies are expensive and require a lot of time to complete. Since this specific study incorporates both a longitudinal and cross-sectional design, it will be more expensive than a cross-sectional design alone.
C. If you remember some of the benefits of a longitudinal study, you will remember that, because you are examining the same individuals at 3 time points, you are able to track their developmental changes. This is not true of a purely cross-sectional design. However, since this is a cross-sequential design, we are able to track developmental changes, therefore this option is incorrect.
D. We define selective attrition as a loss of participants over time leading to a fundamentally different sample being left. The study described in this question has participants return to complete Internet search tasks 3 separate times, so it is possible that there will be some selective attrition. This means that this study is NOT protected from selective attrition, indicating that this option is the correct response.

Key Terms

Active Correlations	Event-Related Potentials	Longitudinal Design
Allele	Evocative Correlations	Maturation
Babbling Principle	Experience-Dependent Growth	Monozygotic Twins
Canalization Principle	Experience-Expectant Growth	Passive Correlations
Cell Division	Extreme Behaviourist Point of View	Phenotype
Chromosome	Genes	Polygenic Trait
Co-Dominance	Genetic Point of View	Preference Method
Competence-Performance Distinction	Genotype	Range of Reaction Principle
Critical Period	Habituate	Recessive Allele
Cross-Sectional Design	Habituation Procedure	Sensitive Period
Development	Heterozygous Condition	Sex Chromosome
Dishabituate	High-Amplitude Sucking Method	Sex-Linked Inheritance
Dizygotic Twins	Homozygous Condition	Simple Dominant-Recessive Inheritance
Dominant Allele	Interactionist Perspective	
	Learning	

Development 1 & 2 – Bottleneck Concepts

Canalization Principle vs. Range of Reaction Principle
Critical Period vs. Sensitive Period
Habituation Procedure vs. Preference Method vs. High-Amplitude Sucking Method
Genotype-Environment Correlations

Canalization Principle vs. Range of Reaction Principle

The canalization and range of reaction principle highlight how both our genes and environment are influential in shaping our phenotype. Both principles suggest that our genotype establishes a range of possible phenotypic expressions. The difference is how wide the range of phenotypes are and how strongly the environment can influence the phenotypic expression. According to the canalization principle, only very extreme environmental conditions can modify the phenotypic expression set out by the genes. As a result, the range of phenotypes are limited and usually unfold in predictable ways. The canalization principle often (but not always) fits with developmental processes such as walking, teething, babbling, menstruating etc. According to this principle, children develop in similar ways at similar times unless there is extreme environmental variability, (i.e., malnutrition, abuse). Alternatively, the range of reaction principle often relates to characteristics that are very different between people (i.e., height, intelligence, language, athleticism, musical ability). The genotype passed on from your parents will dictate a wider range of possible phenotypic expressions, which can be more significantly influenced by the environment. For example, if both of your parents are professional tennis players, there is a greater likelihood that you will be athletic too. However, this likelihood comes with a range of phenotypic expression of being a moderate to advanced tennis player. If you only eat junk food and rarely go to tennis lessons, then you may express moderate tennis playing ability. However, if you eat well and go to tennis lessons regularly you may express advanced tennis playing abilities. Tennis playing ability would not fall under canalization principle because life experiences and your environment plays too big a role in your future tennis abilities. For canalization principle to take place there would have to be very little environmental influence, i.e., unless you were locked away in a dungeon you would express advanced tennis playing abilities.

Test your Understanding

1) Identify whether the scenario is best representing the canalization principle or the range of reaction principle.

a) Infants prefer their own mother's faces and voices over an unrelated female's face and voice	
b) Thomas, who grew up in Britain, learned to speak English while his twin brother John, who grew up in France, learned to speak French	
c) When Jorgie was found severely malnourished at age 15 doctors were concerned that she had not yet begun menstruating	
d) After years of swimming in the ocean, salmon return to the same rivers they were born to lay their eggs	

2) Think of an example from your own life that represent examples of the canalization principle and the range of reaction principle.

Practice case study

Rachel Berry is a child prodigy when it comes to music. At an early age, her parents have encouraged her to take music lessons. She becomes so good at music; developing "Absolute Pitch", a rare ability to name a pitch just by listening to it. It is so rare that only 1 in 10 000 people in North America have it. She earns a scholarship to spend a summer at the *China Conservatory of Music*. When she gets there, she is shocked to discover her amazing gift is fairly common among the other students. In fact, she learns that most individuals from countries that have tonal languages (languages where a change in pitch determines the meaning of the word) have Absolute Pitch.

1) From a developmental level of analysis, how could you explain this phenomenon?

2) What kind of study would you run to test this phenomenon?

3) How would you run this study?

Concept Map: Development 1 & 2

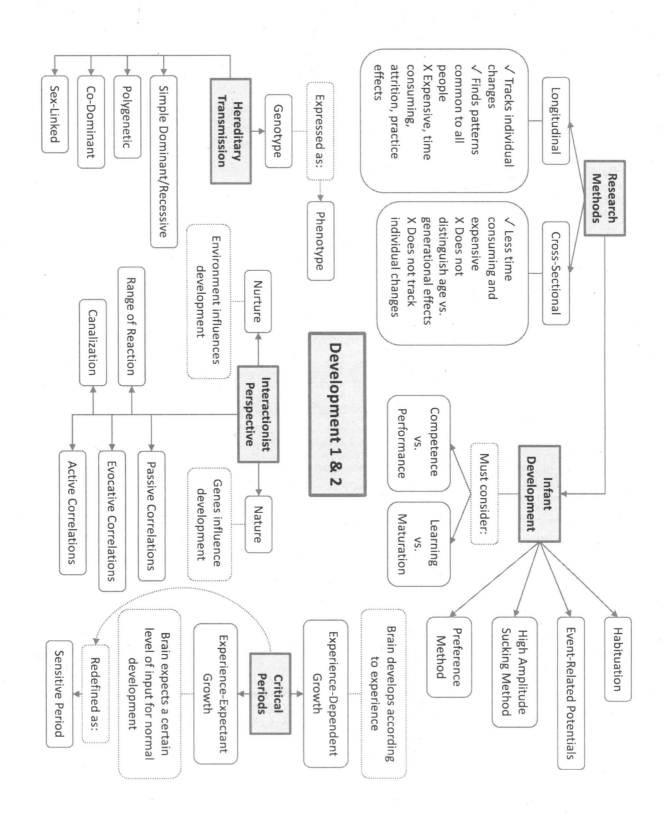

Active Correlations
Development

Allele
Development

Babbling Principle
Development

Canalization Principle
Development

Cell Division
Development

Chromosome
Development

Co-Dominance
Development

Competence-Performance Distinction
Development

A single pair of genes, one inherited from each parent. **Example:** An individual may have one allele for straight hair and one allele for curly hair. **Personal Example:**	An individual's genotype influences the kinds of environments that person seeks out. This correlation plays a larger role in development as an individual begins to make more of their own decisions. **Example:** A child with natural athletic ability may try out for sports teams and choose to play with friends who also enjoy sports. **Personal Example:**
According to this principle, the genotype restricts the phenotype for a species to a small number of possible developmental outcomes. **Example:** In the example of baby babbling, all infants babble the same sounds, regardless of what culture they are born into. **Personal Example:**	An example of the canalization principle, all infants babble the same speech sounds, regardless of which culture they are born into. Their external environment will later shape this babbling to produce different languages. **Example:** Korean infants will process both /ra/ and /la/ phonemes but lose this ability as they become adults unless they are exposed to English. **Personal Example:**
A threadlike structure made up of deoxyribonucleic acid (DNA) and consisting of many genes. A single human cell contains 46 chromosomes, 23 from each parent. **Personal Example:**	The process by which a cell reproduces, known as mitosis for autosomal cells and meiosis for sex cells. In mitosis, the resulting daughter cells will have 46 chromosomes. In meiosis, the resulting daughter cells will have 23 chromosomes. **Personal Example:**
The fact that an individual may fail a task not because they lack those cognitive abilities, but because they are unable to demonstrate those abilities. **Example:** A preverbal infant may not be able verbalize which of two pictures she prefers, but this does not mean she doesn't have a preference. **Personal Example:**	Two dominant alleles are both fully and equally expressed to produce a phenotype that is an intermediate of the two alleles. **Example:** Crossing a white flower with a red flower will produce a flower that has both white and red petals **Personal Example:**

Critical Period
Development

Cross-Sectional Design
Development

Cross-Sequential Design
Development

Development
Development

Dishabituate
Development

Dizygotic Twins
Development

Dominant Allele
Development

Event-Related Potentials
Development

A developmental research design in which different age groups are studied at the same point in time to observe age-related differences. **Example:** To study age-related differences in the ability to discriminate between two speech sounds, children between ages 2 and 10 are tested on their ability to discriminate between these two sounds. **Personal Example:**	A window of time during development in which particular environmental stimulation is necessary to see permanent changes in developmental abilities. After this time, the same environmental stimulation will not have the same developmental benefit. **Example:** A feral child who is raised for the first years of life without exposure to human language will never fully acquire the ability to produce language, even if taught later in life. **Personal Example:**
The changes and continuities that occur within an individual between conception and death. **Personal Example:**	A developmental research design that combines both longitudinal and cross-sectional designs. While it combines the strongest features of both designs, it is also the most costly and time consuming. **Personal Example:**
Twins that result from two different sperm and ova and start off as two different zygotes from conception. They are no more genetically similar than any two biological siblings. **Personal Example:**	An increase in responsiveness to a stimulus that is somehow different from the habituated stimulus. **Example:** If any infant is repeatedly shown a picture of a red ball, her interest in or response to the picture will decrease. If she is presented a picture of a blue ball and shows increased interest and response, she has dishabituated. **Personal Example:**
A method of measuring brain activity evoked by the presentation of stimuli. An electrode cap is placed on an individual's scalp to measure electrical activity across a population of neurons in the brain. **Example:** If you presented an infant with a loud noise, you might expect an ERP in the temporal lobe region, which is an area devoted to sound processing. **Personal Example:**	In a heterozygous condition, the dominant allele is expressed in the phenotype over the recessive allele. **Example:** If the allele for brown eyes is dominant over the allele for blue eyes, a heterozygous individual will have brown eyes. **Personal Example:**

Evocative Correlations
Development

Experience-Dependent Growth
Development

Experience-Expectant Growth
Development

Extreme Behaviourist Point of View
Development

Genes
Development

Genetic Point of View
Development

Genotype
Development

Habituate
Development

The unique way in which the brain develops according to personal experiences. This type of brain growth is specific to each individual. **Example:** A Braille reader will have a specialized area in their brain that responds to specified somatosensory stimulation of the fingertips, which non-Braille readers will lack. **Personal Example:**	In this correlation, traits that an individual has inherited through genes influence how others in their environment behave towards that individual. **Example:** A child who has a naturally happy disposition would cause other people to smile and be happy around that child. **Personal Example:**
The view that nurture is all-important in development and that development is largely independent of genetics. **Example:** The behaviourist Watson suggested that with proper environmental control and training, any individual could become a doctor, musician or criminal, regardless of their genetics. **Personal Example:**	Brain growth that is dependent on a certain amount of environmental input in order to develop properly. **Example:** The brain relies on a certain, ordinary amount of visual input for the visual cortex to develop properly. **Personal Example:**
The opposite extreme to the behaviourist point of view, it is the view that who a person becomes is largely predetermined by genetics with little to no environmental influence. **Example:** In this view, a child with intelligent, successful parents will necessarily become intelligent and successful. **Personal Example:**	Segments of DNA that provide the chemical code for development. **Personal Example:**
A decrease in the responsiveness to a stimulus following its repeated presentation. **Example:** If an infant is presented a picture of a red ball, they will initially show interest. When repeatedly shown the ball, the infant's response will decrease. **Personal Example:**	An individual's roughly 30,000 to 40,000 inherited genes. **Example:** Brent has one recessive allele for blue eyes and one dominant allele for brown eyes at the eye colour locus. **Personal Example:**

Habituation Procedure
Development

Heterozygous Condition
Development

High-Amplitude Sucking Method
Development

Homozygous Condition
Development

Interactionist Perspective
Development

Learning
Development

Longitudinal Design
Development

Maturation
Development

When two alleles at a locus are different, and the dominant allele is expressed over the recessive allele. **Example:** If the allele for brown eyes is dominant and the allele for blue eyes is recessive, the heterozygous individual will have brown eyes. **Personal Example:**	A technique designed to determine whether an infant can detect the difference between two stimuli. **Example:** In determining if an infant can tell the difference between the sounds /ra/ and /la/, a researcher would repeatedly present the /ra/ sound to the infant until they habituate. She will then present the /la/ sound. If the infant's response increases to /la/, it indicates that infant can discriminate between the two. **Personal Example:**
When two alleles at a locus have the same effect on the phenotype. **Example:** An individual who has two recessive alleles for blue eyes will have blue eyes. **Personal Example:**	A technique designed to assess what an infant likes and dislikes using the fact that infants can control their sucking behaviour to influence the presentation of a stimulus. **Personal Example:**
Acquiring neuronal representations of new information which lead to permanent changes in thoughts and behaviours as a result of experiences. **Example:** An individual is likely to automatically look both ways before crossing the street as she was taught to do so by her parents when she was young. **Personal Example:**	The view that most developmental changes reflect the interaction of maturation and learning or between genetics and the environment. **Example:** This view would emphasize the fact that both the cognitive capacity to speak and exposure to human language are important for language development. **Personal Example:**
The biologically timed unfolding of changes within the individual according to that individual's genetic plans. **Example:** If an individual grows up in a healthy environment, he or she is likely to start puberty at a predetermined age based on genetics. **Personal Example:**	A developmental research design in which the same individuals are studied repeatedly over a subset of their lifespan. **Example:** In studying age-related differences in speech sound discrimination ability, the same group of individuals are studied each year from the age of 2 to 10 years old. **Personal Example:**

Monozygotic Twins
Development

Passive Correlations
Development

Phenotype
Development

Polygenic Trait
Development

Preference Method
Development

Range of Reaction Principle
Development

Recessive Allele
Development

Sensitive Period
Development

The environment that your parents raise you in is influenced by their own genes, therefore this environment will likely complement your own genes. **Example:** A couple who are both naturally athletic may choose to raise their child in an environment with toys and games that promote hand-eye coordination and reflexes. **Personal Example:**	Genetically identical individuals who originate from the same sperm and ovum and formed one zygote, then split into two separate zygotes later in development *in utero*. **Personal Example:**
When multiple genes are involved in the expression of a trait. **Example:** Traits such as height and weight are determined by the interaction of multiple genes. **Personal Example:**	The expression of an individual's genotype in terms of observable characteristics. **Example:** Brent has one dominant allele for brown eyes and one recessive allele for blue eyes (genotype), which is expressed in the phenotype of brown eyes. **Personal Example:**
An individual genotype establishes a range of possible developmental outcomes to different kinds of life experiences. **Example:** Your final height is determined by a number of environmental factors but the potential range of your height across various environments is determined by genetic factors. **Personal Example:**	A method of measuring what an infant likes and dislikes. An infant is put into a looking chamber to simultaneously look at two stimuli and the researcher observes whether the infant is directing more attention to one stimulus. **Personal Example:**
This term has come to replace the term critical period. It captures the idea that the brain does maintain some residual capacity for change and growth into adulthood and so there is greater flexibility in the timing and type of stimulation that are required for normal development. **Personal Example:**	In a heterozygous condition, the allele that is not expressed in the phenotype. This allele is; however, still heritable. **Personal Example:**

Sex Chromosome
Development

Sex-Linked Inheritance
Development

Simple Dominant-Recessive Inheritance
Development

The pattern of inheritance that involves genes expressed on the X chromosome. This results in traits more often being expressed in males than in females.
Example: A recessive gene expressed on the X chromosome causes colour blindness.
Personal Example:

The 23rd pair of human chromosomes, which determine a person's sex. A female will carry two X chromosomes and a male will carry an X and a Y chromosome. These chromosomes are heritable.
Personal Example:

A pattern of inheritance in which the expression of a trait is determined by a single pair of alleles. A heterozygote and a homozygous-dominant individual will express the dominant phenotype, while a homozygous recessive individual will express the recessive phenotype.
Example: The type of earwax you have is determined by variation at a single gene.
Personal Example:

Evolution 1 & 2

"It is not the strongest of the species that survives, nor the most intelligent... it is the one that is most adaptable to change."
- Charles Darwin, the author of the Theory of Evolution by Natural Selection

What a Girl Wants

As if men didn't have a hard enough time figuring out what women want; it turns out that a woman's preference in men can change depending on where she is in her reproductive cycle. Evolutionary psychologist Steven Gangestad and colleagues examined women's mate preferences and discovered that when women are ovulating (able to get pregnant), they were significantly more attracted to the masculine-looking, athletic type – the rugged guy. However, when women were not ovulating and not in their fertile phase, they actually preferred men that had more feminine facial features and a kinder disposition – the nice guy. When Gangestad asked what kind of relationship the women wanted to have with presented male faces, they found that women preferred the masculine-looking men more for short-term "hook-ups" rather than long-term relationships. As with nearly everything in our human nature, this proximate change in preference can be ultimately explained by evolutionary theory. When fertile, women are driven to mate with a man that is masculine as this quality is a strong indicator of good genes for their future children. However, when not fertile, women prefer the more feminine, nice guy as this quality is more indicative of someone who will care for you and your offspring. The woman's driving force behind her change in mate preference is so that her offspring has the best chance at surviving, reproducing and ultimately passing on her genes to consecutive generations. See, nice guys don't always finish last...they just have to time their flirt game right!

What do you think of this evolutionary analysis of human reproductive behaviour? Does it make a post-hoc or a priori prediction? Does it justify or explain trends in human behaviour?

Gangestad, S. W., Simpson, J. A., Cousins, A. J., Garver-Apgar, C. E., & Christensen, P. N. (2004). Women's preferences for male behavioral displays change across the menstrual cycle. *Psychological Science*, *15*(3), 203-207.

Weekly Checklist:
- ☐ **Web modules to watch: Evolution 1 & 2**
- ☐ **Readings: Chapter 2**
- ☐ **Pre-Quiz & Quiz 2**

Upper Year Courses
If you enjoyed the content of this week's module, consider taking the following upper year courses:
- PNB 2XC3: Animal Behaviour and Evolution
- Psych 3EVS: Evolution and Mental Health
- Psych 3SE3: Comparative Social Evolution

Evolution 1 – Outline

Unit 1: Introduction to Adaptations

Evolution is the unifying theory of the biological sciences—including psychology.

Unit 2: Adaptations

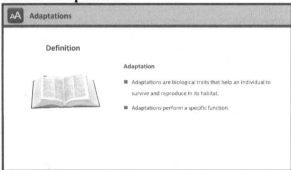

Adaptations are functional traits or characteristics that help an individual survive and reproduce in their environment.

Human eye:

Raccoons:

Bats:

Mental activities, such as memory encoding, can also serve adaptive functions.

Unit 3: Evolution by Natural Selection

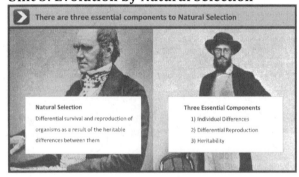

Adaptations arise through the three components of natural selection.
Who?
Natural selection (NS):

1) Individual Differences

2) Differential Reproduction

3) Heritability

Characteristics that help an individual survive and reproduce are selectively transmitted to consecutive generations.

_____
_____
_____
_____
_____
_____
_____
_____
_____

Unit 4: Natural Selection in the Wild

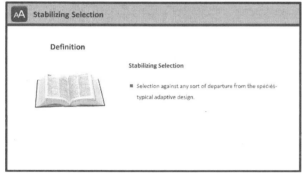

Stabilizing selection selects against any traits that are dissimilar from species-typical adaptive design.

_____
_____
_____
_____
_____

<u>Significant environmental change?</u>

_____
_____
_____

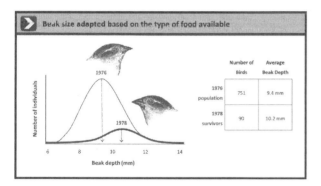

Darwin's finches are an example of rapid evolutionary change following significant environmental change.

_____
_____
_____
_____
_____

<u>Finches: Three requirements for NS to occur?</u>

_____
_____
_____
_____

Observable evolutionary change is most often very subtle.

_____
_____

_____
_____
_____
_____

Unit 5: Reproductive Success = Fitness

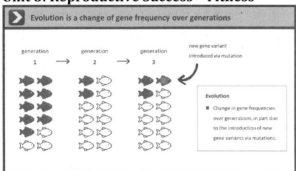

Fitness = one's ability to reproduce and leave copies of their genes in subsequent generations, relative to another individual.

_____
_____
_____
_____
_____
_____
_____

Fitness = competition between genotypes:
_____
_____

Unit 6: Sexual Selection

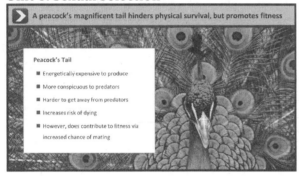

Sexual selection is a type of natural selection that selects for behaviours and traits that increase the likelihood of reproducing.

_____
_____
_____
_____
_____
_____
_____
_____
_____

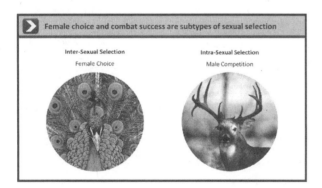

Being chosen by a female and success in combat are two modes of sexual selection.

_____
_____
_____

1) Female choice: _____
_____

2) Success in combat: _____
_____
_____

Signs of sexually selected traits:

1) Differs between the sexes: _____
_____
_____

2) Specific to breeding season: _____
_____
_____
_____

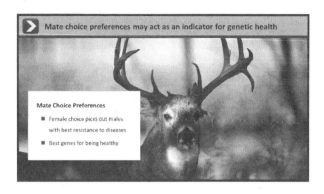

Females are attracted to males whose traits convey that their offspring will be healthy and strong.

Eyespots and symmetry experiment:

Purpose of female choice:

Humans?

Unit 7: Species-Typical Behaviour and the Comparative Approach

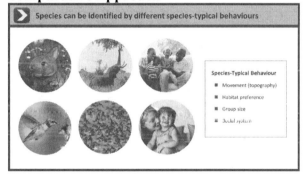

Behaviours have also evolved to serve adaptive functions for individual species.

Sandpiper example:

Species-typical behaviour (4):

By selectively breeding animals with certain extreme behaviours, behavioural geneticists can observe the evolution of behaviours.

Short generation times:

Evolution 1 – Courseware Exercise

Now that you've learned a bit about how natural selection operates in the wild, you can see how the same process that selected for beak size among Darwin's finches could also select for and preserve adaptive mechanisms in the brain, such as behaviour and emotion. For example, to test if a trait such as red eyes will be naturally selected for, experimenters can selectively breed animals that have red eyes for several generations. This will result in a final population of individuals with only red eyes. Experimenters can then allow their red-eyed population to breed with non-modified animals from a particular environment. If the resulting generations continue to show a large number of red-eyed individuals, this would suggest that the red-eye trait may be adaptive in the environment being tested.

1. Design an experiment that tests whether anger is an adaptive trait.

2. What species would you use as your participants? Why?

3. If the results of your experiment support the theory that anger is an adaptive trait, what are some reasons that anger may have been selected for? What adaptive problems would it solve?

4. Can you think of any other emotions that have an adaptive origin? What adaptive problems do they solve?

5. Although a peacock's feathers solve the adaptive problem of attracting a mate, they also make the peacock more conspicuous to predators. What physical characteristic or behaviour do humans possess that attract mates, but may also carry risks? If you can't think of any, you can do a quick search on 'costly signalling in humans'.

Evolution 1 – Review Questions

1. Which of the following is NOT an example of adaptations?
   a) Some species of chameleon are able to change the colour of their skin in order to send signals and camouflage.
   b) In Zambia, there has been a 30% increase in the size of male elephants' tusks due to the rise in poaching.
   c) Camels, which live in the desert, are able to withstand long periods of time without ingesting water.
   d) Some species of birds have the ability to see into the ultraviolet spectrum, allowing them to easily detect fruit.

2. Which of the following can be considered natural selection?
   a) A species of moth can be one of three colours: brown, white and yellow. They live in a habitat with many trees that have either brown or white trunks. The yellow moths are not able to hide from predators among the trees, and eventually no yellow moths are being born.
   b) A turtle is born with the ability to move faster than the other turtles in its population. This turtle is better at obtaining food and evading predators, and has many more offspring than other turtles.
   c) A small sub-group of fish got separated from the rest of their population due to a disruption in their stream of water. This small sub-group contained mostly orange fish, while the larger population contained an even amount of orange and red fish. Many generations later, the offspring of this subgroup now contains only orange fish.
   d) The domestication of horses has led to several different breeds of horse today, bred for different purpose.

3. Which of the following best exemplifies fitness in evolutionary terms?
   a) An individual's ability to survive compared to other individuals.
   b) An individual's ability to survive and reproduce, compared to other individuals.
   c) A genotype's ability to reproduce itself, compared to other genotypes.
   d) The evolution of a new genotype that promotes survival, compared to other genotypes.

4. Which of the following scenarios is least likely to occur according to sexual selection?
   a) Male rock sparrows compete in song to attract females; females prefer and mate with males who sing high pitched, slow songs.
   b) While ovulating, women prefer to mate with a low-pitched, masculine sounding man.
   c) Male giraffes fight for females by swinging their elongated necks at each other; after watching the performance, the female will assert her dominance over the giraffe that is most injured.
   d) Male Northern elephant seals engage in violent fights to establish dominance, the successful male copulates with harems of females, while unsuccessful males are unlikely to mate at all.

Evolution 2 – Outline

Unit 1: Introduction to Social Behaviours

Many social animals appear to help others at a cost to themselves; however, even this behaviour is adaptive.

Honey bees: _____

Ground squirrels: _____

Humans: _____

Selfish gene? _____
_____

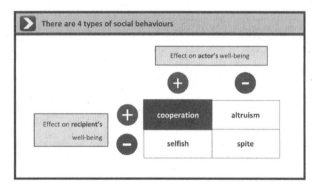

There are four types of social behaviours that individuals can engage in: cooperation, selfishness, altruism and spite.

_____
_____
_____
_____
_____
_____
_____
_____
_____
_____

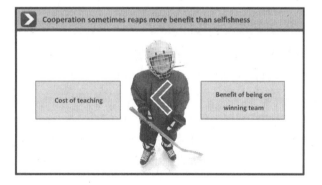

Cost to you < Benefit of your action

_____
_____
_____
_____
_____
_____
_____
_____
_____
_____
_____

Unit 2: Group Selection

For geese, foraging in groups is advantageous to survival and consequently supports future reproduction.

_____
_____
_____
_____
_____
_____
_____
_____
_____
_____

Foraging-vigilance trade-off:

_____
_____
_____
_____
_____
_____
_____
_____
_____
_____
_____

Unit 3: Inclusive Fitness

Altruistic genes can be adaptive if they helped identical copies of themselves continue onto the next generation.

Eusocial hymenoptera (honey bee):

_____
_____
_____

W. D. Hamilton (1960s):

_____
_____
_____
_____

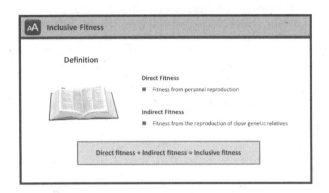

Indirect fitness helps explain the evolution of altruism; NS favours actions that increase the reproductive success of genetic relatives.

Direct fitness:

Indirect fitness:

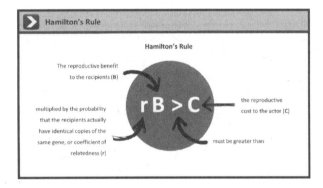

Summarizing inclusive fitness, Hamilton's Rule predicts that an altruistic act is favourable (adaptive) when rB > C.

r:

B:

C:

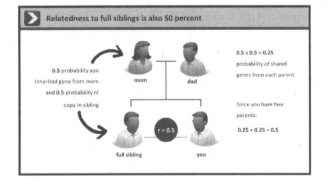

The 'r' value quantifies the genetic relatedness between the actor and the recipient.

Relatedness:

Parents:

Siblings:

Half sibling:
Aunt/Uncle:
First cousin:

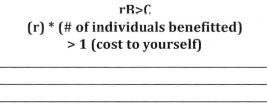

$rB > C$
(r) * (# of individuals benefitted)
> 1 (cost to yourself)

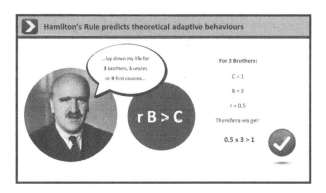

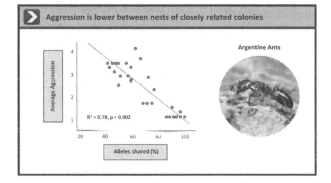

Aggression is low within hymenoptera colonies because members are highly interrelated.

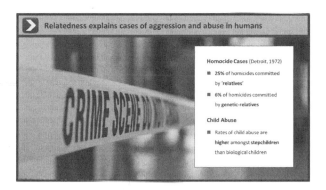

Genetic relatives (high r) are less likely to be victims of abuse than those with lower or no relatedness to the perpetrator.

Unit 4: Kin Recognition

Individuals use kin recognition cues to prevent inbreeding, in addition to targeting altruism and social behaviours towards relatives.

Neighbours:

Mother/Co-residence:

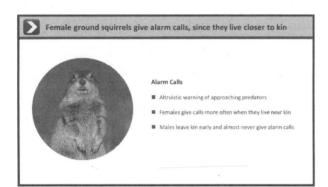

Female Belding Ground Squirrels give alarm calls more often than males.

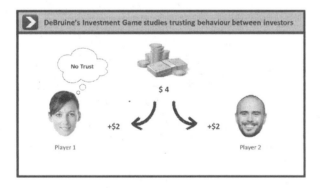

DeBruine's "Investment Game" evaluates the relationship between trust/selfish behaviour and facial resemblance.

P1 & P2 maximize gains?

P1 will be more trusting of:

71

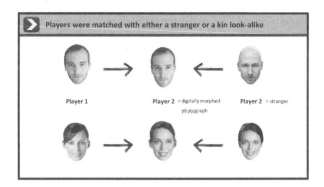

As predicted by inclusive fitness theory, we produce more prosocial behaviours to individuals who resemble us, i.e., potential kin.

_____
_____
_____
_____
_____
_____
_____
_____
_____
_____

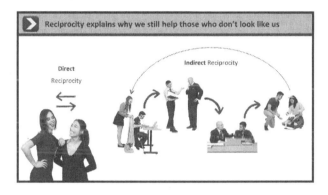

Direct and indirect reciprocity provide an evolutionary explanation for why we act altruistically towards non-kin.

_____
_____

Direct reciprocity: _____
_____

Indirect reciprocity: _____
_____
_____
_____

Evolution 2 – Courseware Exercise

1. In this module, you've learned about a variety of kin identification mechanisms. What is the importance of being able to recognize one's kin?

___

2. For each of the following kin recognition mechanisms, briefly define the mechanism, list a human example and describe the advantages and disadvantages of using that mechanism to identify kin.

Neighbours:
Example:

Advantages:

Disadvantages:

Association with Mother:
Example:

Advantages:

Disadvantages:

Co-Residence with Other Children:
Example:

Advantages:

Disadvantages:

Physical Resemblance:
Example:

Advantages:

Disadvantages:

Evolution 2 – Review Questions

1. Which of the following best exemplifies altruism?
    a) Jamie helps a member of her band learn a song on guitar.
    b) Samantha tutors underprivileged children and earns community service credit.
    c) Chris gives his lunch to his neighbour's child Tim when Tim drops his lunch on the ground.
    d) James offers to help a girl he likes move into her new apartment, and makes a good impression on her.

2. All of the following are true about inclusive fitness, EXCEPT:
    a) It provides an evolutionary explanation for nepotism.
    b) A child-less vervet monkey (in its reproductive prime) should always save herself due to the opportunity for her to have future kin with high relatedness.
    c) It explains why in eusocial hymenoptera, bees are willing to work their whole lives without a chance at reproduction.
    d) It is an important component to consider in Hamilton's rule.

3. You have just learned that there is about to be a flash flood in your city. You can only make one phone call before you must evacuate. According to Hamilton's rule, whom should you call?
    a) Your aunt and her four children (your cousins) who are guaranteed to escape if you call them.
    b) Your brother and his two children (your niece and nephew) who all have a 50/50 chance at escape if you call them.
    c) Your grandma, who is babysitting two of your cousins, and has a 0.8 probability of escape if you call them.
    d) Your sister at the zoo with three of your cousins, who are guaranteed to escape if you call them.

4. Which of the following statements is true?
    a) Altruism involves no benefit to inclusive fitness or reciprocity.
    b) Hamilton's rule examines the cost of an action multiplied by the likelihood of an individual carrying your genes, and compares this with the benefit that individual would receive from your sacrifice.
    c) Female ground squirrels make alarm calls more frequently when they live near kin; this is an example of selfishness, as non-relatives do not receive the same benefit from that individual.
    d) Studies of violence among humans supports the theory of inclusive fitness.

Evolution 1 & 2 – Test Question

In a population of prairie dogs, the males from a certain littler never stray from their nest. In fact, they establish their own nests to raise their offspring in close to the one they themselves were raised in. On the other hand, females travel far away from the nest they were born in to search for a male to mate with. Which of the following is most correct?

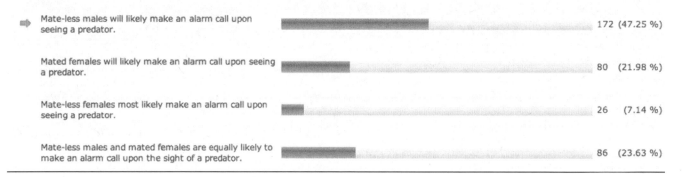

- ➡ Mate-less males will likely make an alarm call upon seeing a predator. — 172 (47.25 %)
- Mated females will likely make an alarm call upon seeing a predator. — 80 (21.98 %)
- Mate-less females most likely make an alarm call upon seeing a predator. — 26 (7.14 %)
- Mate-less males and mated females are equally likely to make an alarm call upon the sight of a predator. — 86 (23.63 %)

This is an actual question from the Evolution quiz that many students struggled with. Fortunately, we are going to go through this question together to identify what sort of errors students were making and how to avoid them in the future. To do so, we will look at each answer option individually and identify why it is correct or incorrect.

In this scenario, it is important to remember that making an alarm call may draw the predator's attention to the actor, so in order for a prairie dog to do this, it would have to be highly beneficial to many individuals that are highly related to that dog.

A. This option suggests that a mate-less male will likely make an alarm call. Notice that males stay close to their birth nests, therefore when the males mate, their offspring are mostly related. If a mate-less male makes an alarm call near his nest, it is likely that he will be warning/protecting his relatives from an oncoming threat. The benefit to helping his relatives survive is greater than the cost to himself, consequently adhering to Hamilton's rule. This makes option A the correct response.
B. In this option, you should remember that the female's only relatives in the nest would be any offspring she might have. She is not related to any other prairie dogs in the nest so she is unlikely to make an alarm call; it would be better to protect her own offspring.
C. This option is similar to option B except this individual is even less likely to make an alarm call because she will not even have a mate or offspring to risk protecting by making an alarm call.
D. We previously determined that a mate-less male is more likely to make an alarm call to benefit his many relatives than will a mated female. As a result we can rule out this answer.

Key Terms

Adaptation	Darwinian Fitness	Mate Choice
Adaptationist Perspective	Direct Fitness	Mate Competition
Altruism	Hamilton's Rule	Natural Selection
Behavioural Genetics	Inclusive Fitness	Phenotypic Matching
Coefficient of Relatedness	Indirect Fitness	Sexual Selection
Cooperation	Kin Recognition	Stabilizing Selection

Evolution 1 & 2 – Bottleneck Concepts

Altruism
Inclusive Fitness & Hamilton's Rule
Natural Selection vs. Sexual Selection
Fitness vs. Adaptation

Inclusive Fitness & Hamilton's Rule

Humans like to believe that we help our family members out of the kindness of our hearts. However, social behaviours almost only evolve if they enhance our fitness. Adaptations evolve if they enhance our inclusive fitness, which is the sum of our direct fitness and indirect fitness. Direct fitness is our personal reproductive success, which includes our ability to survive in order to reproduce. However, indirect fitness refers to our relatives surviving and reproducing to pass on our shared genes to their offspring. Let's consider the movie *Taken* starring Liam Neeson who takes dangerous risks to try to save his kidnapped daughter, played by Maggie Grace. Liam's direct fitness refers to his personal ability to survive this experience and reproduce to have a child in the future. Liam's indirect fitness refers to the survival of his daughter, so she can reproduce and pass on her genes in the future. Given that 50% of Liam's genes are in his daughter, Liam has an interest in saving his daughter's life so there is a chance that she can reproduce and pass on 25% of his genes to a subsequent generation. By acting altruistically to save Maggie, Liam can indirectly increase his own fitness. To calculate whether Liam should risk his own life to save his daughter's, we can use Hamilton's Rule: $rB>C$. 'r' relates to the genetic relatedness the actor has to the person they want to help, i.e., Liam's relationship to his daughter which is $r = 0.5$. 'B' relates to the reproductive benefit that the person who gets saved (Maggie) will receive—we use an arbitrary fitness point of $B = 1$ to account for the one person he is saving (Maggie). 'C' relates to the cost the actor is taking to help the recipient; we use an arbitrary number $C = 1$ to represent Liam giving up all of his fitness potential. The relatedness value of Maggie ($r = 0.5$) multiplied by the benefit to Maggie's fitness ($B = 1$) must be larger than the cost to Liam ($C = 1$) for Liam to act altruistically. Given that $0.5*1 = 0.5$ and 0.5 is less than 1, Liam should not have risked his life to save his daughter. However, while this is not considered via Hamilton's Rule, it's important to consider that Liam is older and unlikely to have more children. Therefore, the fitness cost to himself may actually be lower than the cost presented via Hamilton's Rule. Either way, the movie *Taken* is so far from reality, not following Hamilton's Rule is the least of its worries.

Test your Understanding

1) Who should Liam Neeson save in order to make it worth it to behave altruistically?
    a) His step-daughter, son and daughter
    b) His half-sister and three cousins
    c) His two sisters and daughter
    d) His wife and two daughters
    e) B and C

2) By making reference to inclusive fitness, what is one reason that humans live longer than other species of mammals where the grandparent has no role in child rearing?

Practice case study

The zombie apocalypse is upon us. There are only a few humans left in the world and you are one of them! Zombies have overrun the neighbouring shelter and you can only save one of the following people. You must choose between your sister, a pregnant woman, a super model, or your friend who saved you from being eaten by a zombie last week.

1) How would you go about making this decision?

2) What might be some pros and cons of saving each person?

3) Using evolutionary theory, which concepts could you apply to support your decision to save any of these people?

Over the next 200 years, three more zombie apocalypses occur and there are noticeable differences in the human species that have survived. Humans are now taller, leaner, have highly symmetrical faces, and are fast runners.

4) Why did these changes in the human species occur?

5) Using your knowledge of natural selection and Darwinian fitness, explain this observation.

Concept Map: Evolution 1 & 2

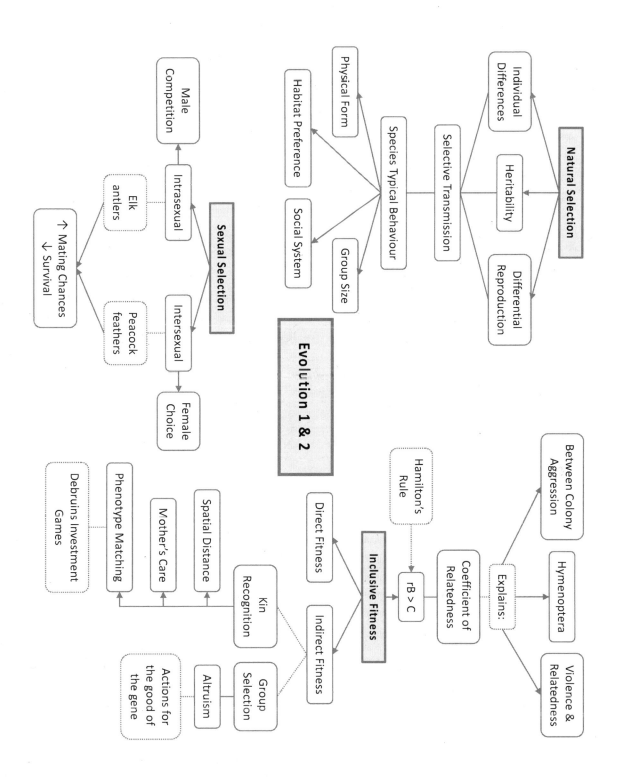

Adaptation
Evolution

Adaptationist Perspective
Evolution

Altruism
Evolution

Behavioural Genetics
Evolution

Coefficient of Relatedness
Evolution

Cooperation
Evolution

Darwinian Fitness
Evolution

Direct Fitness
Evolution

A label to describe how hypotheses about adaptive functions guide scientists' investigations. **Example:** A scientist who wants to study colour perception in humans may research why humans needed to distinguish specific colours during their evolutionary history. **Personal Example:**	Biological traits or characteristics that help an individual survive and reproduce in their habitat. Each adaptation performs a specific function. **Example:** An owl's wide eyes are an adaptation to allow as much as light as possible into the retina during the night. **Personal Example:**
The study of the evolution of genes that code for behavioural traits, rather than physical traits. **Example:** In experiments with fruit flies, it is possible to determine that aggressive behaviour evolves by selectively breeding aggressive individuals only to eventually see a change towards more aggressive behaviour in the population. **Personal Example:**	A social behaviour in which an actor incurs a cost in order to provide a benefit to a recipient. **Example:** When you give money to your friend for lunch, you are performing an altruistic behaviour by incurring a cost to provide a benefit to your friend. **Personal Example:**
According to evolutionary theory, it is the process of an actor working with a recipient to help both themselves and the recipient for personal gain. **Example:** You may help classmates study for an exam so that you can also get a higher grade. **Personal Example:**	Referred to as "r", the mathematic term in Hamilton's Rule that represents the probability that an actor and recipient share the gene in question. **Example:** The probability that you and your mother will share any gene in question is 0.5 (r). This is because you inherit half of your genes from your mother and half from your father. **Personal Example:**
An individual's genetic contribution to the next generation through personal reproduction. **Personal Example:**	The average reproductive success of a genotype relative to alternative genotypes. **Example:** If one genotype leads to brighter colouring in a male bird, relative to another genotype, the bird with the genotype leading to brighter colouring may have a better chance at finding a mate and passing this genotype on to the next generation. **Personal Example:**

Hamilton's Rule
Evolution

Inclusive Fitness
Evolution

Indirect Fitness
Evolution

Kin Recognition
Evolution

Mate Choice
Evolution

Mate Competition
Evolution

Natural Selection
Evolution

Phenotypic Matching
Evolution

Fitness from both direct and indirect sources, including fitness from personal reproduction and the reproduction of close genetic relatives. **Personal Example:**	An equation, which predicts when altruistic behaviour will be performed, defined by the inequality rB>C (benefit to recipient*coefficient of relatedness > cost to altruist). **Example:** According to Hamilton's rule, you would be willing to sacrifice your life for 3 siblings (0.5*3>1) but not for 2 (0.5*2=1) siblings. **Personal Example:**
The ability to recognize the relatedness of other members of a species (through aspects such as location or behavioural activity) and perform altruistic acts accordingly. **Example:** You know you're related to your younger brother because you've seen your mother care for him from birth. **Personal Example:**	An individual's genetic contribution to the next generation through the reproduction of close genetic relatives. **Example:** A mother may help to raise her daughter's children to ensure that the genes of those children survive and reproduce. **Personal Example:**
A subtype of sexual selection in which success in combat with opponents of the same sex drives selection of a particular trait. **Example:** Male elk have antlers that they use to fight other elk; the strongest males will out-survive their opponents to mate and pass their genes on to the next generation. **Personal Example:**	A subtype of sexual selection in which the preference of the opposite sex drives selection of a trait. **Example:** Peahens (female) prefer peacocks (male) whose tails are symmetrical and have more eyespots. Males with these tails are more likely to be chosen by these females to mate and pass on their genes to the next generation. **Personal Example:**
An evaluation of the relatedness between individuals based on an assessment of phenotypic similarity. **Example:** Lisa DeBruine found that graduate students were more trusting of those who resembled themselves. **Personal Example:**	Differential survival and reproduction as a result of the heritable differences between organisms. It requires individual differences within a population, differential reproduction between individuals within that population, and heritability of the traits selected for. **Personal Example:**

Sexual Selection
Evolution

Stabilizing Selection
Evolution

Selection that acts against any sort of departure from the species-typical adaptive design. **Example:** Average neck length in giraffes will remain long over generations because it is adaptive as long as their food is available on the tops of tall trees. **Personal Example:**	The component of natural selection that acts on traits that influence an organism's ability to obtain a mate. **Example:** Peacock tails evolved even though they elevate chances of death because females prefer to mate with peacocks with more elaborate tails. **Personal Example:**

Neuroscience 1

"A typical neuron makes about ten thousand connections to neighboring neurons. Given the billions of neurons, this means there are as many connections in a single cubic centimeter of brain tissue as there are stars in the Milky Way Galaxy."
- David Eagleman, American neuroscientist and New York Times bestselling author

Cannabis and the Brain

Cannabis is the most commonly used drug in Canada. With the recent legalization, it is important to explore the neuroscience of Cannabis and how it produces behaviour change. The endocannabinoid (EC) system of the brain processes a molecule called anandamide which binds to cannabinoid receptors (CB1) on neuronal synapses throughout the brain. Naturally occurring anandamide helps to regulate mood, memory, appetite, pain, cognition and emotions. The active ingredient of cannabis, THC, mimics anandamide and also binds to CB1 receptors. When THC binds to CB1 receptors, it reduces the function of an enzyme that helps the neuron depolarize and trigger action potentials. As a result, the neuron is less excitable which ultimately influences the functionality in a variety of brain areas with CB1 receptors, including areas associated with attention, memory, executive function, and hunger. The effects of cannabis may include shortened attention, impaired memory, altered judgment, and increased appetite. Over prolonged cannabis use, CB1 receptors can downregulate. There are open questions on how age, dosage and duration may play into these long-term effects.

In almost every movie with Seth Rogen, smoking cannabis is portrayed as fun and relaxing. How does cannabis act to create these feelings? Like most recreational drugs, cannabis acts via a rewards circuit that uses the neurotransmitter dopamine which controls brain reward centers. THC blocks the action of an inhibitory neurotransmitter, GABA, which means GABA cannot regulate the amount of dopamine released. As a result, an excess of dopamine is processed which is associated with increased feelings of euphoria and relaxation. Over time, the brain requires more cannabis to bring about the same surge in dopamine. As a result, users consume more to achieve the same high. Upon quitting, users may experience withdrawal where dopamine levels fall below normal levels, resulting in the opposite of pleasure and relaxation—anxiety, anguish and depressive symptoms. Emerging research suggests that early and regular cannabis use is associated with an increased risk of mental illness onset and worsening prognosis. As with all things in life, it is important to educate yourself on the risks associated with alcohol and drug use and always reach out for support if needed.

If you or a friend is in need of support, contact the Student Wellness Center at 905-525-9140 ext. 27700 or visit PGCLL 210/201.

Weekly Checklist:
- ☐ Web modules to watch: Neuroscience 1
- ☐ Readings: Chapter 3
- ☐ Pre-Quiz & Quiz 3

Upper Year Courses:
If you enjoyed the content of this week's module, consider taking the following upper year course:
- Neurosci 3SN3: Neural Circuits

Neuroscience 1 – Outline

Unit 1: Introduction to Neuroscience

Descartes' dualistic perspective:

Neuroscience studies how the biological nervous system produces mental processes.

Unit 2: The Neuron

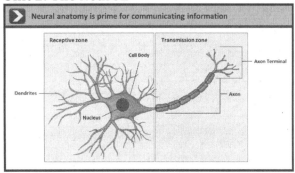

Neurons are communication cells; the receptive zone receives neural signals and the transmission zone passes them on to other cells.

Receptive zone & dendrites:

Transmission zone & the axon:

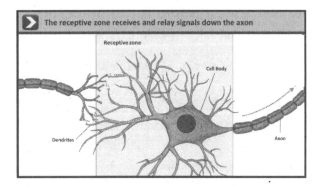

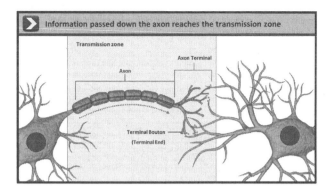

The neural signal is transmitted from the axon to its terminal boutons, and further to the receptive zone (dendrites) of nearby neurons.

Glial cells:

Neural communication requires that certain ions move across the cell membrane depending on the charge of the cell.

Selective permeability:

Protein channels:

Resting potential (-70 mv):

Unit 3: The Action Potential

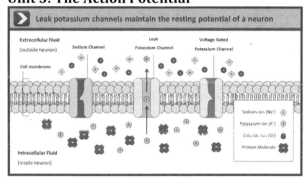

Electrostatic force (Chloride):

Diffusion (Sodium):

Movement of potassium ions (2):

1) Leaky K+ channel:

2) Voltage gated K+ channel:

An action potential is an all-or-nothing event.

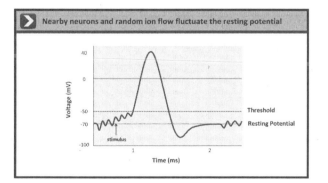

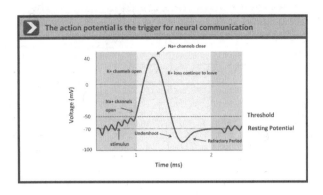

Upon reaching threshold, an action potential will be triggered and continue until completion.

The rise:
Na+ influx? Channel? Force?

K+ outflux? Channel? Force?

During the refractory period, the neuron is unable to fire another action potential until the cell becomes more positive

Peak at +40 mV? VG-Na+ channel?

The fall:
K+ fast outflux? Overshoot towards -100 mV?

The sodium-potassium pump helps to maintain ion balance and restore resting potential following an action potential.

Speed and energy?

Role:

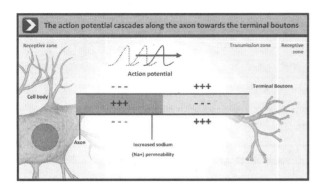

Action potentials cascade via saltatory conduction to neighbouring neurons' dendrites.

Myelin:

Saltatory conduction:

Nodes of Ranvier:

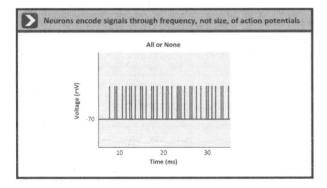

The frequency and pattern of action potentials is what communicates the intended neural message.

Strong/weak signal?

Unit 4: The Synapse

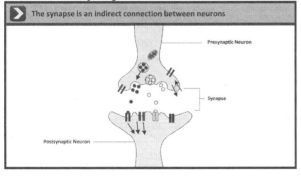

Neurotransmitters from the presynaptic neuron help facilitate the relay of a signal to the receptors on the post-synaptic neuron.

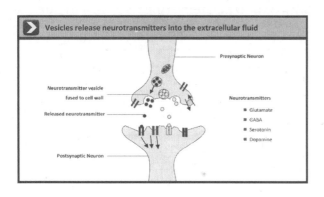

There are hundreds of neurotransmitters—each capable of many varied functions.

1) Vesicles:

2) Synaptic cleft:

3) Receptors:

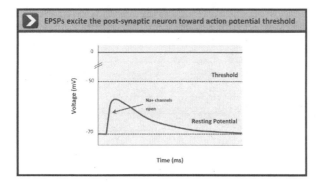

An EPSP depolarizes the neuron making it more positive and closer to firing threshold.

Na+ influx:

Depolarization:

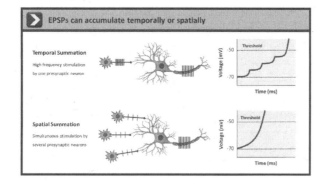

There are two ways that single EPSPs can be summed in order to trigger an action potential.

1) Temporal summation:

2) Spatial summation:

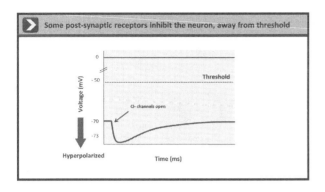

IPSPs help streamline neural signals to ensure the appropriate signals are transmitted.
_____
_____

Cl- influx: _____
_____

Hyperpolarization: _____
_____
_____

Unit 5: Neural Development

Following conception, the brain develops dramatically into the first few years of life.
_____
_____
_____
_____
_____

Four stages of neural development:
1) Neurogenesis
2) Migration
3) Differentiation
4) Maturation

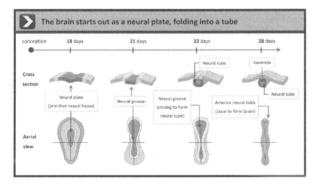

Neurogenesis is the growth and development of the nervous system.

18 days: _____

21 days: _____

28 days: _____

Week 20: _____

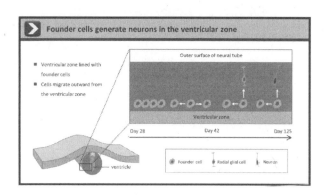

The ventricular zone within the neural tube is lined with founder cells.

Symmetrical division:

Asymmetrical division:

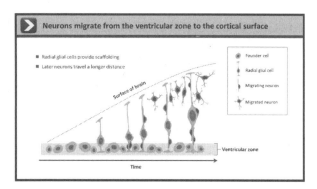

Neurons migrate from the inside out.
Timeline:

Radial glial cells:

Neuronal differentiation is determined by both genetics and experience.

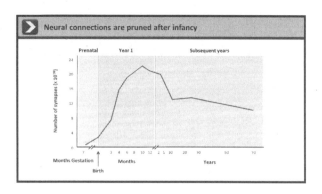

Maturation requires neurons to compete and make connections, or risk dying.
When?

Neural connections peak at age 1:

Plasticity:

Neurons that fire together wire together!

Neuroscience 1 – Courseware Exercise

The following diagram shows the change in voltage that occurs within a cell during an Action Potential. At each of the numbered stages, fill out the following information.

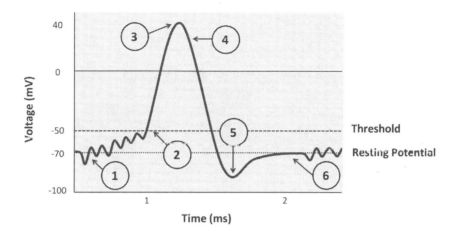

1. Resting State, Voltage=
Ion Placement:

State of Channels (open/closed):

2. Depolarization (Sodium's Role), Voltage=
Movement of Ions: Change in Voltage (increase/decrease):

State of Channels (open/closed):

3. Peak, Voltage=
Ion Placement:

4. Repolarization (Potassium's Role), Voltage=
Movement of Ions: Change in Voltage (increase/decrease):

State of Channels (open/closed):

5. Hyperpolarization, Voltage=
Movement of Ions: Change in Voltage (increase/decrease):

State of Channels (open/closed):

6. Return to Resting Potential, Voltage=
Movement of Ions: Change in Voltage (increase/decrease):

State of Channels (open/closed):

7. What is occurring between Step 1 and 2? Why does this not always result in an action potential?

8. How would a neuron convert a strong stimulus into a strong signal using action potentials?

Neuroscience 1 – Review Questions

1. Which of the following statements is true regarding neurons?
   a) The dendrites directly transmit electrical signals toward other neurons.
   b) Neurons are cells that are specialized for communication.
   c) Glial cells house the voltage gated ion channels and are crucial to sending electrical signals.
   d) Dendrites are part of the reception and transmission zone in a neuron.

2. During resting potential, the inside of a neuron has _____ potassium (K+), _____ sodium (Na+), _____ organic proteins (O-), and _____ chloride (Cl-).
   a) more, less, more, less
   b) more, more, less, less
   c) more, less, less, more
   d) more, less, less, less

3. Which of the following events occurs during the action potential?
   a) Electrostatic forces are responsible for pulling sodium into the cell.
   b) Diffusion forces are primarily responsible for pushing potassium outside of the cell.
   c) A combination of EPSPs and IPSPs alters the membrane potential to reach threshold.
   d) The sodium pump intakes two sodium ions into the cell and replaces them with three potassium ions.

4. An action potential can only occur if the inside of a cell reaches -50 mV. Which of the following is NOT one of the ways to reach this threshold?
   a) A number of EPSPs fire simultaneously from multiple presynaptic connections to the receptive zone of one postsynaptic neuron.
   b) Spatial summation: A number of EPSPs fire one after the other from different presynaptic connections to the receptive zone of the same postsynaptic neuron.
   c) Temporal summation: multiple EPSPs fire consecutively from the same presynaptic connection.
   d) IPSPs compliment spatial and temporal summation of EPSPs to send appropriate electrical signals.

5. Which of the following is true about neural development?
   a) While neural migration continues into adulthood, all neurons in the brain are born by the time a baby is 6 weeks.
   b) A neuron is differentiated to take on a specific function partly based on genetics.
   c) Neurotrophic molecules select which neurons will survive and make connections by actively binding to the neuron; all other neurons are trimmed away.
   d) Radial glial cells extend throughout the brain and give birth to neurons; this allows neurons to migrate.

Neuroscience 1 – Test Question

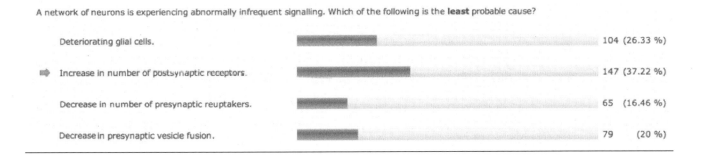

This is an actual question from the Neuroscience 1 quiz that many students struggled with. Fortunately, we are going to go through this question together to identify what sort of errors students were making and how to avoid them in the future.

This question is assessing whether students understand the steps involved in neuronal signalling, and it is important to note that we are looking for the LEAST likely cause of a deficit in signalling. In order for a signal to be transmitted, the presynaptic neuron must have vesicles fuse to the membrane to release neurotransmitters into the synapse. From there, the neurotransmitters either bind to the postsynaptic receptors, or are removed from the synapse by reuptakers where they would again be stored in the presynaptic neuron. When neurotransmitters bind to the postsynaptic neuron's dendrites, it allows for the signal to pass through the axon to the terminal bouton where it can be sent along to another neuron. Now that we understand the steps in neuronal signalling, let's look at each option in turn to see whether it can explain why infrequent signalling may be occurring.

- A. This option was an attractive choice for students, but if we consider how deterioration of a glial cell would affect signal transmission, we can see why it is incorrect. The deterioration of a glial cell indicates that the myelin is wearing off, which would mean slower or worse transmission of the signal. This could explain the infrequent signalling because signals would take longer to travel through the network of neurons.
- B. This option discusses an increase in the number of postsynaptic receptors. This option would be unlikely to cause infrequent signalling because having more receptors would allow for more neurotransmitters to be detected by the postsynaptic neuron and more signals to be transmitted.
- C. This answer discusses an increase in the number of presynaptic reuptakers. An increase in reuptake would mean less neurotransmitters being left in the synapse. With less neurotransmitters available to bind to postsynaptic receptors, a decrease in signalling is plausible, therefore ruling out option C.
- D. This option can also be ruled out because a decrease in presynaptic vesicle fusion would lead to less neurotransmitters in the synapse and thus a decrease in signalling.

Key Terms

Action Potential	Maturation	Refractory Period
Axon	Migration	Resting Potential
Differentiation (cellular)	Neurogenesis	Spatial Summation
Diffusion	Neuron	Synapse
Electrostatic Force	Neurotransmitters	Synaptic Cleft
Excitatory Postsynaptic Potential	Postsynaptic Neuron	Temporal Summation
Glial Cells	Presynaptic Neuron	Threshold
Inhibitory Postsynaptic Potential	Receptive Zone	

Neuroscience 1 – Bottleneck Concepts

Temporal vs. Spatial Summation
EPSP vs. IPSP
Diffusion vs. Electrostatic Force
Hyperpolarize vs. Repolarize vs. Depolarize

Hyperpolarize vs. Repolarize vs. Depolarize

In its resting state, a neuron is said to be polarized given that the inside of the cell is negative relative to the outside of the cell. The prefixes hyper-, re- and de- are all in reference to the neuron's resting polarized state. During the rise, positive sodium ions rush into the cell and the inside of the cell becomes more positive relative to the outside. The prefix 'de-' means to remove. In reference to the action potential, we are removing the negative charge from the inside of the cell—therefore, depolarization.

During the fall, positive potassium ions rush out of the cell leaving the inside of the cell more negative relative to the outside. At resting state, the inside of the cell was also more negative than the outside. The prefix 're' means occurring again. In reference to the action potential, we are returning back to the polarized resting state—therefore, repolarization.

During the undershoot phase, too many positive potassium ions rush out of the cell and as a result the resting potential of -70 mV is passed and the cell continues on to become even more negative relative to the outside (-100 mV). The prefix 'hyper-' means excess or over and given that we are always referencing the negative polarized resting state, hyperpolarization means excessively negative relative to the outside of the cell. Hyperpolarization can also occur during an inhibitory post-synaptic potential (IPSP) when negative chloride ions enter the cell resulting in the cell, becoming more negative than resting potential.

Again, when the cell is returning to resting potential following the undershoot, it is said to be repolarizing. The cell is returning back to its polarized resting state to start this process all over again!

Test your Understanding

1) Which of the following statements is <u>false</u> regarding the action potential?
   a) During hyperpolarization, the cell becomes more negative relative to the outside as a result of potassium ions rushing out of the cell quickly
   b) An EPSP repolarizes the neuron making it more positive and closer to firing threshold
   c) During depolarization, the cell moves away from resting potential because positive ions are rushing into the cell faster than negative ions are leaving it

d) During repolarization, positive potassium ions leave the cell and bring the voltage of the neuron back towards resting potential

2) What would happen if a cell was injected with a chemical that stopped the inflow of sodium ions? Make sure to reference the various types of polarizations.

Practice case study

Brian, a long-retired football player, and his wife Annie recently gave birth to a new baby girl, Brianna. A few years later, Brian seems to rapidly lose his motor coordination and begins to have vision problems. Brian remembers that he once had a serious concussion in high school and wonders if these symptoms are related to that event. He visits a doctor and the doctor discovers that some of his nerves are propagating action potentials abnormally slowly.

1) What might explain Brian's condition?

2) Annie notices that Brianna develops better and better motor coordination as she grows up. What might myelination have to do with this?

3) Myelination continues in humans until at least 30 years of age. How might this help to explain why people become better at something with practice?

4) How does myelin speed up an action potential?

Concept Map: Neuroscience 1

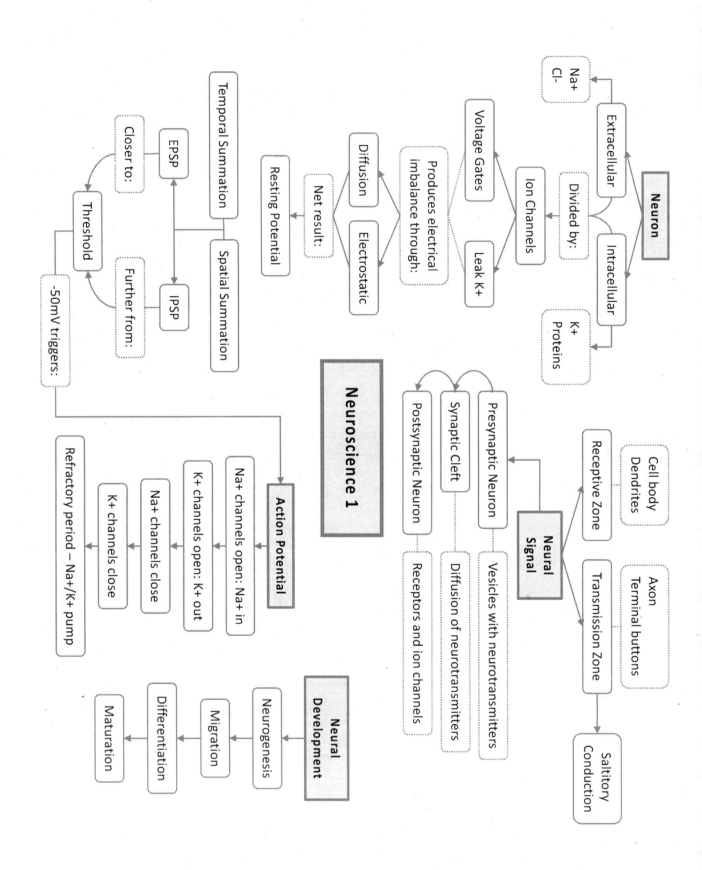

Action Potential
Neuroscience 1

Axon
Neuroscience 1

Differentiation
Neuroscience 1

Diffusion
Neuroscience 1

Electrostatic Force
Neuroscience 1

Excitatory Postsynaptic Potential
Neuroscience 1

Glial Cells
Neuroscience 1

Inhibitory Postsynaptic Potential
Neuroscience 1

A long fibre that projects from the receptive zone of a neuron, through which the electrical signals of an action potential pass. At the end of the axon is the transmission zone, whereby the signal is passed to neighbouring neurons. **Personal Example:**	The fundamental unit of communication for neurons. It involves a series of ionic events along the axon: reaching the threshold potential of -50 mV, a rapid increase in membrane potential, a decrease in membrane potential and ending with the refractory period. **Personal Example:**
The tendency for molecules to distribute themselves evenly through a medium. This is one of the forces controlling the resting potential of a neuron. **Example:** If you put a drop of food colouring in a glass of water, the food colouring will distribute itself evenly throughout the water. **Personal Example:**	The transformation of unspecified cells into specialized cell types that differ in structure and function, usually occurring after migration. **Example:** A particular group of unspecialized cells may become a part of the frontal cortex while another group of unspecialized cells becomes a part of the Broca's area. **Personal Example:**
An event in the post-synaptic neuron in which the Na+ channels open, allowing positive ions to flow into the cell, depolarizing it above the -70mV resting potential and bringing it closer to the -50mV threshold to fire an action potential. **Personal Example:**	The repulsion between ions of the same charge. This is one of the forces controlling the resting potential of the neuron. **Example:** Sodium ions and potassium ions repel one another because they are both positively charged. **Personal Example:**
An event in the post-synaptic neuron in which Cl- channels open, allowing negatively charged chloride ions to flow into the cell, hyperpolarizing it below the -70mV resting potential. This event brings the resting potential further from the -50mV threshold to fire an action potential. **Personal Example:**	Non-neuronal cells in the nervous system that provide structural support, nourishment and insulation to neurons. **Personal Example:**

Maturation
Neuroscience 1

Migration
Neuroscience 1

Neurogenesis
Neuroscience 1

Neuron
Neuroscience 1

Neurotransmitters
Neuroscience I

Postsynaptic Neuron
Neuroscience I

Presynaptic Neuron
Neuroscience 1

Receptive Zone
Neuroscience 1

The travelling of neurons from the ventricular zone to their correct location on the surface of the cortex along radial glial cells. **Personal Example:**	The growth of neurons by establishing connections with other neurons. This is an important process for a neuron, as those that do not make connections will be pruned away. **Personal Example:**
A type of cell found throughout the nervous system, specialized for communication throughout the body. The neuron's unique structure is made up of receptive (dendrites and cell body) and transmission (axon and terminal boutons) zones which make it especially good at communication. **Personal Example:**	The process by which neurons are created in the nervous system. **Personal Example:**
At a synapse, the neuron to which signals are sent from the presynaptic neuron. **Personal Example:**	A variety of signalling chemicals found in vesicles in the presynaptic neuron. They're released by the presynaptic neuron at a synapse and send signals to the postsynaptic neuron, causing varying effects dependent on the type of neurotransmitter. **Example:** Serotonin is believed to be a contributor to the feeling of happiness. **Personal Example:**
The part of the neuron that consists of the cell body and dendrites. This is where electrical signals are received from other neurons. **Personal Example:**	At a synapse, the neuron from which a signal is sent to a postsynaptic neuron. **Personal Example:**

Refractory Period
Neuroscience 1

Resting Potential
Neuroscience 1

Spatial Summation
Neuroscience 1

Synapse
Neuroscience 1

Synaptic Cleft
Neuroscience 1

Temporal Summation
Neuroscience 1

Threshold
Neuroscience 1

The baseline potential difference between the intracellular and extracellular fluid of a neuron, commonly stated as -70 mV of the inside relative to the outside of the cell. At this voltage, no electrical signals are being sent. **Personal Example:**	A period of time following the action potential during which it is harder or impossible to fire a new action potential. **Personal Example:**
The region consisting of the transmission zone of a presynaptic neuron and receptive zone of a postsynaptic neuron, through which electrical signals may be passed from neuron to neuron. **Personal Example:**	When multiple EPSPs occur simultaneously from several different presynaptic neurons at the receptive zone of the postsynaptic neuron, causing it to reach the -50mV threshold required to fire an action potential. **Personal Example:**
When multiple EPSPs occur one after another on the receptive zone of the postsynaptic neuron from the same presynaptic connection, causing a slow climb towards the -50mV threshold required for an action potential to fire. **Personal Example:**	The space between two neurons in which neurotransmitters float freely with other molecules. **Personal Example:**
	The -50mV potential difference across the neuronal membrane that must be reached in order for an action potential to fire. **Personal Example:**

Neuroscience 2

"Before brains there was no color or sound in the universe, nor was there any flavor or aroma and probably little sense and no feeling or emotion."
- Roger Wolcott Sperry, a Nobel Prize winning neuropsychologist conducting split-brain research

The Woman with No Fear

Imagine walking through a dark alley alone at night. All of a sudden you hear rustling behind you and turn around to find a person holding a knife. He moves toward you and as you wrestle to get free you feel the edge of the knife against your face. How does it feel reading that? Now imagine being there, are you scared? For "the woman with no fear" this scenario happened and she did not even flinch. In fact, she went back down that same dark alley in the weeks that followed. S.M. is a female patient with a rare genetic condition leading to a complete bilateral destruction to her amygdala. Researchers have used S.M.'s unique experiences to uncover the role of the amygdala. The amygdala is a key brain structure that processes fear and anxiety and helps us avoid experiences that will bring us pain, sickness or death. Without an amygdala, S.M. does not show any fear response or heightened anxiety when faced with scenarios that would make most people fearful! Experiments revealed that S.M. showed no fear in response to handling snakes and spiders, walking through a haunted house, or watching horror movies; rather, she was interested, curious and excited. While having no fear may seem like a handy trait to have, it is extremely dangerous. Fear has evolved to keep humans from engaging in activities that could harm them. We avoid handling snakes because they may be venomous. We avoid high ledges because we could fall off and die. We avoid dark alleys because a predator may be lurking. Fear is adaptive and while too much may be maladaptive, just the right amount keeps us safe and alive to continue on with the business of living.

Weekly Checklist:
- ☐ **Web modules to watch: Neuroscience 2**
- ☐ **Readings: Chapter 4**
- ☐ **Pre-Quiz & Quiz 4**

Upper Year Courses:
If you enjoyed the content of this week's module, consider taking the following upper year course:
- Psych 2NF3: Clinical Neuropsychology

Neuroscience 2 – Outline

Unit 1: The Structure of the Brain

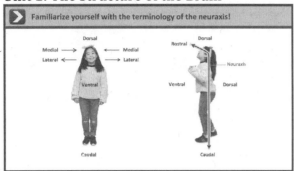

The neuraxis is used to describe the position of structures in the central nervous system.

_____
_____
_____
_____
_____
_____
_____
_____
_____
_____
_____

Unit 2: Studying the Brain

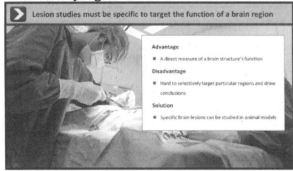

The brain has specialized structures for complex behaviours.

Phineas Gage: _____
_____

Natural lesion studies (pro/con): _____
_____

1) Induced lesion studies: _____
_____
_____
_____
_____

Penfield used electrical brain stimulation to pair function with brain anatomy.

Penfield's Montreal procedure: _____
_____

2) Stimulation & observation: _____
_____

3) Single cell recording: _____
_____

Hubel & Wiesel: _____
_____

107

Structural and functional neuroimaging are used to study the overall brain's structure and function.

1) CT Scan – Structural Neuroimaging

Purpose:

Pro:

Con:

2) MRI – Structural Neuroimaging

Purpose:

Con:

3) PET Scan – Functional Neuroimaging

Active brain areas?

Purpose:

Con:

4) fMRI – Functional Neuroimaging

Purpose:

Pro:
Oxygen?

Con:

5) EEG & ERP

EEG purpose/con:

ERP:

Average EEG waves:

ERP marker signals: EEG purpose/con:

ERP + EEG =

Hint: More information is available in the textbook for the above section

Unit 3: The Brain Regions – Hindbrain and Midbrain

Found in nearly every vertebrate species, the hindbrain was likely the first brain region to evolve.

Hindbrain: medulla, pons, reticular formation & cerebellum

Purpose:

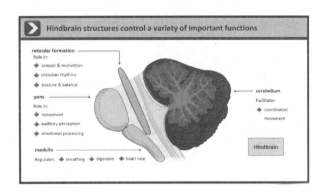

Medulla: _____

Pons: _____

Reticular formation: _____

Cerebellum: _____

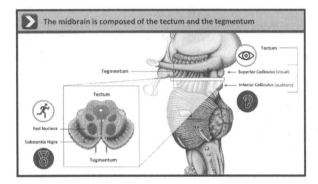

The midbrain is divided into the tectum and tegmentum.
1) Tectum: _____

a) Superior colliculus: _____

b) Inferior colliculus: _____

2) Tegmentum:
a) Red nucleus: _____

b) Substantia nigra (NT?): _____

Unit 4: The Brain Regions - Forebrain

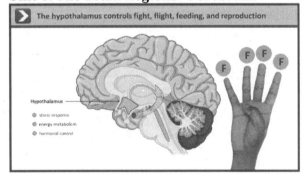

The forebrain is the largest and uppermost region of the brain.

Limbic System (subcortical):
1) Hypothalamus: _____

Four F's: _____

Regulatory? _____

109

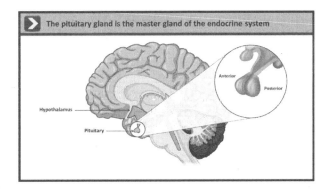

The pituitary gland is considered the master gland of the endocrine system.

2) Pituitary gland: _____

a) Anterior pituitary: _____

b) Posterior pituitary: _____

Oxytocin? _____

Vasopressin? _____

3) Thalamus: _____

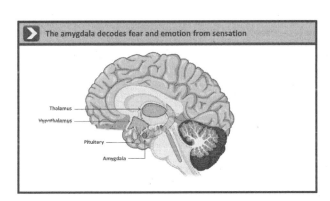

4) Amygdala: _____

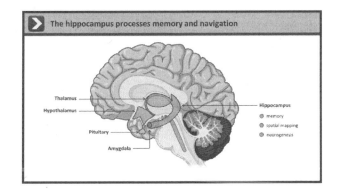

The hippocampus is involved in memory formation/storage and is vital for navigation.

5) Hippocampus _____

Neurogenesis & Alzheimer's Disease: _____

Note: **Interconnectivity!**

Unit 5: The Brain Regions - Cortex

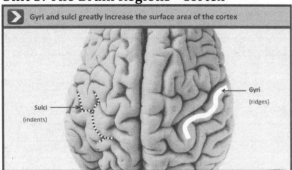

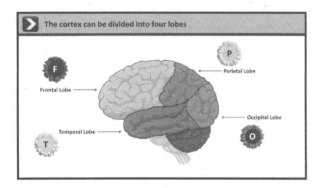

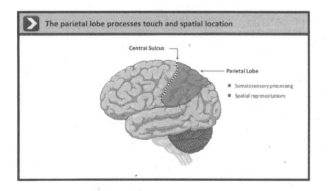

The cerebral cortex is the newest part of the brain and contributes to the behaviours that make us uniquely human.

Cortex: _____
_____
_____

Gyri & sulci: _____
_____
_____
_____
_____

Fissures: _____
_____

The cortex is divided into four lobes: frontal, parietal, temporal and occipital.

1) Occipital lobe: _____
_____
_____

Damage? _____

2) Temporal lobe: _____
_____
_____
_____
_____

Damage? _____
_____

3) Parietal lobe
_____
_____
_____
_____
_____
_____

Damage? _____
_____
_____
_____

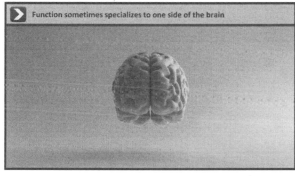

4) Frontal lobe

_____
_____
_____
_____
_____
_____
_____
_____

Damage?
_____
_____

Unit 6: Brain Lateralization

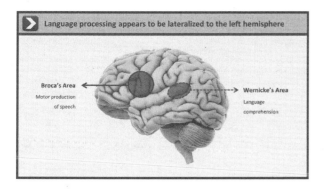

Mirrored brain regions often perform a unique function in their respective hemisphere.

Symmetry: _____
_____

Asymmetry/brain lateralization: ___
_____
_____
_____

Dissociation?
_____
_____
_____

The left hemisphere is most important for language production and comprehension.

_____
Broca's Area: _____
_____
_____
_____

Wernicke's Area: _____
_____
_____
_____

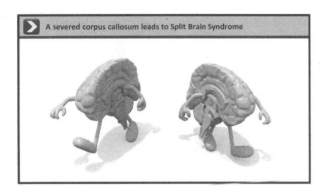

Individuals with Split Brain Syndrome have two independently functioning brain hemispheres.

Corpus callosum: _____

Sperry & Gazzaniga – Split Brain Syndrome: _____

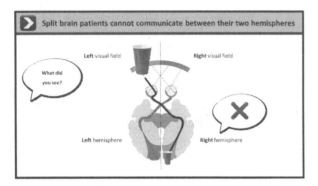

Split Brain experiments: _____

Cup to left visual field → travels to right brain: _____

Name (language)? _____

Touch (spatial)? _____

Cup to right visual field → travels to left brain: _____

Brain lateralization: _____

Neuroscience 2 – Courseware Exercise

1. Describe three experimental methods that could be used to understand cerebral lateralization of function. Include the advantages or disadvantages for each method.

a) _____

_____

Advantages: _____

Disadvantages: _____

b) _____

_____

Advantages: _____

Disadvantages: _____

c) _____

_____

Advantages: _____

Disadvantages: _____

2. Test your understanding of Split Brain patients.

a) Mark is a split brain patient. He is shown the word "bird" in his right visual field. He is asked to identify the bird from a collection of toys.

What information is being tested and where is it processed? _____

Will Mark be able to complete this task? _____

Is he able to say the word that he saw? _____

b) Jane is a split brain patient. She is shown an image of a trumpet in her left visual field. She is asked to mimic the sound that this instrument produces.

What information is being tested and where is it processed? _____

Will Jane be able to complete this task? _____

If she is played a number of different instrumental sounds, can she correctly identify the sound of a trumpet? _____

c) Sue is a split brain patient. She is shown a multiplication question in her right visual field. She is asked to verbally state the answer and write it down with her left hand.

What information is being tested and where is it processed? _____

Will Sue be able to verbally state the answer? _____

Will Sue be able to write it down with her left hand? _____

Neuroscience 2 – Review Questions

1. Brain lesion studies allow researchers to:
   a) Conclusively test specific predictions regarding brain function
   b) Examine the general relationship between structure and function
   c) Examine how neurons fire in relation to stimuli
   d) Examine functions such as vision and motor skills, but cannot examine personality

2. A researcher is interested in getting a clear and detailed view of the hypothalamus, which technique should they use?
   a) either CT or MRI
   b) either MRI or fMRI
   c) CT only
   d) MRI only

3. After a car accident, Thomas had trouble communicating with his wife, Cindy. While Thomas knew what he wanted to say, he was unable to communicate effectively—Cindy did not understand what he was saying. What brain area and location did Thomas likely suffer a lesion?
   a) Wernicke's area; left temporal lobe
   b) Broca's area; left temporal lobe
   c) Broca's area; left frontal lobe
   d) Wernicke's area; left frontal lobe

4. Caleb quit his job and began his own limousine driving company. Caleb frequently drove the limos himself for the first 5 years of his business; after those 5 years, Caleb found that navigating around the city had become very easy. In what area can we expect to see changes to Caleb's brain?
   a) Hippocampus
   b) Cerebellum
   c) Amygdala
   d) Pons

5. After experiencing brain trauma, Sharon is a witness to a bank robbery. While all the other witnesses are terrified, Sharon remains calm and collected. In what region of the brain is it most likely that she experienced brain damage?
   a) Hypothalamus
   b) Thalamus
   c) Amygdala
   d) Pituitary

Neuroscience 2 – Test Question

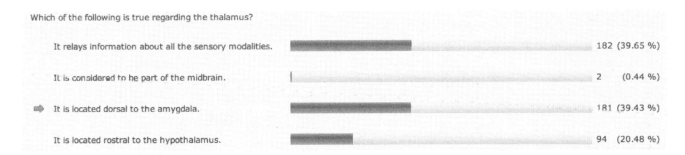

This is an actual question from the Neuroscience 2 quiz that many students struggled with. Fortunately, we are going to go through this question together to identify what sort of errors students were making and how to avoid them in the future. To do so, we will look at each answer option individually and identify why it is correct or incorrect.

A. This was the most popular response given by students and suggests that the thalamus relays information about all the sensory modalities. Often students find a phrase that they are familiar with and conclude it is the correct answer, without thinking critically. It is correct that the thalamus is a relay station for most sensory information, however, the module explicitly states that olfaction (smell) is an exception.
B. This option can be ruled out because the thalamus is part of the limbic system that is located in the forebrain.
C. When examining this answer, we must remember that dorsal is towards the back of the neuroaxis. However at the level of the head, the neuroaxis does a 90 degrees curve, and therefore dorsal denotes "above" or towards the top of the brain. In this case, the thalamus is above the amygdala so this option is correct.
D. Rostral means towards the front of the brain so we can rule out this answer because the thalamus is not in front of the hypothalamus.

Key Terms

Amygdala	Gyri	Positron Emission Tomography (PET)
Cerebellum	Hindbrain	Reticular Formation
Computed Tomography (CT)	Hippocampus	Single-Cell Recording
Corpus Callosum	Hypothalamus	Split Brain Syndrome
Cortex	Lesion Studies	Structural Neuroimaging
EEG	Magnetic Resonance Imaging (MRI)	Sulci
Fissure	Medulla	Tectum
Forebrain	Midbrain	Tegmentum
Frontal Lobe	Occipital Lobe	Temporal Lobe
Functional Magnetic Resonance Imaging (fMRI)	Parietal Lobe	Thalamus
	Pituitary	
Functional Neuroimaging	Pons	

Neuroscience 2 – Bottleneck Concepts

Structural vs. Functional Neuroimaging
Lesion Studies vs. Stimulation Studies
Split Brain Syndrome
Broca's Aphasia vs. Wernicke's Aphasia

Broca's Aphasia vs. Wernicke's Aphasia

Brain injury case studies have told us a lot about the function of the brain. They have revealed that the left hemisphere of the brain is central to language processing. If an individual with a speech deficit (i.e., aphasia) seeks out treatment, a doctor will know to look in the left hemisphere of their brain when investigating a cause. More specifically, the symptomology of the speech deficit can guide the doctor towards a specific brain region. Paul Broca's observations of a patient nicknamed Tan revealed that a region in the left frontal lobe, named Broca's Area, is responsible for the motor production of speech—think Broca/broken speech. An individual with Broca's aphasia (i.e., motor aphasia), understands conversations and even knows what they want to say, but struggles to physically articulate the words with their mouth. Wernicke's observations of a patient revealed that a region in the left temporal gyrus, named Wernicke's Area, is crucial to language comprehension. An individual with Wernicke's aphasia (i.e., receptive aphasia), can articulate words normally, but their speech is out of order, grammatically erred, incoherent and/or not relevant to the topic. Wernicke's aphasia leaves the individual with a deficit in language comprehension, both written and spoken. While an individual may present with a general speech deficit, it is the specifics of the deficit—comprehension or production—that can help the doctor know the region of the brain responsible and work towards an effective treatment plan.

Test your Understanding

1) Is the following situation an example of Broca's or Wernicke's Aphasia and why?
Geoff is in the hospital recovering from a seizure. His doctor asks him to describe what he last remembers before the incident. Geoff pauses for a long time and says what sounds like "ye, I wah eh hom". The doctor asks what he was doing at "home" when he had his seizure and Geoff becomes increasingly frustrated as he tries to answer. He signals to the doctor for a pen and Geoff slowly wrote on a pad of paper, "I felt dizzy while watching TV at home".

2) What kind of treatment do you think someone with Broca's Aphasia would benefit from and why?

Practice case study

Bobby is a volunteer in the brain injuries ward of the hospital. One day, Bobby accidentally mixed up a pile of patient files. The files contained: brain scans, a list of symptoms, and medication information for each patient. These files are critically important for the hospital and the patients. Bobby must figure out which patients' files were which.

Patient names: John, Paul, George, and Ringo.
Symptoms:
-Has difficulty performing physical activities due to excessive clumsiness
-Has difficulty retrieving the correct word from memory
-Is considered very impulsive and is constantly misplacing things.
-Has difficulty going to sleep due to a recurring nightmare.

1) Which areas of the brain may be associated with each of the symptoms listed above?

2) What question or tasks could the patient perform that would help Bobby narrow down which subject has which symptom?

A nurse from the brain injury ward who knows each patient was able to piece together the names of the patients and their symptoms. However, she does not remember which area of the brain was damaged in each patient. Bobby decides that in order to find out which area of the brain is damaged in each patient, he will perform a brain scan on each patient (either fMRI, PET, or EEG).

3) If Bobby only uses one brain scan per patient, which brain scans should he choose? Explain your answers.

Concept Map: Neuroscience 2

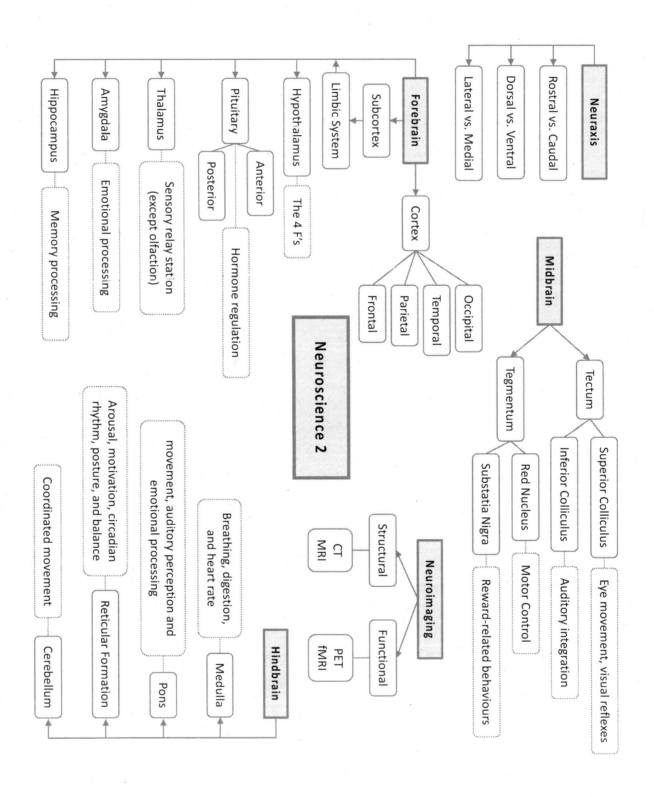

Amygdala
Neuroscience 2

Cerebellum
Neuroscience 2

Computed Tomography (CT)
Neuroscience 2

Corpus Callosum
Neuroscience 2

Cortex
Neuroscience 2

Electroencephalogram (EEG)
Neuroscience 2

Fissure
Neuroscience 2

Forebrain
Neuroscience 2

Translating to "little brain", it is a structure in the hindbrain resembling a miniature version of the entire brain. It coordinates motor movement and so damage to this area can result in exaggerated, jerky movements.
Personal Example:

An almond-shaped structure located below the surface of the temporal lobe that plays a role in decoding emotions (particularly fear).
Personal Example:

A thick bundle of axons passing through the centre of the brain and allowing for communication between the left and right hemispheres.
Personal Example:

A structural neuroimaging technique in which a series of X-ray slices of the brain are taken and pieced together, producing a quick image of the brain. It has poor resolution compared to an MRI but is often used to help diagnose brain injuries.
Personal Example:

A functional neuroimaging technique in which electrical activity of the brain is recorded through the scalp by wearing a cap of very sensitive electrodes. It provides a very rough image of the brain's overall activity from populations of neurons.
Personal Example:

A part of the forebrain, it is the largest part of the brain. It contains the occipital, temporal, parietal, and frontal lobes and is where most of the actual information processing, behaviours and cognitive functions take place.
Personal Example:

The most evolutionarily recent and largest part of the human brain, consisting of the cortex and the subcortical structures of the limbic system.
Personal Example:

Deep groves/crevices found throughout the cortex, which often divide major areas of the cortex.
Personal Example:

Frontal Lobe
Neuroscience 2

Functional Magnetic Resonance Imaging (fMRI)
Neuroscience 2

Functional Neuroimaging
Neuroscience 2

Gyri
Neuroscience 2

Hindbrain
Neuroscience 2

Hippocampus
Neuroscience 2

Hypothalamus
Neuroscience 2

Lesion Studies
Neuroscience 2

A functional neuroimaging technique using magnetic fields to measure the relative use of oxygen throughout the brain, creating a functional map of brain activity. **Personal Example:**	The most anterior part of the cortex, it is the most complex and least understood of the cortical lobes. It is where movements originate (in the motor cortex) and where complex decision-making is performed. **Personal Example:**
Ridges, or outward bulges, on the cortex. These, along with sulci form folds that provide the additional surface area required for cortical processing. **Personal Example:**	A variety of techniques used to learn how brain activity relates to specific cognitive tasks, such as fMRI, PET scans or EEG. **Personal Example:**
A horseshoe-shaped structure in the temporal lobe, it is involved in memory formation and the ability to navigate through the world. **Personal Example:**	The brain's evolutionarily oldest region, lying at the base of the brain and consisting of the medulla, pons, reticular formation, and the cerebellum. **Personal Example:**
Studies of brain activity following damage to a particular area, observing a resulting loss of function. If the occipital lobe is involved with vision, an individual may have impaired vision after experiencing a stroke in their occipital lobe. **Personal Example:**	A part of the limbic system in the forebrain, which regulates the "four F's" (fight, flight, feeding, and reproduction). **Personal Example:**

Magnetic Resonance Imaging (MRI)
Neuroscience 2

Medulla
Neuroscience 2

Midbrain
Neuroscience 2

Occipital Lobe
Neuroscience 2

Parietal Lobe
Neuroscience 2

Pituitary
Neuroscience 2

Pons
Neuroscience 2

Positron Emission Tomography (PET)
Neuroscience 2

The most caudal part of the hindbrain, located directly above the spinal cord. The medulla is vital for functions such as breathing, digestion, and regulation of heart rate. **Personal Example:**	A structural neuroimaging technique using powerful magnetic fields that align the hydrogen atoms in the brain to create an image of the brain. It has good spatial resolution, relative to a CT scan. **Personal Example:**
At the posterior end of the cortex, it is exclusively responsible for visual processing. It contains the primary visual cortex and other visual areas. Damage to it may result in functional blindness. **Personal Example:**	Found between the hindbrain and the forebrain, it contains the tectum and tegmentum, both of which are involved in a variety of functions including perception, arousal and motor control. **Personal Example:**
Referred to as the master gland of the endocrine system, it has two sub-regions. The anterior pituitary receives signals from the brain to release hormones that regulate other endocrine glands such as the thyroid, testes and ovaries. The posterior pituitary is an extension of the hypothalamus and it releases the hormones oxytocin and vasopressin. **Personal Example:**	Located anterior to the occipital lobe, the parietal lobe contains the primary somatosensory cortex, where the processing of touch begins. The parietal lobe is also involved in a number of complex visual and spatial functions. **Personal Example:**
A functional neuroimaging technique that uses a radioactive tracer to observe active areas of the brain, creating a functional map of brain activity. It has better temporal resolution but is more invasive than an fMRI. **Personal Example:**	A small structure in the hindbrain that relays information about movement from the cerebral hemispheres to the cerebellum. It also processes some auditory information and contains nuclei that are a part of the reticular formation. **Personal Example:**

Reticular Formation
Neuroscience 2

Single-Cell Recording
Neuroscience 2

Split Brain Syndrome
Neuroscience 2

Structural Neuroimaging
Neuroscience 2

Sulci
Neuroscience 2

Tectum
Neuroscience 2

Tegmentum
Neuroscience 2

Temporal Lobe
Neuroscience 2

During various human functions, extremely precise electrical recordings are made from a single neuron in the nervous system. The human anatomic map related to human function (somatotopic map), discovered by Doctor Penfield, was discovered using single-cell recordings. **Personal Example:**	An interconnected set of nuclei throughout the hindbrain, it contains the ascending reticular formation (involved in arousal, motivation and circadian rhythms) and the descending reticular formation (involved in posture, equilibrium, and motor movement). **Personal Example:**
A variety of techniques used to study the large-scale structure of the brain and identify structural abnormalities. **Personal Example:**	A condition in which an individual's corpus callosum is severed such that the two hemispheres of the brain cannot communicate with each other. **Personal Example:**
Part of the dorsal midbrain, containing the superior and inferior colliculi, it is involved in perception and action, including eye movements, visual reflexes, and auditory integration. **Personal Example:**	The indents, or gaps, between gyri on the cortex. These, along with gyri, give the cortex its ridged structure and provide more surface area for cortical processing. **Personal Example:**
Lying at the sides of the brain below the Sylvian fissure, the temporal lobe is involved in visual association, memory and language and contains the primary auditory cortex. **Personal Example:**	The part of the midbrain involved in the regulation and production of movement (partly influenced by the red nucleus), motor planning, learning, and reward seeking (partly influenced by the substantia nigra). **Personal Example:**

Thalamus
Neuroscience 2

Part of the forebrain that acts as a "relay station" from the cerebellum, limbic system, and every sensory area (except olfaction) to the cerebral cortex.
Personal Example:

Vision 1 & 2

"The only thing worse than being blind is having sight but no vision."
- Helen Keller, famous blind and deaf activist, author and educator

Night Vision Eye Drops

What would you do if you could see in the dark? Would you explore a dark forest, spy on a stranger, or save money on electricity? A pair of biohackers with the group Science for the Masses dreamed of these possibilities and extended findings from a mice study to test night vision eye drops. It all began with the deep-sea dragonfish and their bioluminescent eyes. The fish's rhodopsin (light-sensitive pigment in rods) absorbs mid-wavelength light, allowing for monochromatic reddish-purple night vision. A derivative of chlorophyll, chlorin e6, was responsible for this night vision and researchers tested the effects of injecting chlorin e6 into the eyes of mice. As expected, these mice demonstrated increased sensitivity to red light, suggesting that they had night vision comparable to that of the dragonfish. Despite this promising finding, dozens of controlled animal studies would be required before any human trials could occur. However, two biohackers from California skipped these animal studies and went straight to injecting chlorin e6 into one of the researcher's eyes. Please don't try this at home: chlorin e6 is a potentially dangerous chemotherapy chemical and the biohackers took a foolish risk. Luckily, the experiment was a success and the researcher's eyesight even returned to normal with minimal side effects. After injection, the researcher was able to see in the dark; identifying various symbols among their background and tracking moving objects in a dark forest up to 50 meters away.

While it seemed like these biohackers had proven the effectiveness of night vision eye drops, their findings had many confounds to consider. First, there was no baseline comparison. The experimental participant's night vision was only tested after the eye drops were applied; perhaps the experimental participant had superior night vision prior to the eye drops. Second, there may have been placebo effects. The experimental participant knew he was getting the experimental eye drops and as a result could have been more confident when interpreting fuzzy shapes in the dark. There needs to be random and blind assignment of eye drops to a large group of participants to ensure the findings are valid. It is important to be a critical reader of whatever you read on the internet and not take findings like, "New Eye Drops Give Humans Night Vision" at face value.

Licina, G., Tibbets, J. (2015, March 25). A review on night enhancement eyedrops using chlorin e6. Retrieved from http://scienceforthemasses.org/wp-content/uploads/2015/03/AReviewonNightEnhancementEyedropsUsingChlorine6.pdf

Weekly Checklist:
- ☐ Web modules to watch: Vision 1 & 2
- ☐ Readings: Chapter 5
- ☐ Pre-Quiz & Quiz 5

Vision 1 – Outline

Unit 1: Introduction to Vision

What we "see" is a product of our brain activity.

Unit 2: The Stimulus - Light

Wavelength & colour:

Wavelength & frequency?

Visible spectrum (360 nm(violet) – 750 nm(red)):

UV:

Infrared:

Amplitude & brightness:

3) Purity & saturation:

Pure/natural light?

Unit 3: The Eye

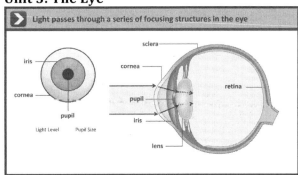

The steps of light travel through the eyes:

1) Cornea: _____

2) Pupil: _____

3) Iris (dilate/constrict): _____

4) Lens: _____

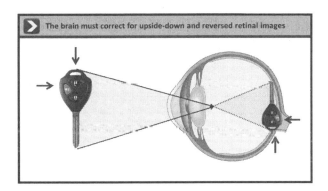

The brain corrects for the effect of the lens' curvature to allow us to perceive a properly oriented image.

_____

Accommodation: _____

Close object? _____

Far object? _____

5) Vitreous humor: _____

6) Retina: _____

Unit 4: The Retina

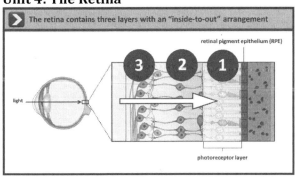

Light is translated from a physical stimulus to a neural signal at the level of the retina.

Retina: _____

Photoreceptors: _____

Retinal pigment epithelium (RPE): _____

Photoreceptors:
1) Cones are used for day vision and allow us to see in colour.

\#: _____

Light intensity: _____
_____

Colour? _____
Acuity? _____

Location? _____
_____
_____

Photoreceptors:
2) Rods are used for night vision and provide no colour information.

\#: _____

Light intensity: _____
_____

Colour? _____
Acuity? _____

Location? _____
_____
_____

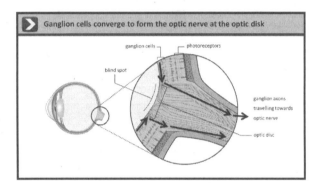

Neural signals are passed from the photoreceptor cells to the bipolar cells and finally to the ganglion cells.

Ganglion axons converge on the optic disc:
_____
_____
_____

Blind spot? _____
_____
_____
_____

Overview of light through the retina:
- Light passes through layers 2 and 3 to reach the photoreceptors
- Neural signals are sent back through layers 2 and 3, then out via the optic nerve to the brain

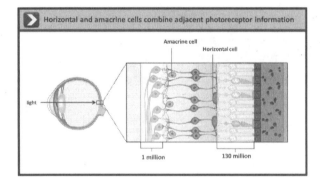

Visual processing begins in the retina.

Horizontal and amacrine cells: _____
_____
_____
_____

130 to 1 million? _____
_____
_____
_____
_____

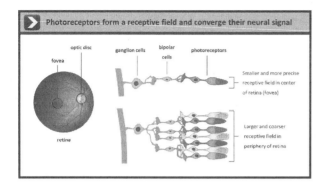

Cones share a more direct link with ganglion cells than rods do—translating to a higher visual acuity.

Cones grouping:

Rods grouping:

Receptive field:

Vision 2 – Outline

Unit 1: Visual Pathways

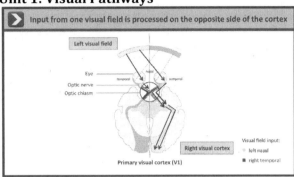

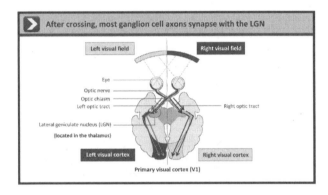

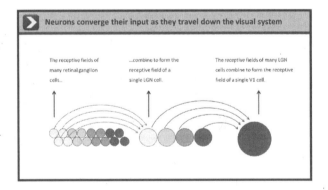

Each hemisphere of the brain receives information from both eyes.

RVF: _____

LVF: _____

Inner eye axons? _____
_____
_____

Optic chiasm: _____
_____

Most visual signals relay information in the thalamus towards the occipital lobe.

Main pathway: _____
_____
_____
_____

Primary visual cortex (V1) (aka?): _____

Extrastriate cortex: _____
_____

With every further synapse, the receptive fields of many cells converge onto fewer cells

_____
_____
_____
_____

Topographic map: _____
_____
_____
_____
_____

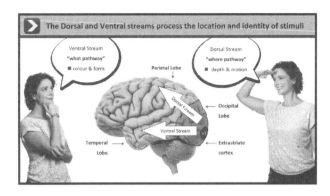

Information compression: _____
_____
_____

Unit 2: Evolution of the Eye

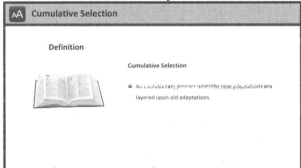

Visual information is processed in either the dorsal or ventral stream of the extrastriate cortex.
_____

Dorsal (where) → parietal lobe: _____
_____
_____

Ventral (what) → temporal lobe: _____
_____
_____
_____
_____

The eye evolved through a process of cumulative selection.
_____
_____
_____
_____
_____
_____
_____
_____

The advantages of an adaptation must outweigh the metabolic costs.
_____
_____
_____
_____

Different designs for different environments:
_____
_____
_____
_____

There are two types of image-forming eyes.

1) Simple eyes vary their design in accordance to the environment that the species lives in.

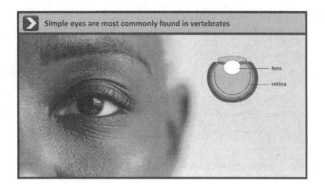

Vertebrates and mollusks: _____

Eyeball, lens & retina _____

Vary widely: _____

2) Compound eyes are good at detecting movement, but only at close distances.

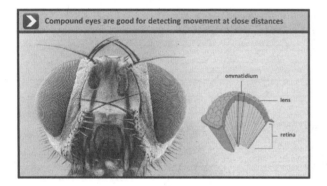

Made of ommatidia: _____

Larger eyes tend to have higher visual acuity or sensitivity.

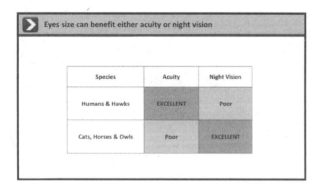

Two functions: _____

Hawks & humans: _____

Cats, horses & owls: _____

Deep sea? _____

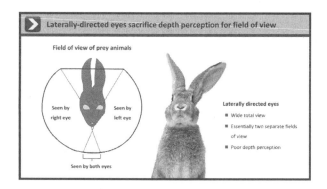

Eye placement is associated with a trade-off between depth perception and field of view.
_____
_____

Lateral = prey: _____
_____
_____

Forward = predator: _____
_____
_____

Note: "good" is a subjective term

Unit 3: Development of Visual Architecture

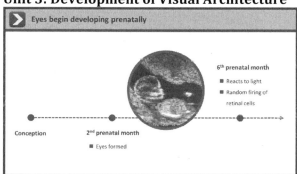

Vision is the least developed sense at birth.

Eyes form: _____
_____

React to light: _____
_____
_____

Organized wiring: _____
_____
_____
_____

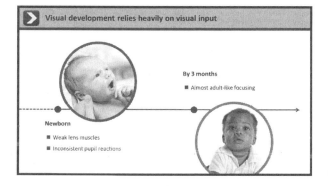

The visual system requires visual stimulation to fully develop.
_____
_____

Newborn: _____
_____
_____
_____

3 months: _____
_____
_____

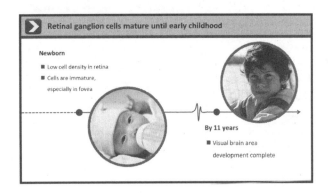

The development of the visual brain area is not fully complete until ~ 11 years of age.

Retina (+fovea):
_____
_____
_____
_____
_____

Optic nerve & visual cortex:
_____
_____
_____
_____
_____

Visual acuity reaches adult levels around 4 to 6 years of age.

Birth (20/600):
_____
_____
_____
_____
_____
_____

6 months (20/100):
_____
_____
_____

Age 1 → Age 4 to 6:
_____
_____
_____

Vision 1 & 2 – Courseware Exercise

1. The eye is composed of a variety of smaller parts, each with its own role. These small parts contribute to an individual's ability to see the world. Write down the path of a photon of light as it travels into the eye and state the function of that part. *Include the iris and the three layers of the retina.*

1.
2.
3.
4.
5.
6.
7.
8.
9.

2. Compare and contrast rods and cones. Consider quantity, location, visual acuity and responsiveness to light.

Rods	Cones

3. In this module, you learned about the environmental attributes that lead toward selection for various elements of a species' eye. Imagine that you encounter a new species that lives in low light levels, but requires vision to hunt other animals that are on the same vertical plane as them. Describe the characteristics that would be expected for this species' eye, as well as the reason why you would expect each to occur.

Vision 1 & 2 – Review Questions

1. Which of the following is true about the physical and psychological properties of light?
    a) Light with a large amplitude is less bright, light with a large wavelength has a high frequency, and light that has low purity is less saturated.
    b) Light with a small amplitude is less bright, light with a small wavelength has a high frequency, and light that has low purity is less saturated.
    c) Light with a small amplitude is less bright, light with a large wavelength has a high frequency, and light that has high purity is less saturated.
    d) Light with a large amplitude is less bright, light with a small wavelength has a high frequency, and light that has high purity is less saturated.

2. A new species of bird is discovered and appears to have a very similar eye structure to humans. However, the bird is nocturnal and demonstrates extreme sensitivity to light and has excellent night vision. Which of the following would likely explain the difference between this species of bird's eye compared to the human eye:
    a) The bird's lens is unable to accommodate and has more rods than cones.
    b) The bird's iris does not function as the human eye does and the rods are organized in the periphery.
    c) The bird's iris does not function as the human eye does and has an even greater proportion of rods relative to cones.
    d) The bird's lens is unable to accommodate and the bird's iris does not function as the human eye does.

3. This new bird species was examined further and researchers found that in fact the rods are found near the bird's fovea and the cones are found in the periphery. Which of the following is true based on this new information:
    a) The bird is best able to see its prey at night while looking at it from the side with its head tilted.
    b) The bird is best able to see its prey during the day and identify what color it is while looking directly at it.
    c) The bird is best able to see its prey at night while staring directly at it.
    d) The bird is best able to see its prey during the day while staring directly at it.

4 Which of the following is the accurate path of the visual signal as it exits the eye towards the brain?
    a) Photoreceptors, ganglion cells, bipolar cells, optic nerve
    b) Ganglion cells, bipolar cells, photoreceptors, optic nerve
    c) Optic nerve, ganglion cells, bipolar cells, photoreceptors
    d) Photoreceptors, bipolar cells, ganglion cells, optic nerve

5. Sally recently suffered from a stroke that damaged fibres on the left side of her optic chiasm. However, the fibres that cross over were left untouched. Which of the following demonstrates where Sally has lost her vision?
    a) The medial right visual field
    b) The lateral right visual field
    c) The medial left visual field
    d) The lateral left visual field

6. A newborn baby is sleeping in her mother's arms in a dark room. Suddenly, the lights turn on and the baby is being kissed and admired by her visiting relatives. Which of the following is true regarding the baby's visual experience at this moment?

    a) She is able to find her mother's face in the crowd of blurry faces.
    b) She is unable to find her mother's face in the crowd of blurry faces.
    c) She is able to find her mother's face and is able to focus on the other faces.
    d) She is unable to find her mother's face because her pupils won't let any light in.

Vision 1 & 2 – Test Question

Tabitha is undergoing a physical examination at her doctor's office where a light is shone into Tabitha's eyes from various points. Tabitha has trouble seeing the light when in her far left visual field, but she can see it everywhere else. When Tabitha can see the light, she cannot tell the doctor what colour it is. Where would you expect Tabitha to have damage?

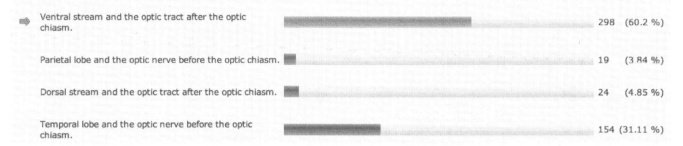

This is an actual question from the Vision quiz that many students struggled with. Fortunately, we are going to go through this question together to identify what sort of errors students were making and how to avoid them in the future. To do so, we will look at each answer option individually and identify why it is correct or incorrect.

This question is testing two aspects of visual processing presented to you: where damage can occur along the path to the primary visual cortex (V1) and where further processing such as colour information takes place.

A. This is the correct answer. We know that the ventral stream processes colour information, half of this answer matches so far. Next, we know that damage to the right optic tract (*after* the optic chiasm) could lead to visual deficits in the left visual field.

B. This option can easily be ruled out because we know that colour information is processed along the ventral stream which leads to the temporal lobe. The parietal lobe is the endpoint of the dorsal stream which processes movement and location of visual stimuli. Additionally, if damage had occurred before the optic chiasm, Tabitha would lose *all* sight from that eye.

C. This option can be ruled out because we know that the dorsal stream processes movement and location of visual stimuli, not colour information.

D. Although it is true that colour information is processed in the temporal lobe, having damage to the optic nerve before the optic chiasm is inconsistent with Tabitha's symptoms. Notice that the question does not specify whether the right or left optic nerve is damaged; therefore, you must assume that both optic nerves (for either the right or left eye) could be damaged. If damage occurred before the optic chiasm, she would have trouble seeing anything with her left eye, which would lead to a deficit in *both* the left and right visual fields.

Key Terms

Accommodation	Horizontal Cells	Receptive Field
Amacrine Cells	Iris	Retina
Amplitude	Lateral Geniculate Nucleus (LGN)	Retinal Pigment Epithelium (RPE)
Bipolar Cells	Lens	Rods
Compound Eyes	Light Sensitive Patch	Saturation
Cones	Ommatidia	Sclera
Cornea	Optic Chiasm	Simple Eye
Cumulative Selection	Optic Disc	Topographic Map
Curved "Cup" Eye	Optic Nerve	Ventral Stream
Dorsal Stream	Photoreceptors	Visible Spectrum
Extrastriate Cortex	Primary Visual Cortex	Vitreous Humor
Frequency	Pupil	Wavelength
Ganglion Cells	Purity	

Vision 1 & 2 – Bottleneck Concepts

Dorsal vs. Ventral Stream
Information Compression in the Visual Pathway
Rods vs. Cones
Visual Acuity Development

Information Compression in the Visual Pathway

The process of convergence or information compression allows our brain to process the extensive number of stimuli present in the world. Convergence occurs at nearly all levels of the visual pathway and is defined as multiple neurons synapsing onto one neuron. Trillions of light photons are processed by over 125 million photoreceptors which converge onto nearly 1 million ganglion cells. A single ganglion cell receives neuronal input from approximately 120 rods, whereas on average, 6 cones converge onto one ganglion cell. As a result of this lower convergence ratio, cones allow for much higher visual acuity than rods do. Instead of having to process the visual input from 120 photoreceptors, the ganglion cell can focus on processing the input from only 6 photoreceptors. Rods, however, are more sensitive in the dark; less light is required to stimulate the ganglion cell because there are so many more rods available to sense the light. Further converging at the optic disk and onwards along the optic nerve, one LGN cell receives input from multiple ganglion cells and one V1 cell receives input from multiple LGN cells. With this convergence also comes specialization. For example, layer 4 of the LGN will process the visual input from parvocellular ganglion cells of the contralateral eye. The LGN then processes and groups the information and sends some information to the V1 area that processes colour and sends other information to the V1 layer that processes form. Furthermore, the V1 will converge the information and send even more specific information about the lines and orientation of the image to the temporal cortex where it is further converged and processed specifically. Finally, our brain combines all of this input to help create the visual scene we see before us. Incredible!

Test your Understanding

1) What quality allows the fovea of our retina to have such high visual acuity?

2) What does this 1:1 cone-to-ganglion cell convergence in the fovea suggest about the amount of light that will be needed to activate its connected ganglion cell?

Practice case study

Hank is the quarterback for McMaster's football team, and has been training hard for the big playoff game against Western. During the big game, he suffers a massive blow to the head. That night, Hank gets up to go to the bathroom, but for some reason he cannot see anything. He waits for his eyes to adjust to the darkness but they never do. When he turns on the lights, he can see fine except that there appears to be a black dot in the inner section of his left visual field in which he cannot see anything. He turns on the tap to splash water on his face, but the water seems like it is frozen in time, even though he can hear it running.

1) What are the visual deficits that Hank is suffering from?

2) At which level of the visual system do you think each problem lies?

3) Using your knowledge of the visual system, what other types of visual deficits do you think head trauma could cause? Describe what the visual deficit would be and in which part of the visual system the associated damage would occur.

Concept Map: Vision 1 & 2

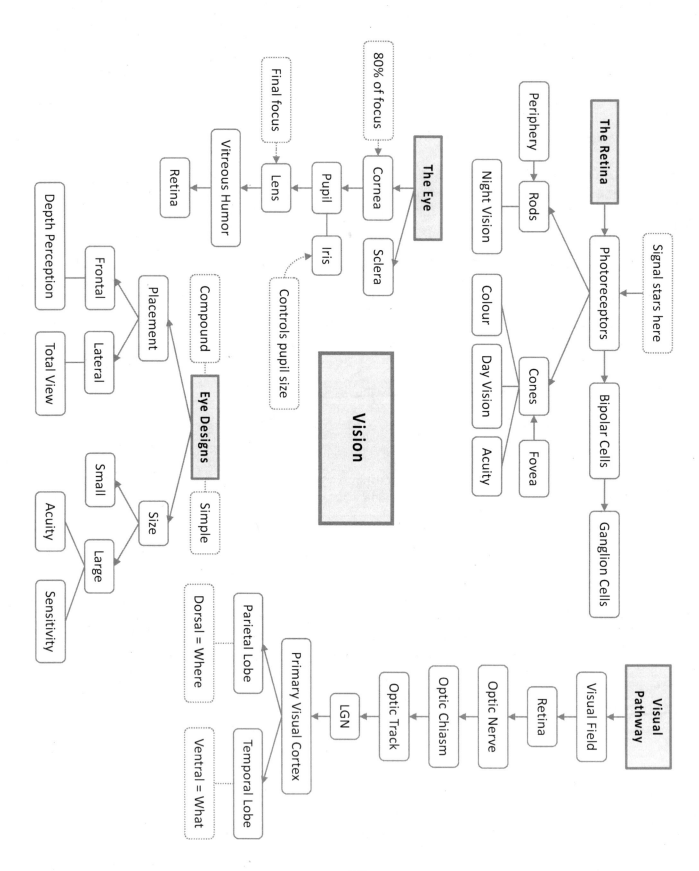

145

Accommodation
Vision

Amacrine Cells
Vision

Amplitude
Vision

Bipolar Cells
Vision

Compound Eyes
Vision

Cones
Vision

Cornea
Vision

Cumulative Selection
Vision

Similar to the horizontal cells, these cells allow adjacent photoreceptors to combine their information such that 130 million photoreceptors converge on 1 million axons in the optic nerve. **Personal Example:**	The process in which the lens of the eye changes shape to focus on objects at varying distances. It becomes rounder when looking at closer objects and flatter when looking at further objects. **Personal Example:**
A layer of cells in the retina that receive information from photoreceptors and then send that information to the ganglion cells. **Personal Example:**	The height of a wave. For light, amplitude corresponds to the perception of brightness. Larger amplitude corresponds to a brighter colour *(Vision)*. For sound, it corresponds to the perception of loudness. Waves of larger amplitudes correspond to louder sounds. **Personal Example:**
A class of photoreceptors, which transmit information about colour at high light intensities. In comparison to rods, they provide better acuity and are much less populous. They are concentrated in the fovea. **Personal Example:**	The type of eye found in arthropods. These are made up of an arrangement of tubular units called ommatidia, each pointing in a slightly different direction to gather light. Signals from each ommatidium combine to form a single image. **Personal Example:**
The evolutionary process whereby new adaptations are layered upon old adaptations, gradually increasing the sophistication of a trait. The human eye is an example of cumulative selection. **Personal Example:**	The transparent window at the front of the eye allowing light to first pass through and where the focusing of light begins. It is the most external structure of the eye. **Personal Example:**

Curved "Cup" Eye
Vision

Dorsal Stream
Vision

Extrastriate Cortex
Vision

Frequency
Vision

Ganglion Cells
Vision

Horizontal Cells
Vision

Iris
Vision

Lateral Geniculate Nucleus (LGN)
Vision

The "where" pathway in vision, which begins in the occipital lobe and terminates in the parietal lobe. It processes information regarding movement and spatial location of objects. **Personal Example:**	The primitive design of the eye that can still be found today in clams. It allows only for basic functions of vision but has an advantage over the light sensitive patch as it allows the organism to sense the direction of the light. **Personal Example:**
A measure of the distance between peaks of a wave. A higher frequency corresponds to a smaller wavelength because there is less distance between successive peaks. **Personal Example:**	Visual processing areas in the occipital lobe that are outside of the primary visual cortex (V1). Processing of more complex visual information occurs here, as well as the beginning of associations and integration with other sensory areas. **Personal Example:**
Similar to amacrine cells, these cells allow adjacent photoreceptors to combine their information such that 130 million photoreceptors converge on 1 million axons in the optic nerve. **Personal Example:**	The layer of cells in the retina that bipolar cells send their information to. They are the front layer of the cells in the retina. Their axons converge on a single point of the eye called the optic disc. **Personal Example:**
The part of the thalamus that receives visual information from retinal ganglion cells after they cross at the optic chiasm and relays it to the primary visual cortex. **Personal Example:**	The coloured part of the eye. It consists of a band of muscles that receive signals from the brain to dilate and constrict the pupil depending on the amount of light reaching the eye. **Personal Example:**

Lens Vision	**Light Sensitive Patch** Vision
Ommatidia Vision	**Optic Chiasm** Vision
Optic Disc Vision	**Optic Nerve** Vision
Photoreceptors Vision	**Primary Visual Cortex** Vision

An example of what primitive eyes may have started out as. Jellyfish and worms have something like this form of eye today. **Personal Example:**	A transparent, flexible structure that does the final focusing of light onto the retina. It may change in shape (accommodate) to focus on objects at different distances, contributing to depth perception. **Personal Example:**
The point at which the optic nerves from the inside half of each eye cross over to the opposite hemisphere. **Personal Example:**	The tubular units that make up the compound eye of arthropods. These point in slightly different directions to gather light directly in front of them and when multiple units are put together, make up a single image that is perceived by the organism. **Personal Example:**
One of the cranial nerves, it is a bundle of ganglion cell axons that transmit visual information out the back of the eye to the brain. **Personal Example:**	The point on the eye at which the axons of the ganglion cell converge and exit to the optic nerve. It is responsible for the human visual blind spot, as this area contains no photoreceptors. **Personal Example:**
Labeled as area V1 in the occipital cortex, it is the first major visual relay area in the cortex where basic visual information is processed. The receptive fields of many LGN cells combine to form the receptive field of a single V1 cell. **Personal Example:**	Cells located on the retina that convert the physical stimulus of light into a neural impulse that is passed to the brain. There are two types of photoreceptors: rods (black and white vision) and cones (colour vision). **Personal Example:**

Pupil
Vision

Purity
Vision

Receptive Field
Vision

Retina
Vision

Retinal Pigment Epithelium (RPE)
Vision

Rods
Vision

Saturation
Vision

Sclera
Vision

A physical characteristic of light, which affects the perception of the saturation, or richness of colours. A pure light wave is composed of a single wavelength of light, while impure light is a mixture of several wavelengths. **Personal Example:**	The round window that appears as a black dot in the middle of the human eye. It is here that light passes through to the lens after it has passed through the cornea. **Personal Example:**
The neural tissue that lines the back of the eye. It consists of photoreceptors where the physical stimulus of light is translated into neural impulses. **Personal Example:**	The collection of rods and cones in the retina that, when stimulated, affect the firing of a particular ganglion cell. Certain receptive fields are responsive to different colours, shades, and shapes. **Personal Example:**
The class of photoreceptors that are primarily used for night vision, provide no colour information and have poor visual acuity. They are more populous than cones and are located in the periphery of the retina. **Personal Example:**	A layer of cells at the very back of the retina to which photoreceptors are connected. The RPE cells provide the photoreceptors with the nutrition required to survive and are the reason for the inside-out arrangement of the eye. **Personal Example:**
A tough structural membrane that covers the portion of the eye not covered by the cornea. The sclera provides the eye with its white appearance. **Personal Example:**	A psychological characteristic of light, corresponding to the purity of a light stimulus. Saturated colours are richer than de-saturated colours and de-saturated colours make up the majority of the natural world. **Personal Example:**

Simple Eye
Vision

Topographic Map
Vision

Ventral Stream
Vision

Visible Spectrum
Vision

Vitreous Humor
Vision

Wavelength
Vision

Retinal coordinates are topographically mapped onto the visual cortex. Neighbouring locations in the visual field correspond to neighbouring locations in the retina, which project to neighbouring locations in the visual cortex. **Personal Example:**	The type of eye found in vertebrates and molluscs that contains an eyeball, lens and retina. This type may vary in exact design by species and environment but is the type of eye that we think of when we think of eyes. **Personal Example:**
The portion of the total range of wavelengths of electromagnetic radiation to which humans are visually sensitive, or, what humans can see. The shortest wavelength of the visible spectrum is 360 nanometers (violet) and the longest is 750 nanometers (red). **Personal Example:**	The "what" visual pathway that starts in the occipital cortex and terminates in the temporal lobe. It processes information about object identity (including form and colour). **Personal Example:**
A physical characteristic corresponding to the distance between peaks of a wave. It corresponds to the psychological characteristic of colour. On the visible spectrum, the shortest wavelengths appear purple while the longest appear red. **Personal Example:**	The clear, jelly-like substance comprising the main chamber of the eyeball. Light passes from the lens, through the vitreous humour, to the retina. **Personal Example:**

Colour Perception

"A colour is as strong as the impression it creates."
- Ivan Albright, renowned American magic realist painter

Claude Monet was Half Honeybee

Colour does not exist in the world but is created by your brain. At face value, this is a difficult statement to accept. While at the Art Institute of Chicago, I came across a wing dedicated to Claude Monet (1840), a French painter, considered to be the father of impressionism—an art style that attempts to portray a fleeting impression of a scene (usually outdoor) using bold and vibrant colours. Uniquely, Monet's paintings are a reflection of how his colour vision changed throughout his lifetime. Later in Monet's career he developed cataracts that gave his eye's lens a yellow-tinge. As explained through subtractive colour mixing theory, the yellow lens subtracted short wavelength colours (blues and purples) from his perceptual scene and left him perceiving mostly long wavelength colours such as yellows, reds, oranges and greens. As a result, Monet's paintings took on this reddish colour palette. Three years before his passing, Monet underwent a surgery to remove the lens from his affected right eye which led to his recognition as "half a honeybee". Bees can see colours into the UV spectrum, which translates to seeing bluer blues and more violet violets. The human eyes' lens filters out this UV light to protect the retina. Therefore, when it was removed, Monet could see shorter UV rays that he could never see before. As a result, his paintings took on a bright blue and purple vibrancy that likely could not even be captured by paint pigments. In 1924, Monet painted the same scene twice, once with each eye shut. Through his remaining cataract eye it was dark, red and yellow and through his lens-less eye it was vibrant blue and violet. Visit the YouTube video cited below for a look! Colour perception is not a unified and unchanging experience. You may perceive colour differently than your friend does and your colour vision may change throughout your lifetime.

Hanson, J. (2014, January 20). Claude Monet Was Half Honeybee: It's Okay to Be Smart, PBS Digital Studios [Video file]. Retrieved from https://www.youtube.com/watch?v=sZ8yMYvHc5E

Marmor, M. F. (2006). Ophthalmology and art: Simulation of Monet's cataracts and Degas' retinal disease. *Archives of Ophthalmology, 124*(12), 1764-1769.

Samu, M. (2004, October). Impressionism: Art and modernity. In Heilbrunn timeline of art history. New York: The Metropolitan Museum of Art. Retrieved from http://www.metmuseum.org/toah/hd/imml/hd_imml.htm

Weekly Checklist:
- ☐ **Web modules to watch: Colour Perception**
- ☐ **Readings: Chapter 6**
- ☐ **Pre-Quiz & Quiz 6**

Colour Perception – Outline

Unit 1: Introduction to Colour Perception
_____
_____
_____
_____
_____

Colour is a creation of our minds.
_____
_____
_____
_____
_____

Unit 2: Evolution of Colour Vision

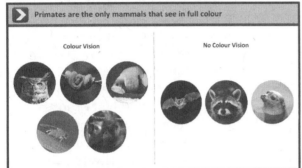

Colour Vision is not universal
_____
_____

Animals with colour vision:
_____
_____
_____

Animals without colour vision:
_____
_____
_____
_____

Colour vision can help with foraging and mate selection.

Function of colour vision in primates?
_____
_____
_____

Function in birds?
_____
_____

Function in bees?
_____
_____

Unit 3: Colour Mixing

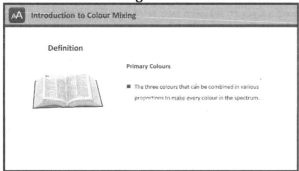

The eye only needs a few colour receptors to perceive millions of colours.
_____
_____
_____
_____

Primary colours:
_____
_____
_____
_____
_____

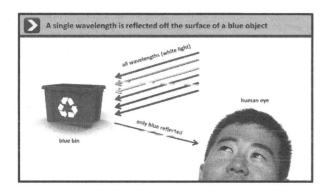

Subtractive colour mixing occurs when a pigmented surface absorbs the colours that are not reflected/perceived.
_____
_____
_____
_____

Blue?
_____
_____

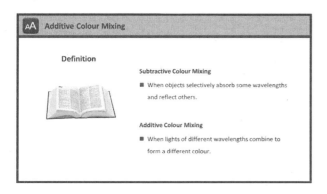

Additive colour mixing occurs by adding the effects of different wavelengths together in our nervous system.

Additive colour mixing:
_____
_____
_____

Primary/ complementary colours:
_____
_____

White?
_____

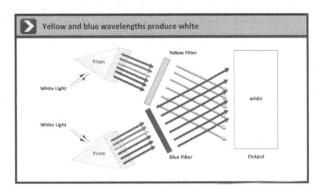

Mixing coloured lights: _____
_____
_____
_____
_____

RGB TV screen: _____
_____
_____
_____
_____

Unit 4: Theories of Colour Vision

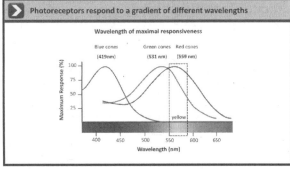

Trichromatic theory (Young-Helmholtz): Retina contains three different kinds of receptors/cones.
_____
_____

Maximally responsive: _____
_____
_____
_____
_____

Yellow: _____
White: _____
_____
_____
_____
_____
_____

The trichromatic theory was developed from empirical observations.
_____
_____
_____
_____

The trichromatic theory could not explain all colour observations.

Pros: _____
_____
_____
_____

Cons: _____
_____
_____
_____
_____

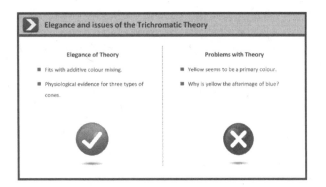

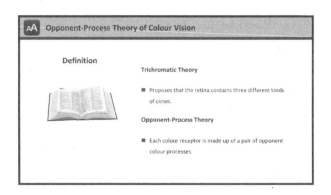

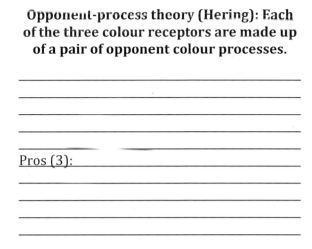

Opponent-process theory (Hering): Each of the three colour receptors are made up of a pair of opponent colour processes.

Pros (3):

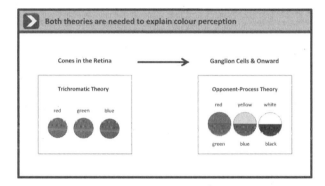

Both theories are accurate in explaining different components of colour perception.

Hurvich & Jameson:

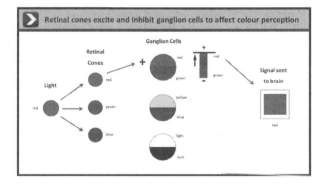

Red:

Green:

Blue:

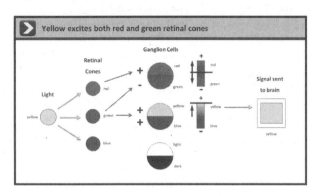

Yellow light causes equal activation of both the red & green cones.

Unit 5: Colour Processing in the Brain

The rate of firing faster or slower than baseline signals to the brain what colour is being seen.

Afterimages:

Rebound effect:

A green-red cell is not the same as a red-green cell. The same is true for blue-yellow and yellow-blue cells

Receptive fields:

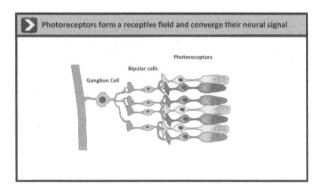

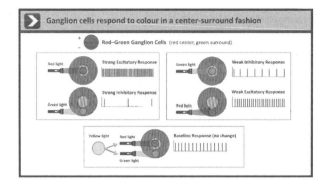

The receptive field of ganglion cells are colour sensitive and respond in a center-surround fashion.

___

Note:* A green-red ganglion cell would have the opposite center-surround colour behaviour compared to red-green ganglion cell.

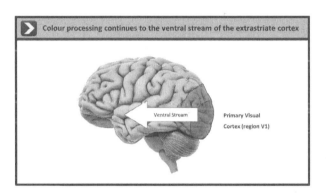

Colour information is analyzed further in the ventral stream of the extrastriate cortex.

___

Unit 6: Colour Blindness

___

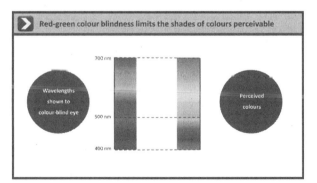

Inherited red-green colour blindness (CB) is the most common form of CB.

<u>Monocular CB case study:</u>

___

<u>Causes of CB:</u>

___

162

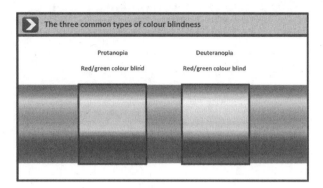

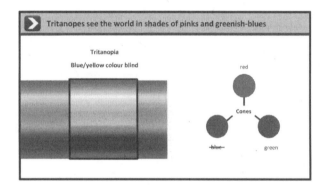

Three types of colour blindness:

1) Protonopia

2) Deuteranopia:

Similarities:

3) Tritanopia

Prevalence?

Colour Perception – Courseware Exercise

1. You have heard about the two types of colour mixing. Describe both types of colour mixing and give examples of how each type of colour mixing is used in everyday life (use new examples not presented in the module).

Subtractive Colour Mixing:
_____

Example:
_____

Additive Colour Mixing:
_____

Example:
_____

2. You also learned about two theories that were developed to explain colour perception. Compare and contrast the trichromatic theory and the opponent-process theory. Include the problems that each theory could and could not solve.

Trichromatic Theory	Opponent-Process Theory

3. How were these theories resolved?
_____
_____
_____
_____
_____
_____
_____

Colour Perception – Review Questions

1. Which of the following is true?

    a) Bees can see in the UV spectrum in order to determine the health of a mate
    b) Bees can see in the Infrared spectrum in order to distinguish important regions of a flower for food
    c) Bees can see in the Infrared spectrum in order to determine the health of a mate
    d) Bees can see in the UV spectrum in order to distinguish important regions of a flower for food

2. Which of the following is true?

    a) Adding two colours of paint is an example of additive colour mixing because each colour adds its dominant wavelength to the mix of paints.
    b) Adding two colours of paint is an example of subtractive colour mixing because each paint pigment absorbs all the colours except the one you see
    c) Our visual system works through subtractive colour mixing as our retinal pigments absorb all colours but the perceived light
    d) Our visual system works by additive colour mixing as our nervous system adds the effects of various wavelengths.
    e) b and d

3. A green light striking the middle region of a *green-red* ganglion cell would show a _____ response, while a red light striking the middle region of a *green-red* ganglion would show a _____ response.

    a) weak inhibitory, strong excitatory
    b) strong inhibitory, weak excitatory
    c) strong excitatory, weak inhibitory
    d) strong, weak

4. Michael and Victor cannot distinguish red from green. Which of the following is true?

    a) Both of them have protanopia
    b) Both of them have deuteranopia
    c) Michael has protanopia while Victor has deuteranopia
    d) Michael has deuteranopia while Victor has protanopia
    e) We cannot tell, we would need to know which photopigment is missing

Colour Perception – Test Question

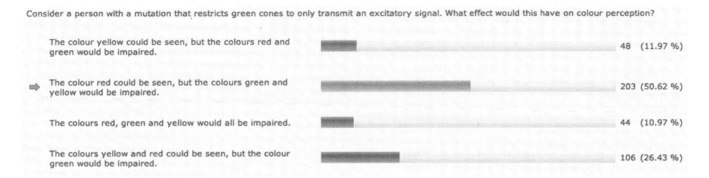

This is an actual question from the Colour Perception quiz that many students struggled with. We are going to tackle this question together.

This is a very common type of test question that has and will continue to appear on your online tests. Rather than testing to see whether or not you can memorize a particular function, this question tests whether or not you understand a function and apply it to a new situation. In this case, identifying the result of green cone mutation on colour perception. To answer this question properly, we need to understand the role of the green cone in processing the different colours presented in the web module. In this way, we can then identify what the result of altering this cone would be.

Which colours, presented in the web module, involve activity of the green cones? Green and yellow. Now, what is the pattern of activity associated with perception of the colour green? Well, green light activates the green cones. Green cones send inhibitory signals to the red-green ganglion cells. The brain interprets the inhibition of this ganglion cell as the colour green. Next, what is the pattern of activity associated with perception of the colour yellow? Well, yellow light activates the red and green cones. Red cones send **excitatory** signals to the red-green ganglion cells and **inhibitory** signals to blue-yellow ganglion cells. Green cones send **inhibitory** signals to red-green ganglion cells and **inhibitory** signals to blue-yellow ganglion cells. Activity from the green and red cones upon the red-green ganglion cells causes no activation of the red/green ganglion cell (remember this ganglion cells is receiving an **inhibitory** and **excitatory** input). This leaves only activation of the yellow-blue ganglion cell (remember it received two excitatory inputs). As a result we see yellow.

With a firm understanding of how we perceive the colour green and yellow, we are now properly equipped to identify the result of "messing" with a green cone. Let's begin by examining the answer options.

A. Remember, we need an inhibitory signal to be sent from the green cone, to cancel out the effect of the red/green ganglion, in order to perceive the colour yellow. The mutation, however, allows only transmission of excitatory signals from the green cones. This option, therefore, is incorrect.
B. Is the green cone involved in the perception of red? No, so red would be unaffected by the mutation. Is the green cone involved in the perception of the colour green? Yes, green light activates the green cone and causes an inhibitory signal to be sent to the red-green ganglion cell. The mutation allows for only transmission of excitatory signals from the green cones. Therefore, green perception would be impaired. What about perception of the colour yellow? We need an inhibitory signal to be sent from the green cone in order to perceive the colour yellow. Yellow must also be impaired as a result of the mutation. This answer seems to be correct.

C. Is the colour red impaired by a mutation to the green cones? No. This option is incorrect.
D. Remember that we need an inhibitory signal to be sent from the green cone to the red-green ganglion cells in order to perceive the colour yellow. The mutation, however, allows only transmission of excitatory signals from the green cones. This option, therefore, is incorrect.

These types of application style questions are a great way to test a student's understanding of a particular phenomenon or function. If you already understand the pathway associated with colour perception then this question should be a piece of cake. If you didn't, fear not! For we have just reviewed this pathway in the current walkthrough! Although the online tests are open book, make sure you take the time to fully understand each and every cognitive process or phenomenon you are exposed to in this course. With a 20 minute time limit, you will not have time to review complicated concepts like colour perception while completing your online tests.

Key Terms

Additive Colour Mixing	Opponent-Process Theory	Subtractive Colour Mixing
Afterimages	Primary Colours	Trichromatic Theory
Complementary Colours	Protanopia	Tritanopia
Deuteranopia	Rebound Effect	

Colour Perception – Bottleneck Concepts

Additive vs. Subtractive Colour Mixing
Trichromatic Theory vs. Opponent Process Theory
Protanopia vs. Deuteranopia

Additive vs. Subtractive Colour Mixing

When we think about colour mixing, we usually think about mixing paints as a child, but this is only one side of the coin. The mixing of pigments is referred to as subtractive colour mixing. It is called 'subtractive' because the surface of the object absorbs (or subtracts away) some of the wavelengths of light, while reflecting others. On the other hand, we have additive colour mixing. This is when colours of light are combined. It is called additive because when lights are mixed, they add their dominant wavelengths together to form a new colour.

Both additive and subtractive colour mixing have primary and secondary colours. Additive colour mixing's primary colours are red, blue, and green. Note that these are the same colours as the cones in your eye. The secondary colours are yellow, magenta, and cyan. For subtractive colour mixing it is the opposite. The primary colours are yellow, magenta, and cyan, while the secondary colours are red, blue, and green. The opposites don't stop there. When you combine the primary colours of light you get white, but when you combine the primary colours of pigments you get black.

The final important term for colour mixing is "complementary" colours. The complementary colour of any primary colour is always the secondary colour produced by mixing the remain two primary colours. For example, in additive colour mixing, the complementary colour of blue is yellow (which is created by mixing red and green together). Interestingly, complementary colours are the same in both additive and subtractive colour mixing. If you look at the complementary colour for yellow in subtractive colour mixing, it would also be blue (which is the result of mixing cyan and magenta).

Test your Understanding

1) Fill in the two colour wheels for additive and subtractive colour mixing. You can use either different coloured markers or just indicate which colour goes where.

Additive   **Subtractive**

2) Which of the following is correct regarding additive and subtractive colour mixing?
   a) Additive and subtractive colour mixing have different primary colours but the same secondary colours.
   b) Additive colour mixing describes mixing paint colours while subtractive colour mixing involves mixing light.
   c) Additive and subtractive colour mixing have the same primary colours but different secondary colours.
   d) Additive and subtractive colour mixing have the same complementary colour parings.

Practice case study

1) Read each scenario and determine:
   i. What type of colour blindness the individual suffers from
   ii. What is happening at the level of the cones that leads to this deficit
   iii. Why the individuals would have difficulty with these particular tasks

Melanie is a 38-year old mother of two, and recently has encountered several issues that have led her husband to suggest that she be tested for colour blindness. During a recent trip to the beach, Melanie did not notice her youngest child becoming sunburned and forgot to reapply his sunscreen. The battery on her camera died soon after reaching the beach, as Melanie can never tell when the battery is getting low. The other night at dinner, Melanie became very sick after eating a piece of meat that was much too rare. When driving in the very bright sunlight or in foggy weather, Melanie is unable to distinguish between the coloured traffic lights.

Roger was diagnosed with a form of colour blindness when he was seven years old, but despite this has had only minor repercussions in his everyday life. While playing Frisbee with his friends, Roger found it difficult to find the blue Frisbee in the grass, and Roger often asks the advice of his girlfriend when deciding which pieces of clothing to match for an important event. Roger also wishes he could see the full spectrum of colours in a sunset, as they do not seem as exciting or beautiful as he hears people describe.

Anthony is a 6-year-old child who has always been a very picky eater, much to the frustration of his parents. He complains that his food always looks yucky, and is particularly put off by bright coloured fruits and vegetables. Anthony plays on a soccer team, and often has trouble differentiating who is on his team. During a recent game of mini-golf, Anthony became frustrated when he could not find his orange ball in the grass. When his mother suggests that Anthony could be colour blind, his father responds that he definitely is not, as Anthony can accurately identify the colour of any object by name.

Concept Map: Colour Perception

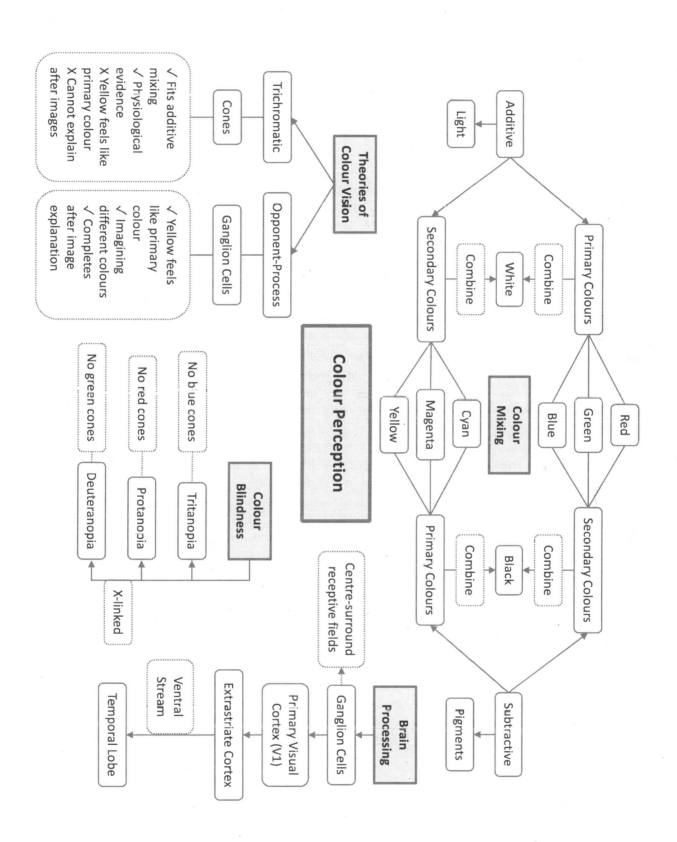

Additive Colour Mixing
Colour Perception

Afterimages
Colour Perception

Complementary Colours
Colour Perception

Deuteranopia
Colour Perception

Opponent-Process Theory
Colour Perception

Primary Colours
Colour Perception

Protonopia
Colour Perception

Rebound Effect
Colour Perception

A phenomenon in which the complementary colours of an image are seen after staring at the image, and then viewing a white surface. Afterimages occur when a colour receptor that has been excited for a prolonged period of time while viewing the image habituates, causing the relevant ganglion cell to go into the opposite, inhibited state, resulting in the perception of the complementary colour. **Personal Example:**	When lights of different wavelengths combine to form a different colour. This is the colour system used by the visual system, where the effects of different wavelengths are added together. **Personal Example:**
A form of red/green colour blindness in which the green cones are missing. **Personal Example:**	Pairs of colours that, when mixed, produce black in subtractive colour mixing and white in additive colour mixing. These pairs are opposite each other on a colour wheel **Personal Example:**
The three colours that can be combined in various proportions to produce every colour in the visual spectrum. They are base colours that cannot be reduced into other colours. **Personal Example:**	A theory in colour vision that argues that there are three classes of colour receptors, each made up of a pair of opponent processes. Each receptor is capable of being in the following opponent states: black-white, blue-yellow, and red-green. This theory explains colour vision at the level of ganglion cells. **Personal Example:**
When a colour receptor is excited for a prolonged period of time, it habituates, causing the relevant ganglion cell to go into the opposite, inhibited state, resulting in the perception of the complementary colour. **Personal Example:**	A form of red-green colour blindness in which the red cones are missing. **Personal Example:**

Subtractive Colour Mixing
Colour Perception

Trichromatic Theory
Colour Perception

Tritanopia
Colour Perception

A theory of colour vision, based on the proposal that the retina contains three different kinds of receptors that are maximally responsive to different wavelengths of light – red, green and blue. This theory explains colour vision at the level of retinal cones. **Personal Example:**	A form of colour mixing in which coloured pigments selectively absorb (or subtract) some wavelengths and reflect others. This type of colour mixing applies to pigments, dyes or paints. **Example:** A blue object looks blue because all wavelengths are being absorbed by the object except blue, which reflects back to the eyes **Personal Example:**
	A form of colour blindness in which the blue cones are lacking or defective. It is a very rare form of colour blindness that causes people to see in shades of pinks and greenish-blues. **Personal Example:**

Form Perception 1 & 2

"There are wholes, the behaviour of which is not determined by that of their individual elements, but where the part-processes are themselves determined by the intrinsic nature of the whole"
- Max Wertheimer, one of the three founders of Gestalt Psychology

You're a Wizard, Harry

Anyone who has ever seen a Harry Potter film can recall they first time we laid eyes on Hagrid the half-giant wizard. Hagrid busted down the door to The Dursley's vacation home to gift Harry a birthday cake and spoke the famous words, "you're a wizard, Harry". In a world where giants don't actually exist, Warner Brothers' had to take advantage of form perception and visual illusions to make Hagrid appear larger than life. Forced perspective is an optical illusion that utilizes size constancy to make objects appear smaller or larger than they really are. During filming, Harry would stand approximately two times as far from the camera than Hagrid would. The further Harry was from the camera, the smaller he appeared. However to make this simple trick more believable, the film makers had to ensure that the brightness and focus on the more distant Harry was the same as that on Hagrid. Interestingly, Hagrid and Harry never once filmed while making direct eye contact; Hagrid was always closer to the camera than Harry was. Therefore, the actor's had to adjust their eye gaze and mannerisms to ensure that it appeared like they were interacting directly with one another. Additionally, the size of the actors' props had to be modified depending on who was holding it. For example, the birthday cake box that Hagrid held was much smaller than the box that Harry held. As a result, the box looked tiny in Hagrid's hands but insanely large in Harry's.

A recent example is from TV series Game of Thrones, when the Stark characters interact with their car-sized dire wolves. The dire wolves are not computer simulated, but are rather real wolves that are positioned closer to the camera than the characters. As a result, the audience perceives them to be giant-sized man-eating wolves, when they are actually just normal sized man-eating wolves. Perceptual constancies help humans understand and interact with our regular mundane world, but can also help us see the mystical and imaginary. The film and television industry can manipulate our minds to see things the way they want us to.

[Tyler Haslett]. (2009, December 8). *Movie Magic Episode 5: Forced Perspective Discovery Channel.* [Video File]. Retrieved from https://youtu.be/htWY43bEYA4

Weekly Checklist:
- ☐ Web modules to watch: Form Perception 1 & 2
- ☐ Readings: Chapter 7
- ☐ Pre-Quiz & Quiz 7

Form Perception 1 – Outline

Unit 1: Introduction to Form Perception

_____
_____
_____

Unit 2: Gestalt Principles

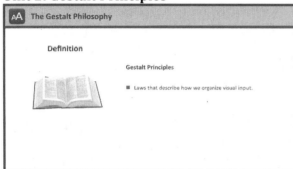

Gestalt psychologists believe that the human experience should not be reduced into its elements, but rather observed as a whole.

_____
_____
_____
_____
_____

Movie example: _____
_____

There are six Gestalt principles that help describe how we group visual input.

_____
_____
_____
_____

1) Figure-ground _____
_____
_____
_____
_____
_____

2) Proximity _____
_____
_____
_____
_____
_____
_____
_____
_____

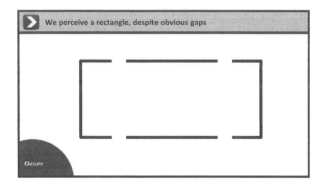

3) Closure

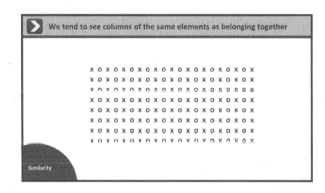

4) Similarity

5) Continuity

6) Common fate

Unit 3: Pattern/Object Recognition

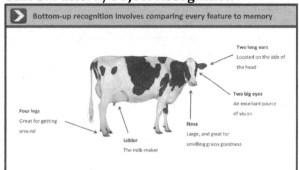

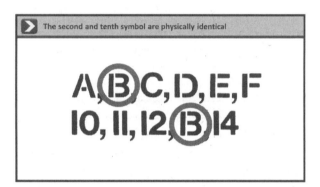

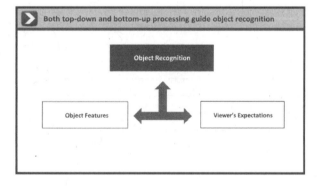

Bottom-up and top-down processing help guide object recognition.

Bottom-up processing (Cow):

Top-down processing (THE CAT & B/13):

Top-down and bottom-up processing both play an important role

1) Geon Theory:

_____
_____
_____
_____

Criticisms (2):
_____
_____
_____
_____
_____
_____

2) Template Theory:

Evidence:
_____
_____
_____
_____

Criticism:
_____
_____
_____

3) Prototype Theory:

Evidence:
_____
_____
_____
_____

Criticism:
_____
_____
_____

Note: **Parallel processing:** _____

Unit 4: Perceptual Constancies

Perceptual constancies help us recognize objects despite a changing visual image.

_____
_____
_____

1) Shape constancy:
_____
_____
_____
_____
_____
_____

2) Location constancy:

3) Size constancy:

4) Brightness constancy:

Checker shadow illusion:

5) Colour constancy:

Reasons for perceptual constancies:

1) Existing knowledge:

2) Cues in a scene:

Unit 5: Visual Illusions

Visual illusions can occur when the brain has to process ambiguous or partial visual information.

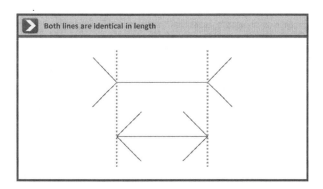

Müller-Lyer Illusion:

Experience dependant?

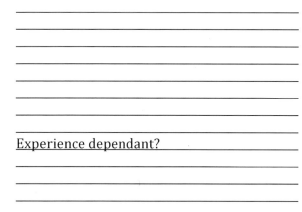

Ames Room Illusion:

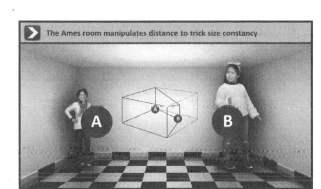

Ponzo Illusion:

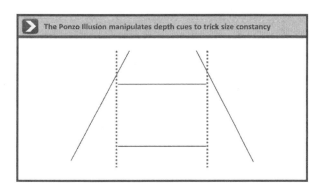

The way we *see* the world is not really the way the world *actually* is.

Form Perception 1 – Courseware Exercise

You have now learned about each Gestalt principle and understand how they relate to vision in our everyday lives. Often, however, one part of the visual scene will incorporate several of these effects, and amazingly our brains are able to easily interpret what we are seeing.

1. In this vein, it is important to understand how our brains treat more ambiguous visual scenes; scenes that contain two or more organizational rules (Gestalt principles). Imagine you want to find out how we perceive stimuli that can be organized by both similarity AND proximity. What would a potential research question be?

_____
_____

2. An important factor when discussing Gestalt principles is the stimuli being observed. Draw a simple sketch of the stimuli that you could present to participants to test your question. How could you experimentally manipulate these stimuli to examine the interplay between similarity and proximity, especially when they are working in opposition to one another?

_____
_____
_____

3. You've now learned about the five perceptual constancies that enable us to recognize the same object in different scenarios. Describe the everyday situation where the following perceptual constancies will be relevant, i.e., when I'm driving in a car, the buildings appear to move.

Shape Constancy: _____

Location Constancy: _____

Size Constancy: _____

Brightness Constancy: _____

Colour Constancy: _____

Form Perception 1 – Review Questions

1. _____ groups small enclosed regions to portray a distinct form among formless surroundings, while _____ is used when there is a discontinuity in a shape's edges.

   a) closure, continuity
   b) figure-ground, closure
   c) continuity, closure
   d) closure, figure-ground

2. After a long night of drinking, Jorge wakes up very groggy and does not know where he is. Using his senses he smells manure, feels straw, and hears cows mooing. He concludes he must have woken up in a barn. This is an example of what type of processing?

   a) Top up processing
   b) Top down processing
   c) Break down processing
   d) Bottom up processing

3 While walking through the forest, Tommy witnesses a strange but familiar looking bird fly by. He scans his memories and finds a bird that mirrors the bird he saw in the forest. Which of the following theories would best explain this scenario?

   a) Availability theory
   b) Template theory
   c) Prototype theory
   d) Geon theory

4. Which of the following is true about the Muller-Lyer illusion?

   a) It is due to a misattribution of size constancy leading to an inaccurate interpretation of size and is unaffected by cultural experience
   b) It is due to a misattribution of size constancy leading to an inaccurate interpretation of depth and is unaffected by cultural experiences
   c) It is due to a misattribution of size constancy leading to an inaccurate interpretation of depth and is affected by cultural experiences
   d) It is due to a misattribution of size constancy leading to an inaccurate interpretation of size and is affected by cultural experience

Concept Map: Form Perception 1

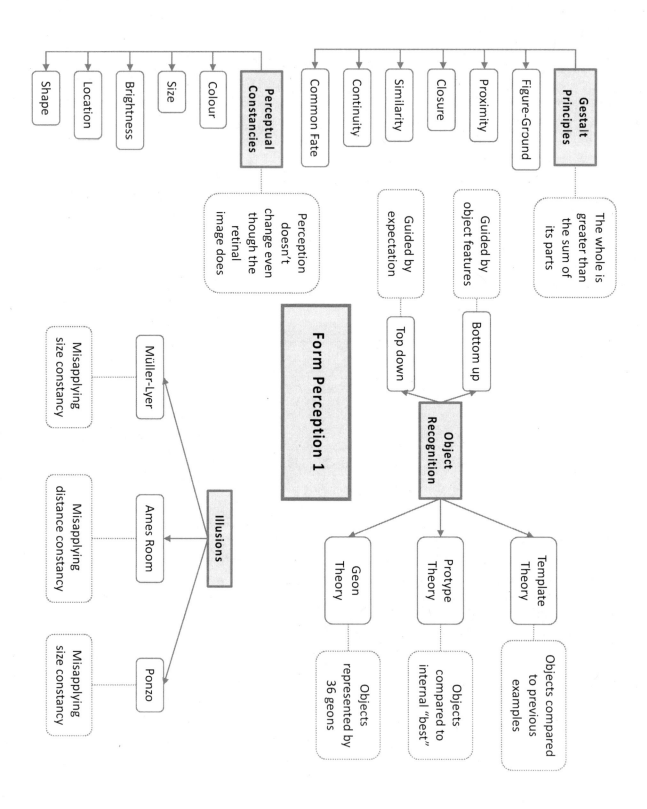

Form Perception 2 – Outline

Unit 1: Feature Detectors

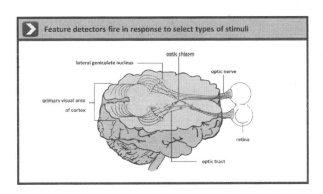

Hodgkin & Huxley (1952): _____

Lettvin et al. (1959): _____

Hubel & Wiesel: _____

Form is processed along the ventral stream of the visual pathway.

Ganglion cells are the crucial first step to object recognition

Not all neurons fire maximally to the same stimuli; the shape, size, position and movement of the stimuli matters.

Simple Cells – orientation

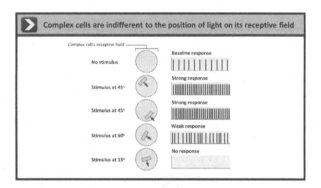

Complex Cells – orientation & direction

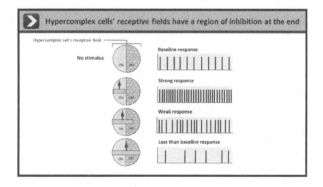

Hypercomplex Cells – orientation, direction & length

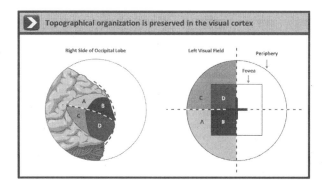

The layout of the visual scene on the retina is preserved in the occipital lobe.

Retinotopic mapping: _____
_____
_____
_____
_____

Parallel processing? _____
_____
_____
_____
_____

Unit 2: Ventral Stream

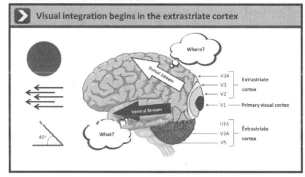

The varied visual information from specific cells must be combined in the visual association cortex.
_____
_____
_____
_____
_____
_____
_____
_____
_____

Dorsal stream: _____
_____
_____
_____

Ventral stream: _____
_____
_____
_____

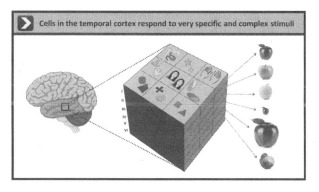

The neurons housed in the columns of the temporal cortex respond to very complex stimuli.
_____
_____
_____
_____
_____

Activity patterns? _____
_____
_____

Unit 3: Development of Pattern/Object/Face Recognition

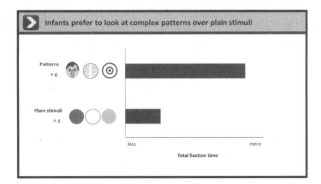

Infants will prefer the most complex stimuli they are *able* to perceive.

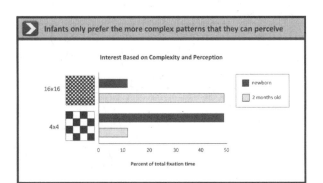

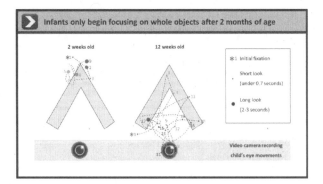

At 2 months, infants struggle to perceive objects holistically.

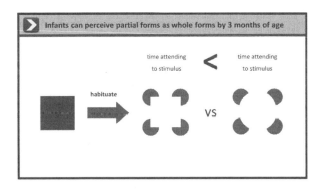

At 3 months, infants can perceive whole forms even when given partial figures.

Habituation?

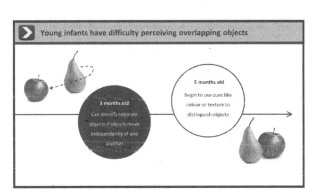

Young infants have trouble differentiating overlapping objects.

Colour/texture?

Movement?

Perceptual constancies in infancy:

4 months?

Ganrud's size constancy study:

4/5 months?

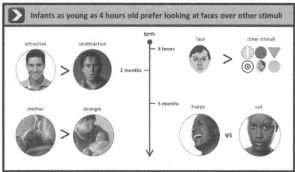

Some findings suggest we have an innate preference for faces.

4 hours:

2 months:

5 months:

Other studies argue that infant face preference is actually just a preference for complex stimuli.

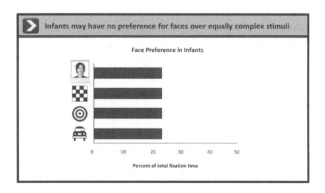

Face tracking studies:

Outer contours:

Inner regions:

Our early experiences shape our preference for faces.

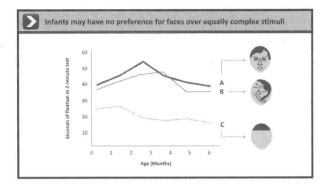

Preferential looking paradigm:

Unit 4: Normal and Abnormal Visual Development

Normal visual development requires an interaction between genes and the environment.

Kitten study:

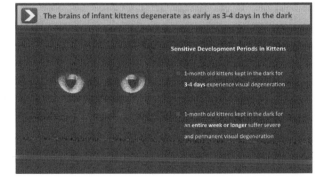

The brain depends on relevant stimulation early in life to maintain certain functions.

1 mo. and 3-4 days of deprivation:

1 mo. and 1+ week of deprivation:

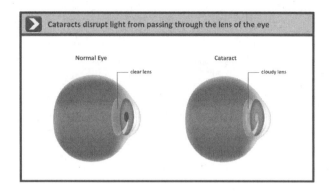

Cataract studies allow us to naturally study the effects of early visual deprivation on human visual development.

_____
_____
_____
_____
_____
_____
_____
_____
_____
_____
_____

Unit 5: Visual Agnosia and Prosopagnosia

Primary visual cortex damage:
_____
_____
_____
_____
_____

Extrastriate cortex damage:
_____
_____
_____
_____
_____
_____

Visual agnosia → 1) Object Agnosia
_____
_____
_____
_____
_____
_____

Exp: The Man Who Mistook His Wife for a Hat:
_____
_____
_____
_____
_____

Visual agnosia → 2) Prosopagnosia
_____
_____
_____
_____
_____
_____
_____
_____
_____
_____
_____

Form Perception 2 – Courseware Exercise

1. In this module, you learned that visual input is not meaningful until visual information is combined in the extrastriate cortex. The extrastriate cortex receives information about the visual scene from the primary visual cortex and beyond. It is within the extrastriate or visual association cortex that information begins to be segregated into two streams according to the type of visual information being processed. Look around your environment, you may be in your room, in the library or outdoors. Using what you know about the dorsal and ventral streams explain how your visual scene is being processed in your extrastriate cortex and beyond.

_____
_____
_____
_____

2. Simple, complex and hypercomplex cells are used for different purposes. State the function of each cell type.

Simple: _____
_____

Complex: _____
_____

Hypercomplex: _____
_____

3. Nancy has a new baby brother, Jamie. After a few days in the hospital, her family takes him home. Excited to play with the baby, Nancy shows him a picture of a big yellow sun she drew for him the day before; she holds the picture next to her face. What will Jamie look at?

_____

4. Nancy's sister Annie also wants to play with her brother. She comes into the room wearing her favourite shirt with four large squares on it. Nancy's also wearing her checkered shirt, but it has 64 squares. Who will Jamie look at more?

_____

5. At three months Jamie is beginning to explore the world around him. What are some principles that he is not able to use yet?

_____
_____

Form Perception 2 – Review Questions

1. You have inserted a microelectrode into a cat's primary visual cortex and are recording the number of action potentials. Which pattern of response would most accurately describe the activation of a complex cell?

    a) Action potentials decrease in frequency when a horizontal bar of light is shifted within the visual field to the right.
    b) Action potentials are most frequent when a bar of light is moved at a consistent angle within the visual field.
    c) Action potentials decrease in frequency when the inhibitory region of the bar of light is shifted outside of the receptive field.
    d) Action potentials are most frequent when the orientation and location of the bar of light remain unchanged.

2. A hypothetical layer in the temporal cortex responds to red cars. Which of the following would be LEAST likely:

    a) The layer above it responds best to green cars.
    b) The layer below it responds best to white trucks.
    c) The entire column responds to variations of vehicles.
    d) The column beside it responds best to blue cars.

3. You use a preferential looking technique on a two-month old infant using various circles. What would you expect the order of circle preference to be from highest preference to lowest?

    a) Circles in the form of faces, completely coloured, black outline with white center
    b) Circles in the form of faces, black outline with white center, completely coloured
    c) Completely coloured, circles in the form of faces, black outline with white center
    d) Completely coloured, black outline with white center, circles in the form of faces
    e) Black outline with white center, completely coloured, circles in the form of faces

4. Tony, who has been in financial distress lately, recently had been in a car accident. He now appears to no longer recognize anything around him. However, his social interactions are relatively unaffected. Tony most likely has _____.

    a) Prosopagnosia
    b) Anosognosia
    c) Object agnosia
    d) Visual agnosia

Form Perception 1 & 2 – Test Question

Jan is reading a book about horses while he and his family travel by train. Jan looks up from his book and sees a tiny horse through his window. When his brother, Mendel, looks out the window he sees that the animal is, in fact, a cow far off in the distance. Why did Jan perceive the animal to be a tiny horse?

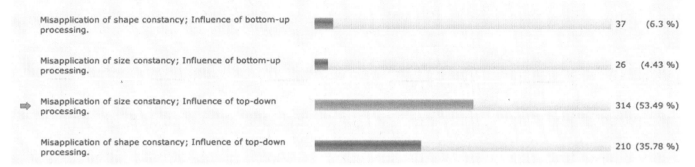

This is an actual question on the Form Perception quiz that many students struggled with. We are going to spend a little bit of time going through this question together.

This is a challenging question because it really requires you to have a strong understanding of perceptual constancies. That is, you must really know exactly how each constancy is defined rather than having only a general idea about how each one works. This will make more sense when we examine option D, but first, let us begin with A.

A. This option involves influence of bottom-up processing. Bottom-up processing is the ability to recognize an object based on the features of that object. Is that what is happening in this scenario? Well it is hard to tell without some additional information and for that, we can go to the question stem. We know that Jan is reading a book about horses. The question provides no information about how Jan is identifying the object in the distance. However, we do know that Jan is reading a book about horses and then perceives a distant animal as a tiny horse. This suggests that the book likely has a strong top-down influence on Jan when she mistakes the cow for a horse. That is, Jan's expectations have been altered as a result of reading about horses. Top-down influence seems far more likely than bottom-up at this point, so let us eliminate this answer option and B as both deal with bottom-up processing.

B. Eliminated based on previous explanation.

C. Top-down processing is in the running, but let us come back to this one.

D. We now need to identify the correct perceptual constancy. To do so, we must stick to the strict definition of each constancy. In this case, we may think we are dealing with shape constancy. At first glance, you might think to yourself: "Hmm. Jan is misclassifying the shape of the cow as a horse; therefore this mistake is because of her misapplication of shape constancy." Wrong. What is the definition of shape constancy? It is the ability to recognize an object when it is presented in a different orientation without thinking it has changed shape. For example, recognizing a door is still a door as it moves and seems as though it has changed shape, but has really just changed angles. Is that what is happening in this question? No. Jan is misapplying size constancy. He is not accounting for the distance between himself and the animal and therefore assumes that because the animal is forming a small image on his retina, it is because the animal itself is tiny. We have now eliminated option D and know that option C is correct.

When completing the quizzes and exam, it is important you make sure you know exactly how the concepts are defined. This will allow you to apply these concepts to new problems in the future with great ease.

Key Terms

Bottom-Up Processing	Geons	Proximity
Brightness Constancy	Gestalt Principles	Shape Constancy
Closure	Hypercomplex Cell	Similarity
Colour Constancy	Location Constancy	Simple Cell
Common Fate	Necker Cube	Size Constancy
Complex Cell	Object Agnosia	Template Theory
Continuity	Perceptual Constancy	Top-Down Processing
Dorsal Stream	Priming	Topographical Organization
Figure-Ground	Prosopagnosia	Ventral Stream
Geon Theory	Prototype Theory	Visual Illusion

Form Perception 1 & 2 – Bottleneck Concepts

Prototype vs. Template Theory
Top-down vs. Bottom-up Processing
Simple vs. Complex vs. Hypercomplex cells
Infant Face Recognition

Top-down vs. Bottom-up Processing

We are constantly using top-down and bottom-up processing when engaging with the world. These processing styles help us perceive and understand the stimuli present in our environment. Top-down processing is guided by our experiences and expectations. A pharmacist may be better able to understand a doctor's messy prescription if she is told what the medication is treating before reading the prescription. For example, an expectation that the prescription is to treat tonsillitis may prime the pharmacist to quickly understand the messy writing as a prescription for amoxicillin—reducing processing time and improving accuracy. Top-down processing may also be facilitated through experience. If Henry thinks all nurses are women, he may be more likely to think a woman at a hospital is a nurse and not a doctor. However, his friend Geoff's mother is a doctor, so Geoff may be more likely to think a woman at the hospital is a doctor and not a nurse. Given that top-down processing can be tailored to one's own personal experiences, it is a more flexible processing style that may differ between individuals. Bottom-up processing is more about perceiving the stimuli's features and taking what is seen at face value to guide perception. As a result, bottom-up processing is more rigid and more similar between individuals. Specifically, bottom-up processing is data-driven. It relies on the information collected by our sensory organs (eyes, ears, nose...). Bottom-up processing is a mostly automatic process that requires little conscious thought. Both bottom-up and top-down processing are used constantly and simultaneously. Top-down processing uses expectation and experience, while bottom-up processing is mostly feature-driven and automatic.

Test your Understanding

1) Which of the following best represents bottom-up processing?
   a) After growing up in Mexico and moving to Ontario, Juan thought he saw an iguana rustling through the trees by his pool
   b) Thinking he was going to see a rock concert, Jose struggled to come up for the name of the on-stage instrument which turned out to be a cello
   c) Camellia quickly found the big dipper by identifying its seven characteristic stars in the shape of a handle
   d) Jennifer knew that the little dipper was near the big dipper and found it easier when she looked near it

2) Look around your visual scene and identify three examples of top-down processing and three examples of bottom-up processing.

Practice case study

John is a Japanese exchange student studying at McMaster University. When he first came to Canada, he had trouble recognizing people and making friends because to him, everyone seemed to look the same! However, he did notice that some individual features of each person's face were different from others. As he spent more time in Canada, he gradually got better at differentiating between students.

1) What are some possible reasons for John's inability to differentiate between different students? How could you run an experiment to test your hypothesis?

2) What does this suggest about face processing? Is it more likely that John is using featural or holistic face processing to recognize faces of other races?

3) How can prototype theory or exemplar theory be used to explain this phenomenon?

4) How could the cross-race effect, which is the ability to more easily recognize faces belonging to one's own racial group, influence someone's relationships with other people?

Concept Map: Form Perception 2

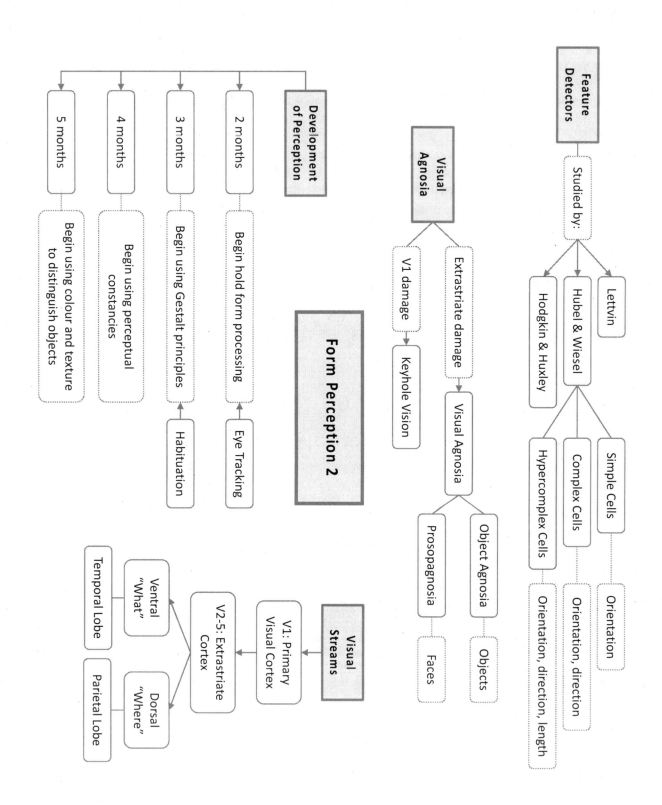

Bottom-Up Processing
Form Perception

Brightness Constancy
Form Perception

Closure
Form Perception

Colour Constancy
Form Perception

Common Fate
Form Perception

Complex Cell
Form Perception

Continuity
Form Perception

Dorsal Stream
Form Perception

The ability to perceive the brightness of objects as unchanging despite changes in ambient lighting. **Example:** A leaf is viewed in sunlight, in a dark room and under clouds and rain, yet is always perceived as being the same brightness. **Personal Example:**	Object recognition guided by features present in the stimulus itself. **Example:** If you saw a yellow face and hands, white t-shirt, blue jeans and a plump belly, you could use these features to identify the object as being Homer Simpson. **Personal Example:**
The ability to perceive objects as being of a constant colour even though the light stimulus reaching the retina changes with different illuminations. **Example:** You will still recognize your white mug if it is under a red light and looks reddish. **Personal Example:**	The Gestalt Principle that refers to our ability to fill in gaps in the contours of a shape, thus perceiving the whole object. **Example:** If a ball is partially occluded by a rock, an individual will still perceive it as a whole ball. **Personal Example:**
A visual cortical cell that responds maximally to a bar of light of a particular direction and orientation, regardless of where it is located within the receptive field. **Example:** One visual cell may respond to a bar that is rotated 45 degrees moving from left to right. **Personal Example:**	The Gestalt Principle that describes our tendency to group together objects that change in the same way. **Example:** If a flock of crows suddenly change course in the same direction, one would assume that they are part of the same group. **Personal Example:**
The "where" pathway in vision, which begins in the occipital lobe and terminates in the parietal lobe. It processes information regarding movement and spatial location of objects. **Personal Example:**	The Gestalt Principle that describes our tendency to perceive objects as having a simple, continuous form rather than a combination of disjointed forms. **Example:** An X is perceived as two diagonal lines that cross in the middle rather than a "v" shape on top of an inverted "v". **Personal Example:**

Figure-Ground
Form Perception

Geon Theory
Form Perception

Geons
Form Perception

Gestalt Principles
Form Perception

Hypercomplex Cell
Form Perception

Location Constancy
Form Perception

Necker Cube
Form Perception

Object Agnosia
Form Perception

The theory of object recognition that suggests we have 36 different geons stored in memory that make it possible to recognize over 150 million different objects. **Example:** An ice cream cone is made up of a sphere and a cone. **Personal Example:**	The Gestalt Principle that describes our ability to determine what aspect of a visual scene is part of the object itself and what is part of the background. **Example:** If a white flower is in field of tall green grass, you would be able to determine that the flower is the object, separate from the grass background. **Personal Example:**
A set of principles that collectively suggest that the whole is greater than the sum of its parts when it comes to object recognition. **Personal Example:**	Simple geometrical forms stored in memory that are used to create millions of recognizable objects, as part of the Geon Theory. **Example:** cones, spheres, cylinders, rectangular prisms are some of the 36 geons. **Personal Example:**
The ability to perceive objects as being stationary despite constantly moving around on the retina due to movement of our eyes, head and body. **Example:** When walking past a house, its location on the retina will change but it will be perceived as stationary. **Personal Example:**	A visual cortical cell that responds maximally to a bar of light at a particular orientation and begins and ends at specific points within the receptive field. **Example:** A particular hypercomplex cell will respond maximally to a horizontal bar in the "on" region of the receptive field but gives a weak response if it is rotated or falls anywhere in the "off" region. **Personal Example:**
A type of visual agnosia in which an individual is unable to identify objects by sight, even though they can see the objects perfectly. This individual will be able to perceive characteristics of that object, but not be able to conclude what the object is by simply viewing it. **Personal Example:**	A visual illusion in which the brain can perceive a two dimensional image of a cube as both popping out or going into a page. **Personal Example:**

Perceptual Constancy
Form Perception

Priming
Form Perception

Prosopagnosia
Form Perception

Prototype Theory
Form Perception

Proximity
Form Perception

Shape Constancy
Form Perception

Similarity
Form Perception

Simple Cell
Form Perception

An effect in which we respond more quickly and accurately if we expect or have recent experience with a particular stimulus or category. **Example:** In priming experiments, you may be required to name the letter that is presented to you. Being told that the object is a letter results in being faster at naming what that letter is. **Personal Example:**	The ability to perceive an object as unchanging despite the fact that the visual image the object produces is constantly changing. The five constancies are colour, brightness, size, location, and shape constancy. **Personal Example:**
A theory of object recognition that suggests we store the most typical or ideal member of a category in our memory and compare new objects to this internal average in order to recognize and categorize them. **Personal Example:**	A type of agnosia in which a person cannot recognize faces, despite being able to recognize regular objects. An individual with this disorder is able to perceive facial features, but will not be able to recognize a person by face. **Personal Example:**
Our ability to perceive objects as being a constant shape despite changes in their shape on our retina. **Example:** When looking at a flat screen TV from the front, it is a rectangle. From the side, it may look like a trapezoid but it is still recognized as being a TV. **Personal Example:**	The Gestalt Principle that describes our tendency to group elements that are close together in space as belonging together. **Example:** Logos often use several shapes that are not attached and we see it as a single image. **Personal Example:**
A visual cortical cell that responds maximally to a bar of light of a certain orientation in a particular region of the retina. **Example:** One visual cell may respond to a bar of light that is rotated 45 degrees in the centre of a visual field. **Personal Example:**	The Gestalt Principle that describes our tendency to group together elements that are physically similar. **Example:** When observing a single flamingo among a flock of penguins, one may group the penguins together based on physically similarity. **Personal Example:**

Size Constancy
Form Perception

Template Theory
Form Perception

Top-Down Processing
Form Perception

Topographical Organization
Form Perception

Ventral Stream
Form Perception

Visual Illusion
Form Perception

A theory of object recognition that suggests we store many templates in memory and compare new objects to all these templates. **Example:** When seeing a tall metal cylinder with a narrow black cap, it is compared to a very similar object in memory. **Personal Example:**	Our ability to perceive the size of objects as unchanging despite changes in their size on the retina as distance from the retina varies. **Example:** As a car approaches, its size on the retina increases; however, the car is perceived as being of constant size. **Personal Example:**
The ordered projection of a sensory surface, found in all sensory systems. In the visual system, two objects that are side by side in the visual field will also be projected side by side in the visual cortex. **Personal Example:**	A process of object recognition guided by your own beliefs or expectations. **Example:** People are able to recognize a paragraph of misspelled words when only the first and last letters of each word are correct. They use the context of surrounding words to read. **Personal Example:**
An ambiguous or incomplete image that is perceived as being something different from what it really is. **Example:** the Necker Cube, Muller-Lyer illusion, and the Ponzo Illusion. **Personal Example:**	The "what" visual pathway that starts in the extrastriate cortex and terminates in the temporal lobe. It processes information about object identity (including form and colour). **Personal Example:**

Audition

"Everyone of us is different in some way, but for those of us who are more different, we have to put more effort into convincing the less different that we can do the same thing they can, just differently."
- Marlee Matlin, Academy Award winning actress and prominent member of the deaf community

The Loneliest Whale in the World

Technology once used to scan for Soviet submarines made an odd discovery when it perceived the characteristic song features of blue whale, but in a surprising emitting sound frequency—52 Hz. Blue whales emit sounds at a maximum range of 10 – 40 Hz and a 52 Hz emission was unheard of and much higher than the sounds emitted by regular blue whales. Following 12 years of tracking, leading researcher Bill Watkins made clear that this was the only blue whale to emit sounds in this frequency; proposing that it was unlikely that other blue whales could understand or communicate back to the whale. Media outlets took off on this finding and dubbed '52 Blue' the loneliest whale in the world—swimming in a big blue ocean calling out for lovers and friends and receiving no answer. The idea of a humanistic lonely whale inspired a documentary, some mixtapes and even a Kickstarter campaign.

Some researchers have theorized that 52 Blue may be a rare hybrid between a blue whale and a fin whale. A hybrid such as this would leave the whale with a modified skull structure allowing it to emit and process unique sound frequencies. Whales do not have vocal cords or a phonic lip and rather emit sounds from their larynx, which is further emitted by bouncing off their skull's bones. Unlike humans, whales do not process received sounds through pressure changes. Rather, whales utilize a process called bone conduction. Given that they do not have a functioning ear canal, the returning sound echo passes through the bones of their jaw and skull which amplifies the sound by nearly 10x as much as a pressure-change system can. Additionally, whales have a higher ratio of ganglion cells to each hair cell which allows them to process more complex sound vibrations. 52 Blue likely has a unique skull shape that leads it to produce and process sound stimuli different than other blue whales. In recent years, researchers have observed a small group of whale singing 52 Blues unique song. Scientists question if 52 Blue is a part of an unidentified hybrid species that has yet to be discovered. However, lovers of the whale are simply hopeful that 52 Blue may find his way to a family or lover and not be #foreveralone.

Ketten, D. R. (2000). Cetacean ears. In: W. W. L. Au, A. N. Popper & R. R. Fay (Eds.), *Hearing by Whales and Dolphins* (pp. 43-108). New York, NY: Springer-Verlag, Inc.

The world's loneliest whale may not be alone after all. (2015, 15 April). In BBC News Earth. Retrieved from http://www.bbc.com/earth/story/20150415-the-loneliest-whale-in-the-world

Weekly Checklist:
- ☐ **Web modules to watch: Audition**
- ☐ **Readings: Chapter 8**
- ☐ **Pre-Quiz & Quiz 8**

Upper Year Courses:
If you enjoyed the content of this week's module, consider taking the following upper year course:
- Psych 3A03: Audition

Audition – Outline

Unit 1: Introduction to Audition

_____
_____
_____
_____
_____

_____
_____
_____
_____
_____

Unit 2: The Auditory Mechanisms of Different Species

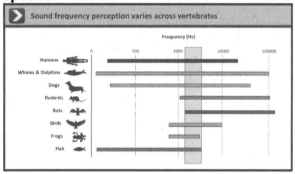

Auditory mechanisms vary across different species depending on their environment and specific needs.

_____
_____

Human audible zone:
_____
_____
_____
_____
_____
_____

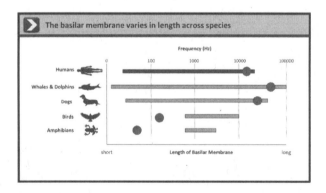

The basilar membrane houses the hearing receptors that process sounds of different frequencies.

_____
_____

Length of basilar membrane?
_____
_____
_____
_____

Unit 3: The Stimulus - Sound Waves

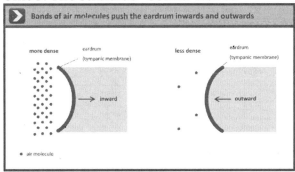

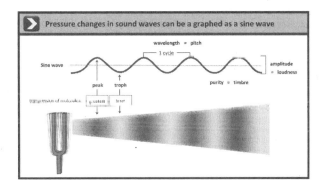

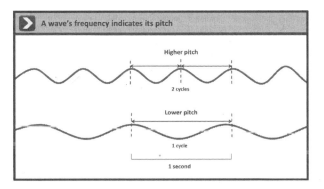

Sound waves are vibrations through a medium of air molecules.

Eardrum:

Pushed inwards:

Pushed outwards:

There are three psychological properties of sinusoidal sound waves.

Sine wave:

1) Amplitude → Loudness (dB):

2) Frequency → Pitch (Hz):

3) Purity → Timbre:

Note: $frequency = \frac{1}{wavelength}$

Unit 4: The Ear

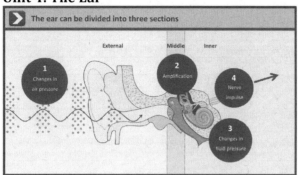

The external, middle and inner ear each conduct sound in a different way.

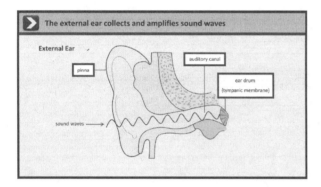

The external ear contains the pinna, ear canal & eardrum.

Pinna:

Ear canal:

Ear drum:

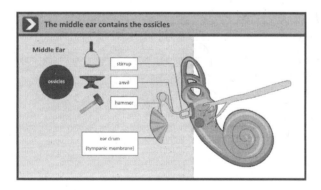

The middle ear contains the three ossicles that amplify the sound signal.

Stirrup:

Anvil:

Hammer:

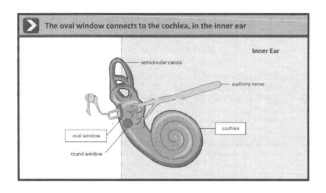

Within the cochlea of the inner ear, physical sound signals are converted into electrical signals destined for the brain.

Cochlea:

Oval Window:

Round Window:

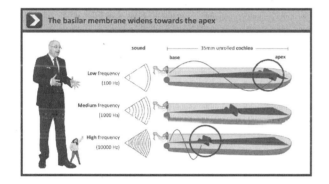

Different frequencies cause different regions of the basilar membrane to vibrate.

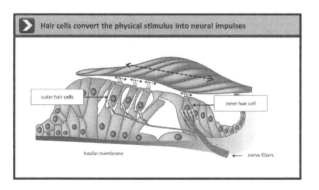

Hair cells are receptors that translate the physical sound signal into neural impulses.

Unit 5: Auditory Pathway – From Receptors to Auditory Cortex

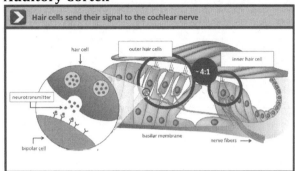

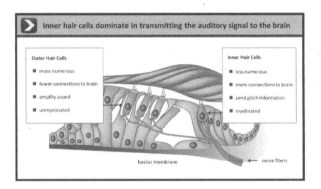

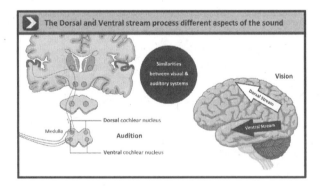

Hair cells synapse with bipolar cells which communicate with the cochlear nerve.

Inner hair cells are primarily responsible for transmitting the electrical signal.

The cochlear nucleus of the hindbrain has separate dorsal and ventral streams.

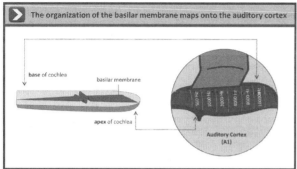

Tonotopic organization maintains frequency information at all levels along our auditory system.

Recall topographic organization: _____
_____

Tonotopic organization: _____
_____
_____
_____
_____

Unit 6: Auditory Localization
_____
_____
_____
_____

There is no direct spatial map for audition; we rely on interaural cues.
_____
_____
_____
_____
_____

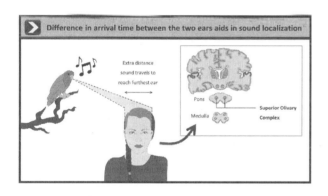

1) Timing of incoming sound between ears
_____
_____
_____
_____
_____
_____
_____
_____

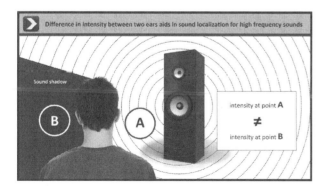

2) Intensity difference between ears
_____
_____
_____

Sound shadow? _____
_____
_____

Superior olivary complex: _____
_____
_____

Sounds in front/behind you are difficult to locate using interaural cues.

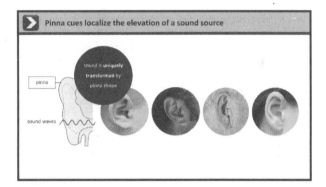

Pinna cues help localize the elevation of a sound source.

Unit 7: Echolocation in Bats

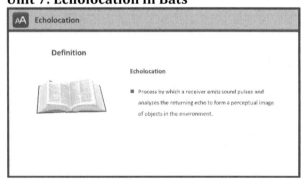

Bats navigate their environment using a system of hearing called echolocation.

Outgoing sound waves & analysis of echo:

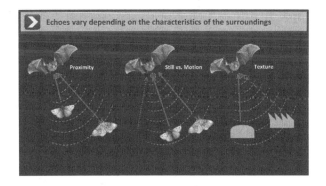

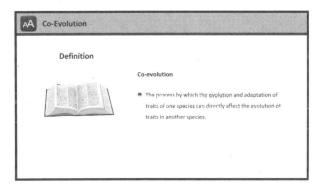

Predators and prey can co-evolve complementary adaptations to increase their respective survival and fitness.

Audition – Courseware Exercise

1. You have now learned the key anatomical features that have evolved to allow humans to accurately locate sounds in their environments. These specific mechanisms are very impressive because they allow us to perceive spatial relations from neural signals!
A participant in an experiment is presented with a sound coming from the lower left hand corner of a room and must identify where this sound originated from using auditory localization. Identify and describe three mechanisms that may aid the participant in localizing this sound.

1) _____

2) _____

3) _____

2. Some sounds that enter your ears are very low with respect to their intensity. In order to pick up these sounds and transmit them to the brain, your ears must amplify these sounds. What are two ways that the ear amplifies sound?

1) _____

2) _____

3. The basilar membrane is the structure that turns the physical signal of sound waves into a neural signal through the hair cells located on its surface. As such, different parts of the basilar membrane are used to transmit different types of sound. State what type of sound the different regions of the basilar membrane respond to.

_____

Audition – Review Questions

1. Which of the following descriptions does NOT match the actual physical property of the sound wave?
   a) Sound waves with larger amplitudes translate to louder sounds measured in decibels (dB).
   b) The more complex a sound vibration, the less pure it is; our perception of timbre allows us to make sense of complex sound vibrations.
   c) With frequency, longer wavelengths result in a perceived higher pitch measured in Hertz (Hz).
   d) Timbre is the combination of the fundamental tone and its overtones that make up an overall perceived tone.

2. Which of the following statements is a correct description of the ear?
   a) As the cochlea gets wider, the basilar membrane also gets wider and vibrates at a lower frequency.
   b) When the basilar membrane is pushed downward, the fluid inside the cochlea causes the round window to bulge outward.
   c) The external ear consists of the pinna, ear canal, eardrum and ossicles.
   d) The differences in an individual's pinna shape does not actually change the perception of sound, it only provides information regarding its location.

3. _____ outnumber _____ at a ratio of about 4 to 1 while the _____ contain more direct links to the brain with _____ axons.
   a) Inner hair cells, outer hair cells, basilar membrane, auditory cortex.
   b) Outer hair cells, inner hair cells, outer hair cells, myelinated.
   c) Inner hair cells, outer hair cells, inner hair cells, unmyelinated.
   d) Outer hair cells, inner hair cells, inner hair cells, myelinated.

4. Which of the following statements is NOT true concerning the processing of sound in the brain?
   a) The cochlear nucleus is located in the hindbrain and contains a ventral AND dorsal stream.
   b) There is a tonotopic organization such that neighbouring regions on the basilar membrane map onto neighbouring regions in the auditory cortex.
   c) The inner and outer hair cells are equally responsible for transmitting the auditory signal to the brain.
   d) The ventral and dorsal streams serve similar purposes as those seen in the visual system.

Audition – Test Question

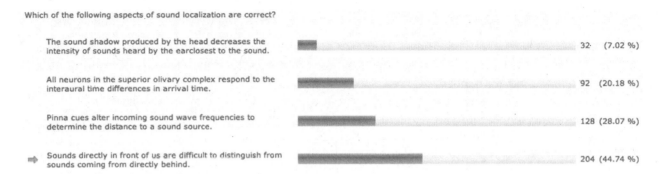

This is an actual question from the Audition quiz that many students struggled with. Fortunately, we are going to go through this question together to identify what sort of errors students were making and how to avoid them in the future. To do so, we will look at each answer option individually and identify why it is correct or incorrect.

A. This answer option is telling us that a sound shadow affects the proximal ear or the ear that is closest to the source. The sound shadow, however, requires sound to pass through the head. Can this affect the ear that is closest to the source? No. It must have an effect on the **distal** ear. Eliminate this option.

B. Be wary when you see descriptive words like: "all" or "every". These will often cause problems for students that are rushing through the test without carefully reading each answer option. If you understand the material presented in the web module thoroughly, you will know that neurons in the superior olivary complex also respond to differences in sound intensity. Eliminate this option.

C. This is a tricky question. Are pinna cues used to determine the distance to a sound source? At first glance you might think this is a reasonable statement as pinna cues are involved in sound localization. Pinna cues, however, are important for identifying the elevation of a sound source. It is a slight, yet important, distinction.

D. Having eliminated options A-C, we know that D is correct. Still, let us examine the answer option. It is, in fact, true that it is hard to localize a sound correctly when it is directly in front or behind us. This should almost make intuitive sense. If something is directly in front or directly behind us, we cannot use interaural sound differences to help us localize the source. This is why we often rotate our head when trying to localize a sound.

It is important that you read the stem and answer options carefully when completing your tests. Doing so may help eliminate careless errors.

Key Terms

Amplitude	Echolocation	Ossicles
Anvil	External Ear	Oval Window
Basilar Membrane	Frequency	Pinna
Cochlea	Hair Cells	Round Window
Cochlear Nerve	Hammer	Sine Wave
Cochlear Nucleus	Inner Ear	Stirrup
Co-Evolution	Interaural Intensity Differences	Timbre
Ear Canal	Interaural Time Differences	Tonotopic Organization
Eardrum	Middle Ear	

Audition – Bottleneck Concepts

Interaural Intensity Differences vs. Interaural Time Differences
Inner Hair Cells vs. Outer Hair Cells
Tonotopic vs. Topographic Organization
Frequencies along the Basilar Membrane

Tonotopic vs. Topographic Organization

In order to make sense of the extensive amount of sensory input, our brain maintains some of the organization presented to it from the outside world. Topographic organization occurs in nearly all sensory and motor systems and occurs when signals remain organized from their origin at the sensing organ all the way throughout the central nervous system. Our auditory system maintains frequency organization through tonotopic organization, while our visual system does so through retinotopic organization. Note, topographic organization is an umbrella term encompassing lots of sensory systems, but is most commonly used to refer to our visual system.

Both tonotopic and retinotopic organization maintain the organization of the physical stimulus all the way through to the primary auditory and visual brain areas. For tonotopic organization, the physical stimulus is the movement of the hair cells as a result of the waves in the cochlear fluid. Depending on the frequency of the wave, different sections of hair cells will be activated. When a high frequency sound is presented, hair cells near the base of the basilar membrane will fire and send a neural signal onwards along the auditory pathway. Those high frequency hair cells will retain their grouped organization along the cochlear nerve until they reach the primary auditory cortex. One region of the auditory cortex will respond specifically to high frequency sounds; this allows us to process specific pitches/frequencies without them becoming muddled by other frequencies. The same thing happens for low frequency sounds, except their hair cells will send an organized signal to a different region of the primary auditory cortex.

For retinotopic/topographic organization, the physical stimulus is the light beam which excites photoreceptors and then ganglion cells which send a neural signal onward along the visual pathway. Retinal cells send information that corresponds to the spatial representation of the light stimulus received. Unlike the auditory system, retinotopic organization does not organize information based on characteristics such as colour or brightness, but rather their spatial location in the physical world. For example, if a bright red light is shone on the right peripheral visual field, then that region of the retina (right nasal retina) will send information about that light to a small region of the occipital lobe. The occipital lobe maintains the spatial organization of the retina so that the information presented in our visual field is spatially maintained in the brain. Specifically, it is maintained upside down and inverted in comparison to the image presented to the eye. This allows us to see our visual scene for what it is and not a jumbled mess of different colours and brightnesses. Rather, we can see that our red apple is to the right of our computer.

Both organizational patterns combine the input from a cluster of cells to a smaller region on its associated brain region. By maintaining organization and converging signals, these processes allow for efficient brain processing.

Test your Understanding

1) Which of the following is true about tonotopic and/or topographic organization?
    a) Tonotopic organization helps us differentiate various frequencies of sounds and identify the direction that each frequency is coming from
    b) In both tonotopic and topographic organization, neural signals are organized in a topographic map which are transmitted from the sensing organ's receptive field throughout the brain
    c) Retinotopic organization, also known as topographic organization, is the mapping of the visual image presented on the retina in a way that the 3D image is maintained in the occipital lobe
    d) Both B and C

2) Which of the following is true about tonotopic organization? The associated regions of the primary auditory cortex process...
    a) Short wavelength sounds that come from the apex of the cochlea and the narrow end of the basilar membrane
    b) Low frequency sounds that come from the apex of the cochlea and wide end of the basilar membrane
    c) Low frequency and high frequency sounds that come from mostly the outer hair cells of the cochlea
    d) High frequency sounds that come from the base of the cochlea and the wide end of the basilar membrane

Practice case study

Matt has been captain of his neighbourhood's ultimate Frisbee team for the past three years. Recently, a few players have suffered from concussions, so the league has instated a new rule. Every player must now wear a tight helmet that covers his or her forehead and ears. Matt agrees with this new rule but is becoming increasingly frustrated with how his new helmet affects his game. He can't seem to respond accurately to other players when they call out his name and he can never seem to locate the correct direction of play.

1) Given your knowledge of audition, why might Matt be having trouble with his game?

Matt's brother Gary plays Frisbee on the team as well. Although he has to wear a helmet too, his Frisbee skills have not declined as much.

2) Why is this?

3) Will Matt's abilities improve over time, even if he must continue to wear his helmet?

Both Matt and Gary have trouble hearing other players on their team if they are directly in front or behind them, as opposed to by their sides.

4) Why might this be?

Concept Map: Audition

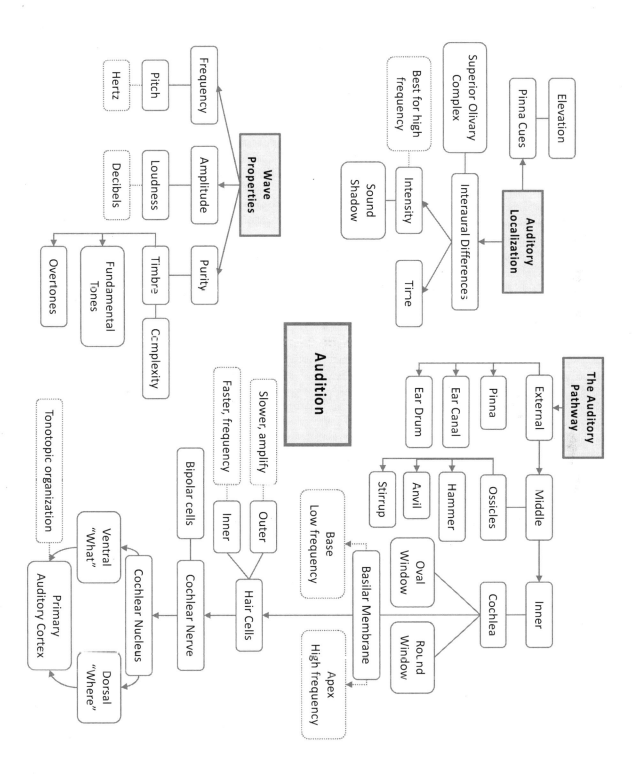

Amplitude
Audition

Anvil
Audition

Basilar Membrane
Audition

Cochlea
Audition

Cochlear Nerve
Audition

Cochlear Nucleus
Audition

Co-Evolution
Audition

Ear Canal
Audition

Also known as the incus, it is the second of the ossicles found in the middle ear. It projects to the stirrup.
Personal Example:

The height of a wave. For sound, it corresponds to the perception of loudness. Waves of larger amplitude correspond to louder sound.
Personal Example:

A coiled, fluid-filled tube in the inner ear containing the basilar membrane.
Personal Example:

The flexible membrane that runs the length of the cochlea, vibrating in different regions along its length in response to different frequencies. It contains the hair cells, which transduce sound into the electrical signals perceived by the brain.
Personal Example:

A region in the hindbrain that serves as the first stop in the brain for axons from the cochlea.
Personal Example:

A bundle of axons carrying action potentials from the hair cells of the cochlea toward the brain, through the cochlear nucleus.
Personal Example:

Part of the external ear, it is used to transmit and amplify sounds from the pinna to the eardrum.
Personal Example:

The process by which the evolution and adaptation of traits in one species can directly affect the evolution of traits in another species.
Example: Prey may become resistant to a toxin used by its predator. In response, the predator may evolve to produce higher levels of the toxin.
Personal Example:

Eardrum
Audition

Echolocation
Audition

External Ear
Audition

Frequency
Audition

Hair Cells
Audition

Hammer
Audition

Inner Ear
Audition

Interaural Intensity Differences
Audition

The process by which a receiver emits sound pulses and analyzes the returning echo to form a perceptual image of objects in its environment. It is a "visual" technique used by some species of animals, including bats and dolphins. **Personal Example:**	Part of the external ear, it is a thin membrane that vibrates at the frequency of incoming sound waves and forms the back wall of the ear canal. **Personal Example:**
The number of waves that pass a fixed place in a given time. It is the inverse of wavelength. With respect to sound, frequency corresponds to pitch, where a larger frequency corresponds to a higher pitch. **Personal Example:**	The part of the auditory system that collects sound from the surrounding environment. It is made up of the pinna, ear canal and eardrum. **Personal Example:**
Also known as the malleus, it is the first of the ossicles found in the middle ear, projecting to the anvil. **Personal Example:**	The auditory receptors found in the basilar membrane that converts sound waves into neural impulses that the brain can understand. **Personal Example:**
A sound localization technique using the difference in intensity caused by the head casting a "sound shadow", which diminishes the sound intensity at the distal ear. **Personal Example:**	The part of the auditory system that contains the neural tissue necessary to transduce sound waves into neural impulses. It is made up of the cochlea, which contains the basilar membrane and hair cells. **Personal Example:**

Interaural Time Differences Audition	**Middle Ear** Audition
Ossicles Audition	**Oval Window** Audition
Pinna Audition	**Round Window** Audition
Sine Wave Audition	**Stirrup** Audition

The part of the auditory system that begins with the structures on the inner side of the eardrum. It is made up of the three ossicles that are used to amplify sound. **Personal Example:**	A sound localization technique that uses the difference in time it takes for sound waves to reach each ear. Sounds can be localized by differences of sub-milliseconds. **Personal Example:**
A small opening in the side of the cochlea that, when made to vibrate, causes the fluid inside of the cochlea to become displaced. It is through here that the middle ear connects to the inner ear. **Personal Example:**	A collection of the smallest bones in the body that are found in the middle ear and used to amplify sound. They consist of the hammer, anvil, and stirrup. **Personal Example:**
An opening located at the end of the cochlea opposite to the round window, which bulges in and out according to the movement of fluid in the cochlea. **Personal Example:**	Part of the external ear, it is the folded cone on the outside of the head that is used to collect sound waves and direct them into the ear canal. **Personal Example:**
Also known as the stapes, it is the last of the ossicles found in the middle ear. It projects onto the oval window of the cochlea in the inner ear. **Personal Example:**	A mathematical curve describing a smooth repetition or oscillation. Sound waves are made up of individual sine waves that vary in wavelength, frequency and amplitude to produce sounds of different pitch and loudness. **Personal Example:**

Timbre
Audition

Tonotopic Organization
Audition

Analogous to the topographical organization of the retina in the visual system, neighbouring frequencies which vibrate on the basilar membrane project to neighbouring areas in the auditory cortex. **Personal Example:**	Our perception of the complexity and purity of a sound wave, related to the unique properties of a sound. Complexity refers to the fact that sounds we hear are made up of multiple sound waves that vary in frequency. **Personal Example:**

Hunger and the Chemical Senses

"The food you eat can be either the safest and most powerful form of medicine or the slowest form of poison"
- Ann Wigmore, pioneering holistic health practitioner and nutritionist

Taste Preferences Explained

Aaliyah and Andre were having trouble pleasing their children's taste palates. Jada loved fruits and vegetables, but Jordan hated them, and both kids hated bitter vegetables. Let's explore how Jada and Jordan's taste preferences were formed through both genetics and their environment. Preferences for bitter tastes are mostly governed by genetics—explaining why both Jada and Jordan have a common hatred. A single gene, TAS2R38, codes for bitter taste receptors on the tongue. There are multiple variations (alleles) of this gene and their combinations dictate how much someone will love or hate something bitter such as coffee. The alleles inform the shape of the receptor protein which determines how strongly it can bind and process the bitter compound, phenylthiocarbamide (PTC). Other bitter foods such as cilantro and broccoli are governed by their own unique set of genes (OR6A2 and HTAS2R38 respectively). The genetic component of taste is expansive with hundreds of genes dictating the types of foods someone will love or hate.

Exposure to different foods while in the womb and while weaning also influence food preferences. In the womb, infants are exposed to their mother's diet through amniotic fluid. The flavours that infants are frequently exposed to shape preferences after birth. Infants whose mothers drank carrot juice during pregnancy preferred carrot-flavoured cereal compared to a control group. Infant taste-preferences can be influenced by the food the mother consumes while *weaning*. Babies whose moms regularly consumed fruits and vegetables during breastfeeding were much more accepting of these foods when it came time to eat them. Infants are also influenced by exposure to a wide variety of food, regardless of initial adverse reactions. Parents should not treat high fat and sugary foods like a reward, with healthy foods as a chore, i.e., "eat your vegetables and then you can have dessert". Healthy eating is crucial to a child's health and worth the investment to establish healthy habits early.

Guo, S. W., & Reed, D. R. (2001). The genetics of phenylthiocarbamide perception. *Annals of Human Biology, 28*(2), 111-142.

Forestell, C. A., & Mennella, J. A. (2007). Early determinants of fruit and vegetable acceptance. *Pediatrics, 120*(6), 1247-1254.

Mennella, J. A., Jagnow, C. P., & Beauchamp, G. K. (2001). Prenatal and postnatal flavor learning by human infants. *Pediatrics, 107*(6), e88.

Weekly Checklist:
- ☐ **Web modules to watch: Hunger and the Chemical Senses**
- ☐ **Readings: Journal Article**
- ☐ **Pre-Quiz & Quiz 9**

Upper Year Courses:
If you enjoyed the content of this week's module, consider taking the following upper year course:
- Psych 3M03: Motivation and Emotion

Hunger and the Chemical Senses – Outline

Unit 1: Introduction to Hunger and Satiety

_____
_____
_____
_____

Unit 2: Hunger and Satiety

Glucose and glycogen balance:

Glucose: _____
_____
_____

Glycogen: _____
_____
_____

Glucose storage as glycogen: _____
_____
_____
_____

Insulin secretion: _____
_____
_____
_____

Hunger? _____
_____
_____
_____

Low blood glucose = glycogen breakdown:
_____
_____
_____

Satiety? _____
_____
_____
_____

NPY is a hunger cue that signals to your body to engage in food seeking behaviours.

_____
_____
_____
_____
_____
_____
_____
_____

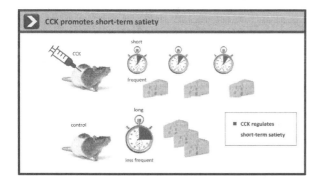

CCK is responsible for short-term satiety and signals to your body to stop eating.
_____
_____
_____
_____

CCK study in mice:
_____
_____
_____
_____
_____

Unit 3: Long-Term Weight Regulation

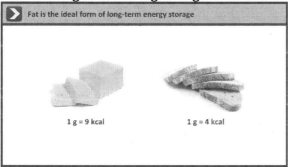

Adipose or fat tissue is crucial for long-term energy storage.
_____
_____
_____
_____
_____
_____
_____
_____
_____
_____
_____

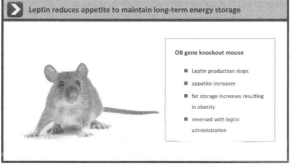

Leptin levels influence both hunger and satiety behaviours.

Leptin: _____
_____
_____
_____

OB Gene knock-out mice: _____
_____
_____
_____
_____

Leptin resistance? _____
_____
_____
_____

Evolutionary significance: _____
_____
_____
_____

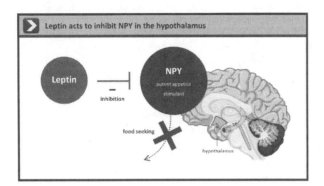

Leptin and NPY interact to regulate your weight to optimal levels.

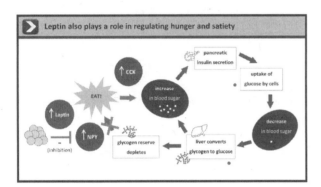

Leptin's role in hunger and satiety

Rat studies of maladaptive feeding:

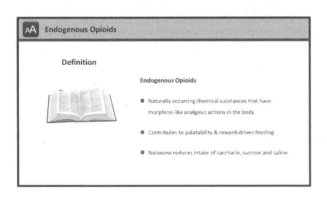

In some people, overeating may be a result of maladaptive opioid-mediated reward-driven feeding.

Endogenous opioids:

Naloxone?

Knock-in mice study:

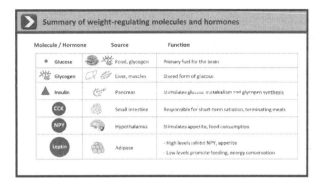

Unit 4: Taste Preferences and Food Selection

Taste is governed by older brain regions:

___

Taste information provides survival benefits.

Bitter/sour:

Sweet/salty/savoury:

Universal taste responses:

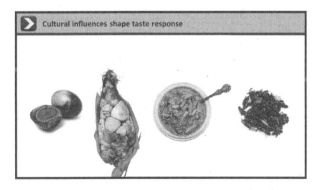

Taste preferences are also shaped by our personal experiences.

Taste sensitivity:

Pregnancy?

Preferences for salty and sweet foods can be maladaptive in modern society.
_____
_____
_____
_____
_____
_____
_____
_____
_____
_____

Unit 5: How Taste is Processed in the Brain

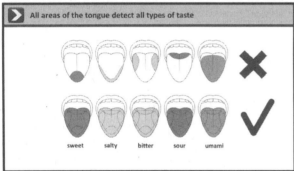

We can distinguish 5 different tastes:
Sweet: _____
_____
Salty: _____
_____
Sour: _____
_____
Bitter: _____
_____
Umami: _____
_____
Flavour? _____
_____

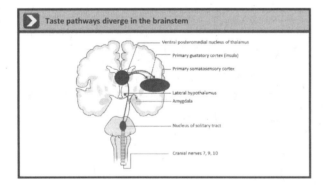

Taste receptor cells → main gustatory nerve → brainstem → two main pathways
_____
_____
_____
Pathway 1: _____
_____
_____
_____
_____
_____
_____

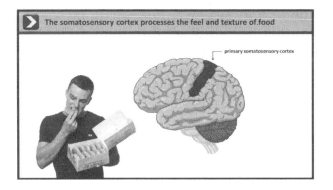

Primary somatosensory cortex: _____
_____
_____

Gustatory cortex: _____
_____
_____

Olfactory cortex: _____
_____
_____
_____

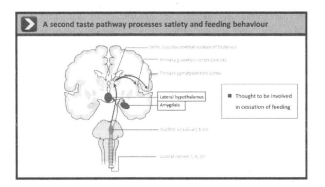

The chemical stimuli of taste and smell interact in the nasal pharynx.

_____
_____
_____
_____
_____
_____
_____
_____

Pathway 2:

_____
_____
_____
_____
_____
_____
_____
_____
_____
_____
_____
_____
_____
_____
_____
_____
_____
_____

Unit 6: How Smell is Processed in the Brain

We can *distinguish* smells better than we can *label* them.

_____
_____
_____
_____

Our sense of smell is unique as it has a direct link to the cortex.

_____
_____
_____
_____

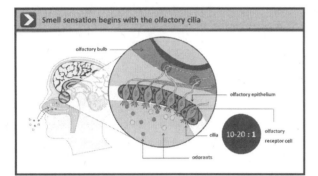

Odorant molecules found in the air bind to our smell receptors.

_____
_____
_____
_____
_____
_____
_____
_____
_____

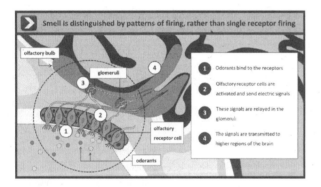

A specific smell activates a unique pattern of firing across olfactory receptor cells.

_____
_____
_____
_____
_____
_____
_____
_____

Olfactory cortices:

_____
_____
_____
_____
_____
_____
_____
_____
_____

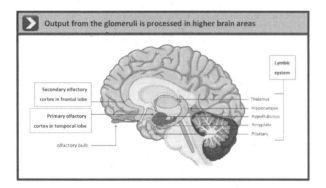

Hunger and the Chemical Senses – Courseware Exercise

1. There are several ways that our bodies indicate hunger and satiety. Name four mechanisms, explaining how each one affects hunger and/or satiety and where it acts.

1) _____

2) _____

3) _____

4) _____

2. You've learned about many of the environmental pressures that caused species to evolve the various taste preferences that they have. Can you think of any specific instances in the last day where innate taste preferences have guided your behaviour?

_____

_____

_____

3. Research has found that moose, which get their necessary sodium from salt licks, are very effective at maintaining balance of this specific nutrient in their diet. Other animals like grasshoppers also show this control. This can be thought of as somewhat analogous to the mechanisms in humans and other animals that cause them to seek food when they are hungry and cease eating when they are satiated.
How do you think that the mechanisms of hunger and satiety evolved in our evolutionary history? You've learned that there are several mechanisms at play—why the need for so many?

_____

_____

_____

_____

_____

_____

_____

Hunger and the Chemical Senses – Review Questions

1. Kinjain has just indulged in a large helping of mango and pineapple. What is likely happening to her insulin levels?
    a) Her pancreas will cease producing insulin allowing her blood glucose to be converted into glycogen.
    b) Her liver releases insulin, which converts her blood glucose into glycogen.
    c) Her hypothalamus releases NPY, which causes her pancreas to release insulin and convert her blood glucose into glucagon.
    d) Her pancreas releases insulin, which converts her blood glucose into glycogen.

2. Which of the following is true regarding our perception of sweet and savoury foods?
    a) Separate sweet and savoury taste receptors on your tongue send information to the thalamus, which then sends information to the gustatory cortex where we perceive flavour.
    b) Sweet and savoury tastes indicate energy rich foods and their flavours are perceived by the gustatory cortex.
    c) Sweet tastes indicate energy rich foods, while savoury tastes indicate glutamate rich foods, with their associated tastes and smells integrated into the perception of flavour by the orbital cortex.
    d) A single taste receptor for both sweet and savoury send information to the gustatory cortex where they are integrated with smell to create our perception of taste.

3. Which of the following is true about leptin?
    a) High leptin levels are an evolutionary adaptation to decrease food intake
    b) Low leptin levels are an evolutionary adaptation to increase food intake
    c) Injecting an obese mouse with leptin will lead to a decrease in weight
    d) Injecting a thin mouse with a OB gene knockout will lead to a decrease in weight

4. Which of the following is NOT true about our perception of taste?
    a) Taste is perceived by the gustatory cortex
    b) Taste signals are integrated with smell signals in the orbital cortex
    c) Receptors in your tongue send taste information to the thalamus
    d) Flavour is synonymous with taste

5. A salty taste helps us detect _____ foods, a sour or bitter taste allow us to detect_____ foods
    a) energy rich, glutamate rich
    b) electrolyte rich, spoiled or toxic
    c) electrolyte rich, aspartate rich
    d) unhealthy, spoiled or poisonous

6. Which of the following is true about the perception of smell?
    a) Each olfactory receptor responds to a specific stimulus, which is integrated by glomeruli cells and sent mostly towards the thalamus
    b) Each olfactory receptor cell responds to a specific stimulus, which is integrated by glomeruli cells and sent mostly towards the hypothalamus.
    c) Olfactory receptor cells respond to a range of stimuli, which are integrated by glomeruli and sent mostly towards the thalamus
    d) Olfactory receptor cells respond to a range of stimuli, which are integrated by glomeruli and sent mostly towards the hypothalamus

Hunger and the Chemical Senses – Test Question

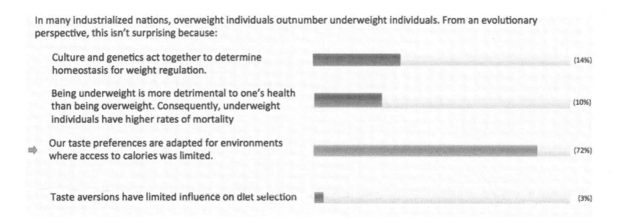

This is an actual question from the Hunger and the Chemical Senses quiz that some students struggled with. We are going to tackle this question together.

A. This option can be ruled out as not being the best explanation of this phenomenon from an evolutionary perspective. Although culture can have an important influence on a person's lifestyle choices, including what is an acceptable weight, it is not likely to have any influence on homeostatic weight regulation. Homeostasis is an automatic physiological mechanism that works to keep our bodily processes in balance. For example, when we intake food, it increases our blood sugar, so our bodies release insulin to counteract this sharp increase.

B. This option can also be ruled out because, whether or not this may be true, it was not presented in the module as an evolutionary explanation for obesity. Remember, we will only test you on content presented in the module or textbook. Both being overweight or underweight can have severe effects on a person's health.

C. This option is correct! As discussed in the module, the environment that our ancestors lived in had limited access to calories and certain minerals that are physiologically important. For example, humans tend to prefer sweet foods because they provide a rich source of energy. Humans also prefer salty foods because they are high in sodium and electrolytes, which are necessary for cellular functions. These nutrients were scarce in our evolutionary past so we have adapted a preference for these tastes to increase our likelihood of consuming them. However, in our current industrialized environment, these nutrients are readily available so it is easy for us to over-consume them, leading to a high proportion of overweight individuals.

D. This option can be ruled out firstly because it has little relevance to what the question is asking, which is why it is so easy to become overweight in our current society. Taste aversion describes the avoidance of certain tastes, likely due to some aversive experience with that taste (e.g. food poisoning). These taste aversions are likely to influence a specific individual's dietary selection (avoiding that specific food), which is not likely to contribute significantly to the tendency of industrialized nations to be overweight.

Key Terms

Adipose	Glycogen	Olfactory Bulb
Cholecystokinin (CCK)	Gustatory Cortex	Olfactory Cilia
Endogenous Opioids	Leptin	Olfactory Epithelium
Glomeruli	Neuropeptide Y (NPY)	Taste Bud
Glucose	OB Gene	

Hunger and the Chemical Senses – Bottleneck Concepts

Glucose vs. Glycogen Balance
Hunger vs. Satiety
Smell vs. Taste
OB Gene Knock-Out Mice Study

Smell vs. Taste

Both taste and smell are similar in that they process chemical, not physical, signals. Physical signals such as light and touch displace air, liquid, or solid to produce a sensation that is perceived by their relative mechanical receptors. Alternatively, the receptors of the olfactory and gustatory senses uniquely bind to chemicals that can dissolve in either gas or liquid. Both taste and smell send information to higher brain regions such as the limbic system to guide responses related to emotion, instinct, and memory.

The process of reaching higher brain regions is quite different between these two chemical senses. For taste, there are five unique receptors which produce the five tastes in the same way every time. For example, to perceive the taste of salt, an amiloride-sensitive channel processes sodium molecules and transmits a signal to the brain to perceive a salty taste. For smell, there are nearly 500 olfactory receptors that process over 10,000 different smells. Each olfactory receptor is covered with approximately 10 cilia which protrude from the receptor neuron into nasal mucous and trap smell molecules. Rather than a specific smell activating a unique receptor cell, a specific smell is transmitted through a number of cilia and result in a unique pattern of firing across many different receptors. The various firing patterns are processed by glomeruli in the olfactory bulb of the brain and perceived as unique smells. A further difference for smell is that once odor molecules react with receptors, a neural signal is sent *directly* to the cortex, specifically to the olfactory bulb. However, taste must first be relayed through the thalamus of the brain before it can reach the cortex. Smell's direct link to the cortex is associated with its more significant evolutionary role in survival and reproduction, i.e., finding food and seeking out mates.

Test your Understanding

1) What do you think are some consequences of losing our ability to taste? What about smell?

2) Leslie is experiencing a massive deficit in her olfactory and gustatory experiences. She sees a specialist and is shocked to discover that her thalamus is not relaying any information onwards through the taste pathway. Which of the following statements is correct?
   a) Since taste and smell molecules are processed in the nasal pharynx and sent directly to the orbital cortex, Leslie is still able to sense flavour
   b) Leslie is still able to feel the difference between a banana and an apple, but cannot identify the fruits by flavour
   c) Leslie is not able to taste or smell anything because all chemical senses must pass through the thalamus before they can be perceived
   d) Leslie will still feel hunger and satiety because this information does not need to be relayed through the thalamus to the hypothalamus and brainstem

Practice case study:

After a recent medical check-up, Darren and his doctor have decided that he should try to lose ten pounds in an effort to lower his elevated blood pressure. Darren concludes that this cannot be that difficult, and decides to skip breakfast in an attempt to lower his caloric intake. Darren finds that he is ravenous by lunchtime, and ends up eating double the portion size that he normally would from the cafeteria lunch buffet.

1) Thinking of the various factors that regulate hunger and satiety (glucose, glycogen, insulin, NPY and CCK), why might Darren have overeaten after skipping breakfast?

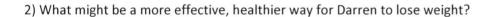

2) What might be a more effective, healthier way for Darren to lose weight?

Darren has been trying to cut unhealthy foods from his diet, but finds that he has the most difficulty limiting his favourite desserts and snacks, such as donuts and potato chips.

3) Considering human evolutionary history, why might Darren find it difficult to control the cravings for these foods?

On week two of his healthy eating, Darren contracts a cold that gives him a stuffed up nose and dry cough. Darren finds that he does not enjoy eating his favourite foods as much when he's sick.

4) Why might Darren's eating preferences have changed while he's sick?

Concept Map: Hunger and the Chemical Senses

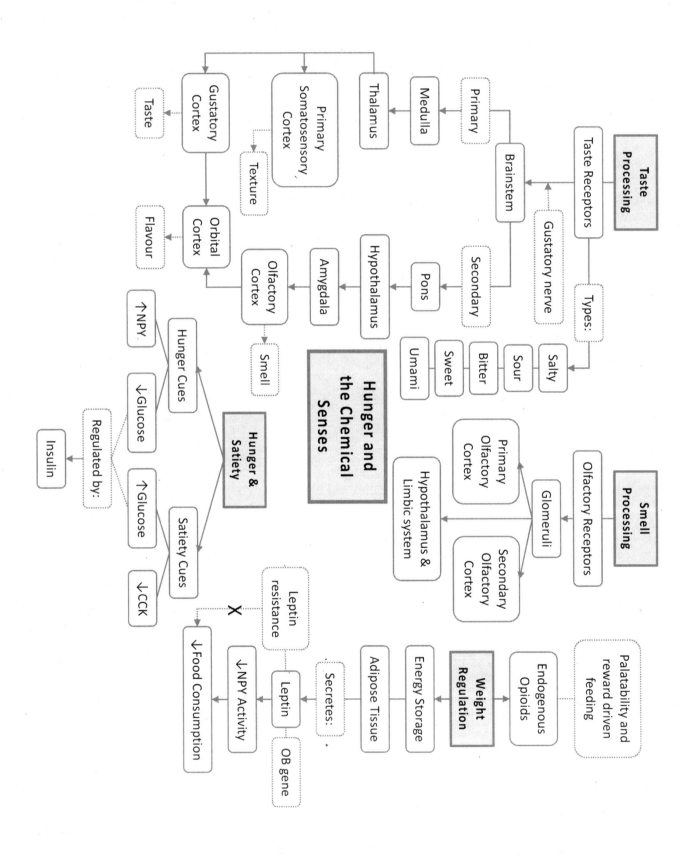

245

Adipose
Hunger and Chemical Senses

Cholecystokinin (CCK)
Hunger and Chemical Senses

Endogenous Opioids
Hunger and Chemical Senses

Glomeruli
Hunger and Chemical Senses

Glucose
Hunger and Chemical Senses

Glycogen
Hunger and Chemical Senses

Gustatory Cortex
Hunger and Chemical Senses

Leptin
Hunger and Chemical Senses

A hormone, produced in the small intestine, which induces satiety (fullness) after eating and serves as a signal to stop eating. **Personal Example:**	An endocrine organ, this tissue acts as a long-term energy source, stored in virtually every part of the body as fat. It is also an active part of regulatory physiology as it produces leptin. **Personal Example:**
A set of cells found in the olfactory bulb that receive and encode smell signals from olfactory receptor cells. Some output goes to the olfactory cortex, whereas others go to the hypothalamus and limbic system that deal with basic drives and emotions. **Personal Example:**	Naturally occurring chemical substances that have morphine-like analgesic effects in the body. They contribute to palatability and reward-driven feeding, which may explain the pleasure that results from eating. **Personal Example:**
A short-term store for the energy found in glucose, which can be converted back to glucose at any time. When you exercise, immediate energy is taken from glycogen stores. **Personal Example:**	An important sugar used for energy in the body. It is the primary source of energy for the brain. The level of glucose in the blood directly relates to feelings of hunger as glucose is obtained from food. **Personal Example:**
A hormone produced by adipose tissue and controlled by the OB gene, involved in long-term energy balance and fat mass. High levels of leptin act on the hypothalamus to reduce appetite. **Personal Example:**	The primary taste area in the brain, containing neurons that respond to each of the five basic tastes. From here, taste information is sent to the orbital cortex, where it interacts with smell information from the olfactory cortex to produce the perception of flavour. **Personal Example:**

Neuropeptide Y (NPY)
Hunger and Chemical Senses

Olfactory Bulb
Hunger and Chemical Senses

Olfactory Cilia
Hunger and Chemical Senses

Olfactory Epithelium
Hunger and Chemical Senses

Taste Bud
Hunger and Chemical Senses

Receives information from the olfactory receptor cells which synapses with the glomeruli contained in the olfactory bulb.
Personal Example:

A hormone in humans and other species. High levels in the hypothalamus lead to increased appetite and food seeking behaviours. Interacts with leptin to regulate weight.
Personal Example:

The receptor surface of the nasal cavity, in which each receptor cell receives input from between 10 and 20 olfactory cilia.
Personal Example:

Hair-like projections covering the receptor surface of the nasal cavity in the nose that interact with olfactory chemicals.
Personal Example:

A raised bump found on the tongue, soft palate and opening of the throat that contains 50 to 150 taste receptor cells. It is the first point at which taste signals start to be converted to electrical nerve signals.
Personal Example:

Psychological Disorders 1 & 2

"The best way out is always through"
- Robert Frost, Pulitzer Prize winning American poet

Mental Health at McMaster

There is a mental health crisis at McMaster University. Feelings of hopelessness, depression and anxiety have become the norm for students on our campus. In the spring of 2016, the National College Health Assessment (NCHA) survey was randomly disseminated to 5500 students with a return of 880 surveys. The survey explored how academic and social factors affect student health. The findings suggest that mental health difficulties are a widespread issue facing the students of McMaster. A jarring 61.9% of students reported feelings of hopelessness and 90.9% of students reported feeling overwhelmed by all they had to do. When there are dozens of assignments, tests and exams to keep up with, hopelessness and feeling overwhelmed can become a normal experience. However, just because it is normal, does not make it fine. Students are encouraged to sign up for a time management workshop through OscarPlus, collaborate with friends, practice positive self-talk or seek professional support to help manage these experiences. Mental illness among university students is growing with 20.8% of students reporting that they have been diagnosed or treated by a professional for anxiety and 17.8% of students for depression. Through psychotherapy, medication or both, mental illness is often manageable. When we hear of the tragedy of a student who has committed suicide, we are understandably shocked. For most of us, feelings of perpetual hopelessness are unimaginable, but at McMaster, this feeling is not uncommon. Out of the 871 McMaster students, 121 students had seriously considered suicide—one hundred and twenty one students who felt that life was not worth living. Of these 121 students, 15 had attempted suicide. We have a mental health crisis at McMaster University and the stigma surrounding mental illness has led many to suffer in silence. But if the results of this survey have told you anything, it is that you are not alone. We accept that physical health is an obvious goal. The next step is to accept that mental health and wellbeing is also an obvious goal.

If you or a friend is in need of support, contact the Student Wellness Center at 905-525-9140 ext. 27700 or visit PGCLL 210/201. Personal counseling and emergency supports are available.

You can also contact the Student Assistance Program: **1-877-234-5327 (For immediate needs)**
- o Psychological counselling services offered by phone 24/7 year-round and toll free. Answered by master's level counselors, of which there are 180 different languages and dialects spoken.
- o https://www.msumcmaster.ca/services-directory/36-health-and-dental-insurance/student-assistance-plan

American College Health Association-National College Health Assessment II: Institutional Data Report McMaster University Web Spring 2016. Hanover, MD: American College Health Association, 2016.

Weekly Checklist:
- ☐ **Web modules to watch: Psychological Disorders 1 & 2**
- ☐ **Readings: Chapter 9**
- ☐ **Pre-Quiz & Quiz 10**

Upper Year Courses:
If you enjoyed the content of this week's module, consider taking the following upper year course:
- Psych 2AP3: Abnormal Psychology

Psychological Disorders 1 – Outline

Unit 1: Introduction

_____
_____
_____
_____
_____

_____
_____
_____
_____
_____

Unit 2: What Is Abnormality

Clinicians use a loose set of criteria, summarized as the Four D's to broadly define abnormality.

_____
_____
_____
_____
_____
_____
_____
_____
_____

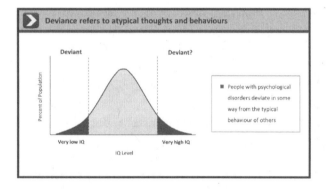

The deviance criterion labels both extremes (ex. very low IQ and very high IQ) as deviant.

Definition: _____
_____
_____
_____

Why is this criterion alone insufficient?
_____
_____
_____
_____
_____

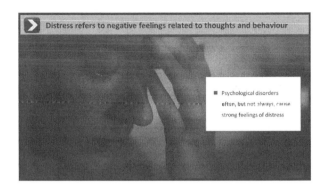

People with psychological disorders often (although not always) experience distress.

Definition: _____
_____
_____
_____

Why is this criterion alone insufficient?
_____
_____
_____
_____
_____
_____

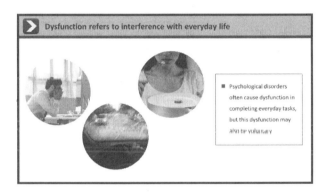

Involuntary dysfunction can be an indicator of psychological disorder.

Definition: _____
_____
_____
_____

Why is this criterion alone insufficient?
_____
_____
_____
_____
_____
_____

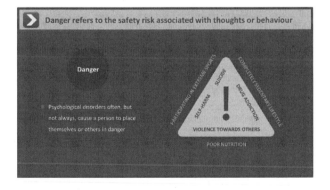

Dangerous behaviours (to the self or others) can be an indicator of psychological disorder.

Definition: _____
_____
_____
_____

Why is this criterion alone insufficient?
_____
_____
_____
_____
_____
_____

Unit 3: Classifying Disorders

The DSM outlines criteria for proper classification and diagnosis of disorder.

Two main functions:
1)

2)

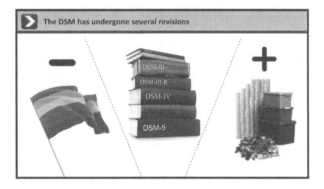

The DSM has undergone many revisions since its first edition, including the addition and removal of several recognized disorders.

Categorical Classification Model:

Dimensional Classification Model:

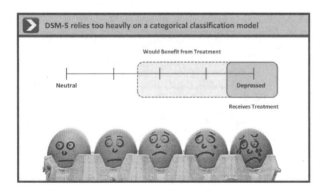

A categorical classification model may prevent suffering people from receiving treatment.

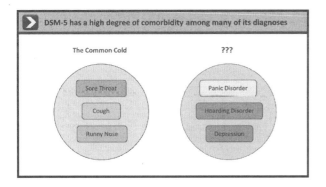

The high degree of comorbidity among DSM disorders may be evidence of an ineffective classification system.

Unit 4: Epidemiology

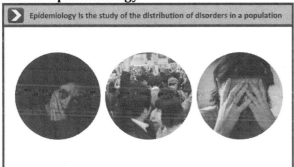

Epidemiology is the study of the distribution of disorders in a population.

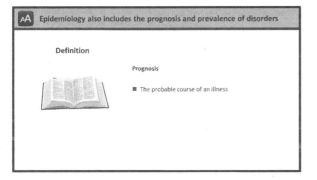

The DSM gives information on the typical prognosis, or probable course of psychological disorders.

Acute:

Chronic:

Episodic:

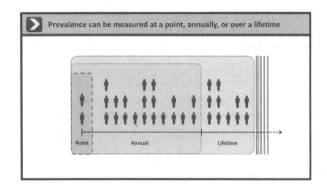

Unit 5: Symptomatology

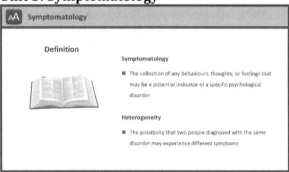

Prevalence can be measured at a point, annually, or over a lifetime.

Point: _____

Annual: _____

Lifetime: _____

Depression is marked by intense, recurrent episodes of sadness.

Symptomatology: _____

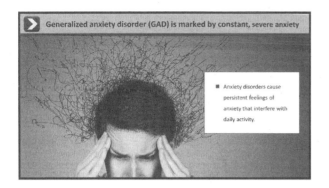

Generalized anxiety disorder is marked by constant, severe anxiety.

Symptomatology: _____
_____
_____
_____
_____
_____
_____
_____

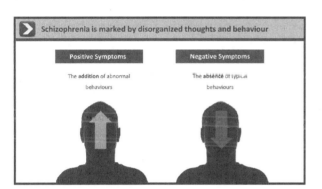

Schizophrenia is describes as having both "positive" and "negative" symptoms

Positive Symptoms: _____
1) Hallucinations _____
_____

2) Delusions _____
_____

3) Disorganized Thinking _____
_____

4) Disorganized Motor Behaviour _____
_____

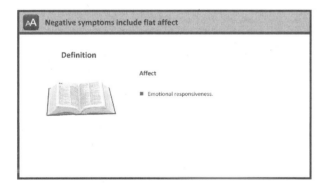

Negative Symptoms: the 5 A's
1) Flat affect _____

2) Alogia _____

3) Anhedonia _____

4) Asociality _____

5) Avolition _____
_____
_____

Psychological Disorders 1 – Courseware Exercise

1. You've now learned about the DSM as a classification system for abnormal behaviour. Abnormal behaviour has been discussed as typically being deviant, distressful, dysfunctional, and dangerous. These unfortunate characteristics of abnormal behaviour mean that an organized grouping system, like the DSM, is incredibly helpful for diagnosticians. However, these criteria are not without fault. Come up with novel examples where a person would meet one of the 4 D's criteria, without necessarily having psychopathology.

Deviance: _____

Distress: _____

Dysfunction: _____

Danger: _____

2. As you've learned, the DSM is not without fault and that is why it is reviewed and updated regularly. Some clinicians take issue with the DSM's categorical labelling system. In such a system, there is a specific threshold at which abnormality is considered symptomatic of a disorder. For instance, imagine a disorder that is characterized by the appearance of up to 10 symptoms. The DSM might define a sufferer of this disorder as someone who has 7/10 of these symptoms. However, where does that leave someone who is very distressed, but suffers from only 6/10 of these same symptoms? Can you think of three problems with this form of classification system?

   1) _____

   _____

   2) _____

   _____

   3) _____

   _____

3. To account for the wide range of symptoms that individuals can present with, the DSM-5 has made some modifications to classify a few disorders on a spectrum (for example, autism and schizophrenia). Outline three advantages of the dimensional classification system.

   1) _____

   2) _____

   3) _____

Psychological Disorders 1 – Review Questions

1) Which of the following scenarios does NOT demonstrate one of the 4 D's of abnormality?
   a) Jim, an avid soccer player, has an above average running speed when compared to the general public.
   b) Joe feels a considerable amount of anxiety because his hobby of collecting lawn gnomes has become very time consuming.
   c) Jack has hurt himself a number of times because of the stress he feels from his marriage
   d) John spends over 14 hours a day cleaning his apartment in order to satisfy his ideals of a clean apartment

2) We discussed 3 different prevalence rates for psychological disorders. Compare and contrast Point, Annual, and Lifetime prevalence.

Rate	
Point	
Annual	
Lifetime	

3) Compare positive and negative symptoms and describe the symptoms of schizophrenia.

Category	Symptomology
Positive Symptoms	
Negative Symptoms	

4) What are some possible causes for schizophrenia?

Concept Map: Psychological Disorders 1

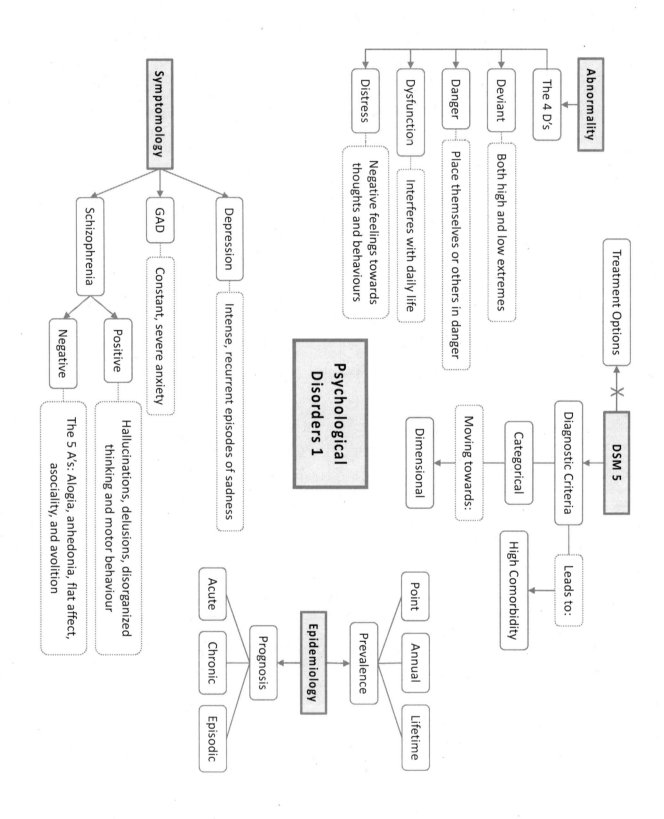

Psychological Disorders 2 – Outline

Unit 1: Introduction

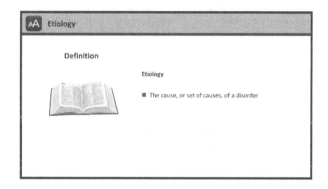

The etiology of disorders directs us to effective treatment methods.

Unit 2: The Biological Model

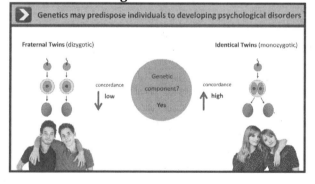

Twin studies determine whether a disorder has a genetic link. Further study is required to determine how specific genes cause disorder.

Concordance:

Specific Genes:

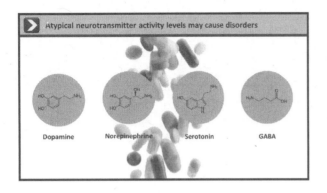

Neurotransmitter activity is part of the etiology of psychopathology, but it is not the whole story.

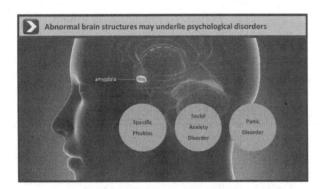

Abnormal brain structures may underlie disorder, but correlation is not causation.

Unit 3: The Environmental Model

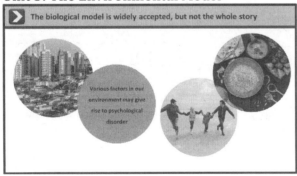

The environmental model considers the effects of environmental factors on causing disorder.

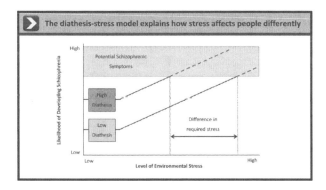

People who are genetically predisposed to schizophrenia only experience symptoms if they are triggered by environmental stress.

_____
_____
_____
_____
_____
_____
_____
_____
_____
_____

Unit 4: The Behavioural Model

According to behaviourists, external factors themselves are not the issue, but rather, our behaviours and emotions in response to them.

_____
_____
_____
_____
_____

How does it explain depression?
_____
_____
_____
_____

Demonstrations of learned helplessness in dogs is evidence in favour of the behavioural model of depression.

_____
_____
_____
_____
_____
_____
_____
_____
_____
_____

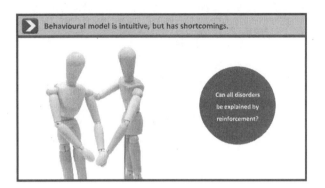

There are several shortcomings to the behavioural model—some are corrected by the cognitive model.

Unit 4: The Cognitive Model

The cognitive model: disorder results from maladaptive interpretations of our environment.

Public Speaking Analogy:

Depressogenic schemata cause people to adopt negative interpretations of life events.

Unit 5: Conclusion

Symptomatology and etiology direct new treatment methods

Psychological Disorders 2 – Courseware Exercise

1. You've learned about 4 different models that help us to better understand the causes of Psychological disorders. Using Generalized Anxiety Disorder as an example, provide a short description on how each of the models could explain the continued disordered behaviour.

Biological: _____

Environmental: _____

Behavioural: _____

Cognitive: _____

2. Each of the 4 models brings a different element into the understanding of disordered behaviour, however, they are not perfect. Provide at least one area where each model is lacking.

Biological: _____
_____

Environmental: _____
_____

Behavioural: _____
_____

Cognitive: _____
_____

3. Looking at a problem from multiple perspectives is usually the best practice. Apply that to the 4 models by explaining how we can get a fully picture of a psychology disorder by combining two or more of the models.

_____
_____
_____
_____
_____
_____

Psychological Disorders 2 – Review Questions

1) Which of the following terms is correctly paired with its definition:
   a) Biological model: Considers the effects of the environmental factors, such as where we live, who we socialize with, and what we consume.
   b) Environmental model: Considering how external factors produce contingencies that lead to disordered behaviours.
   c) Behavioural model: Assumes that a psychological disorder result from malfunction in the brain.
   d) Cognitive model: Suggests that mental disorder result from maladaptive or inappropriate ways of selecting and interpreting information from the environment.

2) Twin studies provide important insight into the etiology of psychological disorders. If a disorder has a strong genetic component, we would expect:
   a) Dizygotic twins to have a higher concordance rate than monozygotic twins.
   b) Monozygotic twins to have a higher concordance rate than dizygotic twins.
   c) Dizygotic twins to have a higher concordance rate than regular siblings.
   d) Monozygotic twins to have a lower concordance rate than regular siblings.

3) Explain the contributions of both the biological and environmental models to the diathesis-stress model.

4) Explain how conditioned responses can produce disordered behaviour according to the Behavioural model.

Concept Map: Psychological Disorders 2

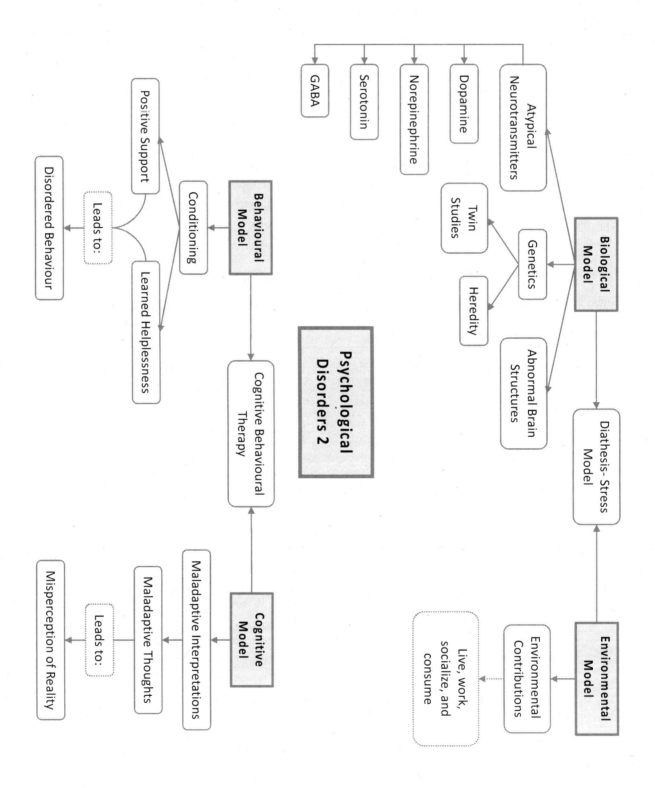

Psychological Disorders 1 & 2 – Test Question

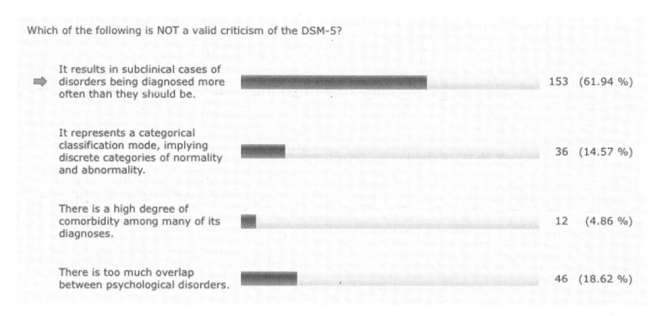

This is an actual question Psychological Disorders Quiz that many students struggled with. We are going to walk through this question together.

This question is asking whether you can understand and recognize the shortcomings of the DSM-5. To answer this question correctly all you need to do is carefully think through each answer option to rule out the incorrect options.

A. In a categorical classification model, individuals are either abnormal, or they are not. As with most traits, it seems that abnormality has variance and exists on a spectrum. The module discusses how people who do not meet the diagnostic criteria for disorders often could still benefit from treatment. Therefore, subclinical cases of disorders are actually being diagnosed LESS often than they should be. Is this a valid criticism? No. So this is the best answer!

B. DSM-5 is often criticized for being too categorical, despite efforts to shift to a more dimensional model. As a result, sub-clinical cases often go undiagnosed and untreated, and people suffer without support. Is this a valid criticism? Yes. This is not the best answer.

C. As we will discuss in D, DSM-5 diagnostic criteria often lead to several comorbid disorders. Is this a valid criticism? Yes. This is not the best answer.

D. The module discusses the issue of comorbidity relative to DSM-5. When the same disorders are frequently diagnosed in the same individual, it seems likely that our current diagnostic criteria must overlap too much. Is this a valid criticism? Yes. This is not the best answer.

After reviewing the answer options, A seems like the best choice. The key here is to weight each answer option carefully, and to pay attention to the "NOT" in the question stem.

Key Terms

Abnormal Psychology	Deviance	Generalized Anxiety Disorder
Behavioural Model	Diagnostic and Statistical Manual	Major Depressive Disorder
Biological Model	Distress	Negative Symptoms
Cognitive Model	Dysfunction	Positive Symptoms
The 4 D's	Environmental Model	Schizophrenia
Danger		

Psychological Disorders 1 & 2 – Bottleneck Concepts

The Four D's
Positive vs. Negative Symptoms
The Four Models

Positive vs. Negative Symptoms

Schizophrenia is a psychotic disorder that is characterized by a wide variety of symptoms that present uniquely in each individual. As outlined by the DSM-5, the symptoms of schizophrenia can be categorized as either positive or negative presentations. A positive presentation describes symptoms that are behavioural excesses or peculiarities, i.e., behaviours that are not present in most people. For example, most people do not see or hear things that aren't there; as a result, hallucinations are a positive symptom. Most people have clear thoughts that are easy to organize and communicate; as a result, disorganized thinking and speech is a positive symptom. Most people do not hold false beliefs or irrational theories; as a result, delusions are a positive symptom. Most people move their limbs normally and smoothly; as a result, grossly disorganized or abnormal motor behaviour is a positive symptom. Individuals with mostly positive symptoms will find that their symptoms come and go throughout the course of their illness. As a result, these individuals experience less impairment in their daily life than someone with predominately negative symptoms.

Negative symptoms are a reduction in or lack of normal behaviours, thoughts, feelings, and drives that would typically be present in most people. For example, most people respond with sadness to the news that someone has died, but the negative symptom of inappropriate or flat affect leads these individuals to show *reduced* emotion (not sad) or an odd emotional response (laughing). When communicating, we usually use many words and compound sentences, but alogia is manifested by using *less* words when communicating and providing brief, empty replies to questions; as a result, alogia is a negative symptom. Most people are relatively energized and interested in doing activities, but someone with avolition has a *lack* of energy and does not want to participate in social activities; as a result, avolition is a negative symptom. Most people show happiness and pleasure when they eat, hang out with friends, or have sex. Someone with anhedonia shows a *reduction in* or *lack* of this normal behaviour; as a result, anhedonia is a negative symptom. The basic drives are feeding, fleeing from danger, fighting to protect ourselves, and seeking out mates. Individuals with negative symptoms show an overall reduction in these basic drives. For example, they may show impaired fear responses and not respond appropriately to threats. Negative symptoms are usually constant throughout an individual's prognosis and as a result are most damaging to their quality of life. Someone with mostly negative symptoms will likely have more difficulty with recovery and need more support to live a relatively normal life.

Test your Understanding

1) Ben has been homeless for 5 years and is known around the neighbourhood as the guy who thinks the government is stealing his thoughts. Police find it very difficult to understand what Ben is saying and find it difficult to help him with his concerns. Ben goes days without eating and has no interest in friends or sexual relationships. It seems like...
    a) Ben is hallucinating that the government is stealing his thoughts
    b) Ben presents with the negative symptom of inappropriate affect because he has no interest in sexual relationships when most men would
    c) Ben is presenting with a positive symptom delusion and negative symptom anhedonia
    d) Ben will likely think the government is stealing his thoughts for his entire life

2) Stephanie's mother is concerned that something is wrong with her teen daughter. For the last two months Stephanie hasn't hung out with friends, doesn't shower or brush her teeth as often, has trouble at school and doesn't cook anymore. Stephanie used to love cooking up recipes, but now says she can't get past the first one or two steps, becomes frustrated, and stops. What diagnosis would you give Stephanie?
    a) Stephanie most likely has Major Depressive Disorder
    b) Stephanie is just a normal teenager
    c) Stephanie most likely has Schizophrenia
    d) Stephanie needs to be monitored further before a diagnosis can be made

Practice case study

Tavangeph's roommate Melissa has recently become concerned for her well-being. Tavangeph has had trouble sleeping, and has woken Melissa with screaming in the middle of the night. In addition, Tavangeph has been very irritable, breaking into tears at any given moment. One day, the two were watching TV in the common room when a mugger attacked one of the characters in the show. Suddenly, Tavangeph started yelling at someone who wasn't there and ran out of the room. Melissa thinks Tavangeph has bipolar disorder.

1) What would make Melissa come to this conclusion? Do you agree with her diagnosis? Why or why not?

Tavangeph meets with a Campus Health Centre psychiatrist, Dr. Smith. Tavangeph reveals that she was mugged two years ago. Although she was upset when it first happened, she is recently experiencing flashbacks and nightmares about the incident for the first time in the past few weeks. Dr. Smith diagnoses her with PTSD.

2) Using what you know about the DSM and the 4 Ds, how do you think Tavangeph's psychiatrist came to this conclusion?

3) In your opinion, are there any cons associated with using the DSM?

Abnormal Psychology
Psychological Disorders

Behavioural Model
Psychological Disorders

Biological Model
Psychological Disorders

Cognitive Model
Psychological Disorders

The 4 D's
Psychological Disorders

Danger
Psychological Disorders

Deviance
Psychological Disorders

Diagnostic and Statistical Manual
Psychological Disorders

Considering how external factors produce disordered behaviours and emotions. External factors themselves are not the issue, but rather, our behaviours and emotions in response to them. Conditioned responses play a large role in our disordered behaviour. **Personal Example:**	A branch of psychology studying the unusual patterns of behaviour, emotion, and thought that vary between people and cultures. Typically, it is summarized with "the four D's": Deviance, Distress, Dysfunction, and danger. **Personal Example:**
Suggests that mental disorder result from maladaptive or inappropriate ways of selecting and interpreting information from the environment. **Personal Example:**	Also known as the medical or disease model, assumes that a psychological disorder results from malfunction in the brain. It usually points to genetics, atypical neurotransmitter activity, or abnormal brain structures. **Personal Example:**
One of "the 4 D's", it is when an individual presents a danger to themselves or others. **Example:** An individual suffering from drug addiction may become dangerous as a result of the anxiety experienced during withdrawal. **Personal Example:**	A set of criteria used to broadly define abnormal behaviour. These criteria are deviance, distress, dysfunction and danger. These must be used with caution as exhibiting one or more is not necessarily indicative of a psychological disorder. **Personal Example:**
A book categorizing and describing mental disorders using a common set of criteria to 1) apply a diagnostic label of symptoms to patients and 2) to communicate with others via a common language. **Personal Example:**	One of "the 4 D's", the experience of thoughts, emotions and behaviour that fall far outside of the standards of what others are doing. **Example:** Most people save their money for rent, so an individual who spends all of their money on excessive shopping sprees and cannot pay their bills deviates from what may be considered normal. **Personal Example:**

Distress
Psychological Disorders

Dysfunction
Psychological Disorders

Environmental Model
Psychological Disorders

Generalized Anxiety Disorder
Psychological Disorders

Major Depressive Disorder
Psychological Disorders

Negative Symptoms
Psychological Disorders

Positive Symptoms
Psychological Disorders

Schizophrenia
Psychological Disorders

One of "the 4 D's", it is the inability to function properly in daily life. **Example:** An individual may have recurring thoughts of a stressful event to the extent that they are unable to focus on work, maintaining a household or building healthy relationships. **Personal Example:**	One of "the 4 D's", the experience of intense negative feelings due to an individual's own behaviour. **Example:** An individual may feel anxiety as a result of performing poorly on a test. **Personal Example:**
Considers the effects of the environmental factors, such as where we live, who we socialize with, and what we consume, on causing psychopathology. **Personal Example:**	An anxiety disorder characterized by excessive and irrational worry about minor things. An individual with GAD may experience minor life stressors as significant sources of anxiety due to their inability to cope. **Personal Example:**
Behaviours that decrease in someone with schizophrenia. They generally point to a decrease in the individual's engagement with the outside world. **Personal Example:**	A depressive disorder characterized by severe decreased mood, loss of motivation, fluctuations in weight, lack of energy, thoughts of suicide, feelings of emptiness, worthlessness, and guilt. **Personal Example:**
The "splitting of the mind" from reality, it is a mental disorder characterized by a breakdown in thought processes and poor emotional responsiveness. Symptoms include but are not limited to delusions, paranoia and auditory hallucinations. **Personal Example:**	Behaviours that increase in someone with schizophrenia. These may include disorders of thought, delusions, hallucinations, and disorganized or abnormal motor behaviour. **Personal Example:**

Psychological Treatments

"The only person with whom you have to compare yourself is you in the past."
- *Sigmund Freud, famed founder of psychoanalytic theory*

A History of Mental Health Care in Canada

Mental health care in Canada has had a long, diverse and complicated history. Indigenous cultures have regarded an individual with mental illness as someone who has lost balance between the four cardinal quadrants of their healing wheel: emotional, physical, spiritual and mental realms. Mental health care was provided through community healing ceremonies where shamans would help to interpret and reenact dreams in hopes of fulfilling the afflicted's needs. In the 17th century and onwards, European settlers believed that mental illness was related to demonic possessions, bodily fluid (humoral) imbalances, or God's will. Mental health care was provided through exorcisms to de-possess the afflicted; bloodletting, purging, or modifying one's diet to balance the humors; or through prayer for a miracle. By the mid-19th century, Canada followed Britain's footsteps to build insane asylums after the burden on at-home care providers became too great. Early on, the goal of these institutions was to cure madness by removing the individual from the homes that caused their troubles and entering a controlled asylum where Freudian therapy and medication could be offered. However, overcrowding became an immediate problem and there were not enough doctors who could provide the necessary care. By the late 19th century, insane asylums were considered to be a last resort option for the incurably ill. In hopes of making asylums more effective, radical treatments such as electroconvulsive therapy and lobotomies were utilized in the early 20th century. Given without anesthesia or muscle relaxants, electroconvulsive therapy induced vicious convulsions and often left patients with fractures and irreparable muscle damage. Additionally, prefrontal lobotomies (incisions) were used to treat severe psychosis and mood disorders. While some individuals had slight improvements in their symptoms, it was almost always at the expense of emotional and intellectual deficits. These radical approaches reduced in use with the rise of the pharmaceutical approach in mid-20th century. Antipsychotics, antidepressants and antianxiety medications helped the mentally unwell rely less on permanent care at psychiatric hospitals which led to the era of deinstitutionalization. Near the end of the 20th century, there was a rapid move from asylum care to community care. Most patients could be served through outpatient psychiatric services and those that needed inpatient care were served at general hospital psychiatric units rather than solely inpatient psychiatric hospitals. Today, outpatient mental health services such as individual and group therapy and psychiatric support are utilized far above inpatient long-term support. While we have come a long way, there is still much room for growth in the mental health care system.

Moran, J. E., & Wright, D. (2006). *Mental health and Canadian society: Historical perspectives.* Montreal, QC: McGill-Queen's University Press.

Weekly Checklist:
- ☐ Web modules to watch: Psychology Treatments
- ☐ Readings: Chapter 10
- ☐ Pre-Quiz & Quiz 11

Upper Year Courses:
If you enjoyed the content of this week's module, consider taking the following upper year course:
- Psych 2AP3: Abnormal Psychology

Psychological Treatments – Outline

Unit 1: Introduction

Unit 2: Barriers to Treatment

> External barriers are systemic obstacles to receiving treatment

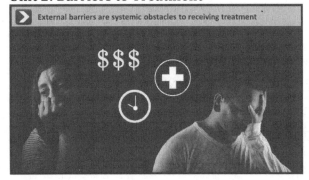

Internal barriers are restrictive beliefs held by the person

Definition

Ego Dystonic
- Having a negative relationship with the disorder

Ego Syntonic
- Having a positive relationship with the disorder

External barriers such as time and money can make accessing treatment difficult.

Ego Dystonic:

Ego Syntonic:

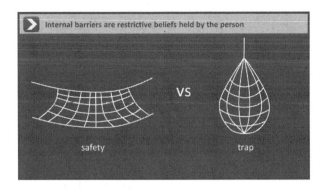

Internal barriers also prevent individuals from seeking help.

_____
_____
_____
_____
_____
_____
_____
_____
_____
_____

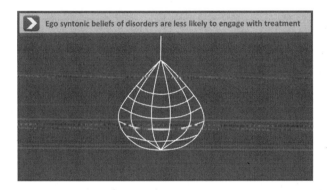

Ego syntonic beliefs can be considered an internal barrier to receiving treatment.

_____
_____
_____
_____
_____
_____
_____
_____
_____
_____

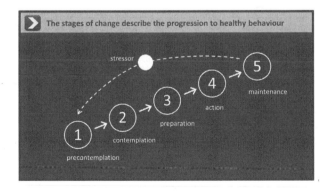

Prochaska and DiClemente's (1983) propose five stages of change.

Precontemplation: _____

Contemplation: _____

Preparation: _____

Action: _____

Maintenance: _____

_____
_____

Unit 3: Treatment Practitioners

Mental health services providers come from a wide range of professional backgrounds and experiences.

_____
_____
_____
_____
_____
_____
_____
_____
_____
_____
_____

Clinical Psychologist: _____
_____
_____

Psychiatrist: _____
_____
_____
_____

Unit 4: Designing Treatment

Efficacy trials occur in very controlled environments.

_____
_____
_____
_____
_____
_____
_____
_____
_____

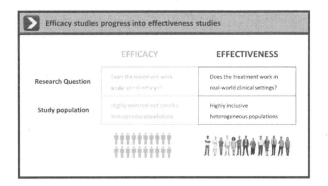

Unit 5: Approaches to Treatment

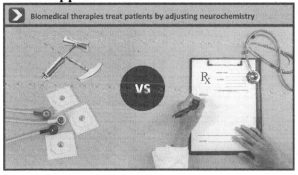

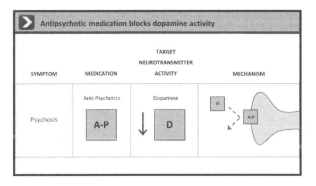

Effectiveness trials occur in more real world settings.

Biomedical therapies are approaches that target physiology and neurochemistry.

Antipsychotic medications attempt to reduce psychotic symptoms by reducing dopamine activity.

Mechanism:

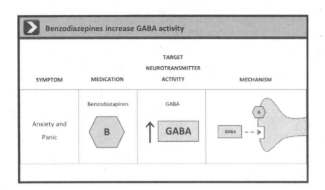

Benzodiazepines increase GABA activity.

Mechanism:

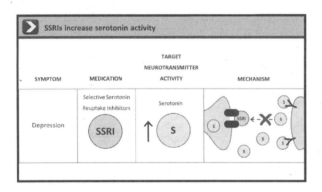

Selective Serotonin Reuptake Inhibitors (SSRIs) combat low serotonin activity

Mechanism:

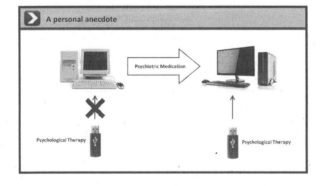

Patients tend to receive the most benefit when psychological and pharmacological approaches are combined.

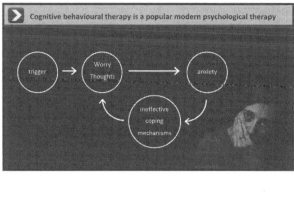

Cognitive Behavioural Therapy is a popular evidence-based psychological therapy.

Dana Example:

Psychological Treatments – Courseware Exercise

Terry has been experiencing persecutory delusions, auditory hallucinations, and several negative symptoms of schizophrenia. After a conversation with his parents, Terry and has decided to pursue professional help.

1. What are some of the specific ways that a psychiatrist might assist Terry?

___

2. What are some of the specific ways that a clinical psychologist might assist Terry?

___

3. Anti-psychotics, benzodiazepines, and selective serotonin reuptake inhibitors are pharmacotherapeutic drugs that target different symptoms via different mechanisms. For each drug, explain which effect it has on its target neurotransmitter, and how this is hypothesized to alleviate the symptoms of interest.

Medication	Target Neurotransmitter Activity	Alleviates Symptoms By:
Anti-Psychotics		
Benzodiazepines		
Selective Serotonin Reuptake Inhibitors		

Psychological Treatments – Review Questions

1) The module discusses a helpful computer-based analogy for how psychiatric medication might improve maladaptive thought patterns. Which of the following incorrectly describes a component of that analogy?
   a) A Hardware Update represents SSRIs
   b) A Downloadable Program represents CBT
   c) Outdated Hardware represents a Therapy-Resistant Patient
   d) Updated Hardware represents a Patient with Adaptive Thought Patterns

2) Which of the following would be the most likely sequence of stages in Prochaska and DiClemente's (1983) stages of change?
   a) Maintenance → Precontemplation
   b) Preparation → Maintenance
   c) Contemplation → Action
   d) Preparation → Precontemplation

3) Compare the similarities and differences in the roles of psychiatrists and clinical psychologists.

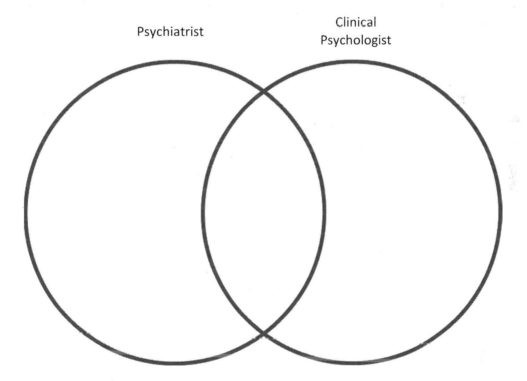

4) Summarize the mechanism of how cognitive behavioural therapy works:

_____

_____

_____

Psychological Treatments – Test Question

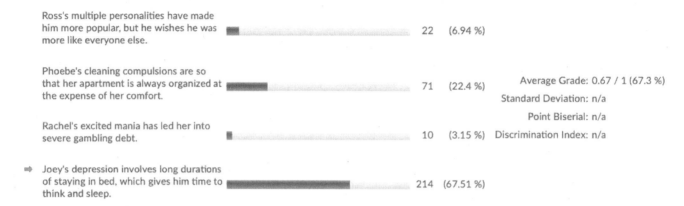

This is an actual question from the Psychological Treatments quiz that many students struggled with. We are going to walk through this question together.

This question is testing your understand of "ego syntonic" and your ability to apply it to novel examples. A person who has an ego syntonic relationship with their disorder perceives their symptoms as valuable or advantageous. This in in contrast to ego dystonic which are symptoms that are perceived by the individual as undesirable.

A. Being more popular is generally viewed as being a positive thing. This could potentially fool you into thinking this is the correct answer. However, the important factor is not whether it is a positive thing to the general population but whether the individual views it as positive. In this case, Ross would prefer he was more like everyone else so he does not see this as a positive benefit. This is not the correct answer.

B. This is similar to option A. Having a clean and organized apartment is a good thing, but Phoebe does not view it as a positive thing as it is causing her discomfort. This is not the correct answer.

C. This option is a negative all around. It is neither viewed as positive by the general population or by the individual in question. This is not the correct answer.

D. In this example, Joey is viewing his time in bed in a positive light. It is allowing him time to think and sleep. This is a good example of on individual viewing a symptom of their disorder, in this case the lack of motivation associated with depression, as advantageous. This is the correct answer.

Key Terms

Anti-Psychotic Medication	Effectiveness	Ego Syntonic
Benzodiazepine	Efficacy	Psychiatrist
Clinical Psychologist	Ego Dystonic	SSRI
Cognitive-Behavioural Therapy	External/Internal Barriers	Stages of Change

Psychological Treatments – Bottleneck Concepts

Efficacy vs. Effectiveness
Clinical Psychologist vs. Psychiatrist
Ego Syntonic vs. Ego Dystonic
Biomedical Therapy vs. Psychological Therapy

Efficacy vs. Effectiveness
Treatments for psychopathology must be tested in both controlled and real-world settings to empirically support their utility. Psychological treatments should demonstrate both efficacy and effectiveness. Efficacy is the ability of a treatment to produce the desired effect within a controlled setting. Efficacy studies are most commonly used in medication research. An efficacy study must utilize a randomized control group through either a single-blind or double-blind format. Consider this example of a hypothetical efficacy study. The participant pool includes 20 participants of European descent, ages 20 – 45, and a sole diagnosis of major depressive disorder. Ten of these participants are randomly assigned to take 10 mg of Cipralex for 4 months, while the other 10 participants take 10 mg of a placebo pill for 4 months. No participant is allowed to take any other drugs or receive any therapy while participating in the study. If the medication group has significantly lower depression scores following the treatment, then the researchers may suggest that the medication had statistically significant effects. Statistical significance means that there is at least a 95% chance that the medication actually lowered depression scores and less than a 5% likelihood that this result was found simply by chance. We would not be able to say that an efficacy study demonstrated clinically significant effects because there are too many controls placed on the participants to suggest it has real-world applicability. Because there are so many controls, sometimes the findings of efficacy studies can be very specific to the group that was used in the study and may not be transferrable to the population as a whole. Efficacy studies require highly controlled treatment manuals, therapist and participant characteristics, control groups and timelines in order to reduce the potential for confounds.

Effectiveness studies are less heavily regulated than efficacy studies. These studies attempt to gauge the usefulness of a treatments in relatively less controlled real-world settings. The real-world does not have control groups, manipulations, restrictions on medication use, or people with only one disorder. Effectiveness studies evaluate how regular people respond to a treatment that is administered as they are living their normal, uncontrolled lives. These studies can tell us if a treatment is clinically significant which means it has a meaningful impact on the lives of people receiving the treatment. Consider this example of an effectiveness study. The participant pool includes 20 people of various ages, ethnicities and mental illnesses who were referred by a free community health clinic. All participants have major depressive disorder, but half also have an anxiety disorder, and a few have an eating disorder. All participants are given 8 weeks of CBT for depression and they find that the participants showed a clinically significant reduction in depressive symptoms. Keep in mind that some participants took medication during their treatment and some even participated in anxiety-focused therapy. How can the researcher know for certain that participating in 8 weeks of CBT for depression was responsible for the group's reduction in depressive symptoms? They can't. Perhaps the individuals who also took medication improved so much that they skewed the results. Additionally, maybe this treatment only works for individuals who are of low socioeconomic status and would need to access free health services. We just don't know.

Because of the limitations of both efficacy and effectiveness studies, you will find that both studies are jointly used to support the usefulness of a treatment. Once efficacy is established and we know that the treatment works in a controlled setting, experimenters can work to establish the effectiveness of the treatment in a real world setting. When efficacy and effectiveness have been supported, the reliability and validity of the treatment is supported and it can be named an evidence-based treatment.

Test your Understanding

1) Which of the following is true about efficacy studies?
    a) A treatment must demonstrate a clinical significance
    b) Efficacy studies control for comorbidity in individuals with psychological disorders
    c) A control group is not needed if the manipulations are administered very carefully
    d) Efficacy is only concerned with the reliability of the findings

2) Fifty participants with anxiety and depression were recruited to receive either cognitive-behavioural therapy alone, or cognitive behavioural therapy combined with anxiety medication. All participants received mindfulness therapy through a group format that was led by either a psychologist or social worker. The therapists were encouraged to respond to the group's needs and focus on things that were relevant to them. The researchers were looking to see how the participants' quality of life, depressive and anxiety symptoms, and mindfulness skills changed over the 12 weeks of sessions. What type of study is this? What are three limitations with this type of study? What would you have to do to make it into the other type of study?

Concept Map: Psychological Treatments

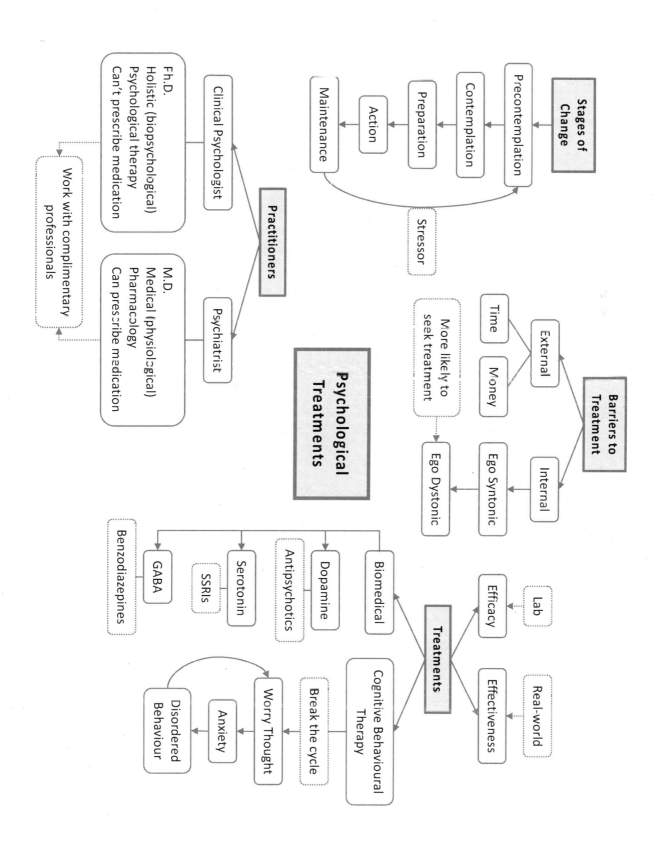

Anti-Psychotic Medication
Psychological Treatments

Benzodiazepines
Psychological Treatments

Clinical Psychologist
Psychological Treatments

Cognitive-Behaviour Therapy
Psychological Treatments

Efficacy
Psychological Treatments

Effectiveness
Psychological Treatments

Ego Dystonic
Psychological Treatments

Ego Syntonic
Psychological Treatments

A drug therapy medication used to alleviate symptoms of anxiety. They work to increase levels of GABA activity in the brain. **Personal Example:**	A drug therapy medication used to alleviate symptoms of psychosis. They work to reduce levels of dopamine activity in the brain. **Personal Example:**
A type of psychological treatment for mental disorders. It aims to make patients aware of how they think and understand how that contributes to the way they feel. It also teaches patients to apply these thought patterns to more productive behaviours. **Personal Example:**	A licenced (i.e. has a doctorate) mental health professional that is formally trained in psychological therapies and typically studies mental health and illness from a holistic perspective. **Personal Example:**
The ability of a treatment to produce a desired effect in real-world settings. **Personal Example:**	The ability of a treatment to produce a desired effect in highly controlled settings. **Personal Example:**
Symptoms of a disorder that are perceived by the individual with the disorder as valued or advantageous. **Personal Example:**	Symptoms of a disorder that are perceived by the individual with the disorder as undesirable. **Personal Example:**

External/Internal Barriers
Psychological Treatments

Psychiatrist
Psychological Treatments

SSRI
Psychological Treatments

Stages of Change
Psychological Treatments

Specialized medical doctors who receive extensive training in pharmacological therapies and are qualified to prescribe medication.
Personal Example:

Mental, physical, and/or sociocultural obstacles that prevent an individual from treating their symptoms; external are systemic and environmental obstacles, while internal manifest as the individual's own restrictive beliefs about treatment.
Personal Example:

The step-wise process that describes the typical progression of treatment, consisting of Precontemplation, Contemplation, Preparation, Action, Maintenance, and sometimes Relapse.
Personal Example:

A drug therapy medication used to alleviate symptoms of depression. They work to increase levels of serotonin activity in the brain.
Personal Example:

ANSWER KEY

Development 1 – Courseware Exercises

1. Two-month old infants have not yet developed language skills and have poor motor coordination. This prevents them from verbally or behaviourally indicating if they can see changes in a visual pattern.
2. These infants are able to demonstrate visual sensitivity through the habituation paradigm, by measuring their breathing or heart rate. This method does not rely on verbal communication or any strong motor coordination. Infants are interested in novel stimuli, which they demonstrate through increased breathing or heart rate. To evaluate whether breathing or heart rate have increased, a baseline level must first be established. Infants are shown a visual stimuli; at first it is novel and they show a burst of activity. However, as the same stimuli is repeated, the infant's breathing and heart rate will return to baseline levels—they have habituated. Following habituation, a different (novel) visual pattern will be shown. If they can perceive a change in the pattern (i.e., view it as a novel stimulus), their breathing/heart rate will increase. If they cannot perceive a difference, their response will remain at baseline.
3. Strong motor coordination allows the use of the habituation paradigm by observing behavioural orienting responses. These babies will habituate to one visual pattern. When their orienting reaction returns to baseline (bored), they will be presented with a novel visual pattern. If they orient to start staring at the novel visual pattern, they are able to tell the two patterns apart.
4. Although this methodology works well for infants, there are more sensitive ways of testing adults. Adults can communicate by being shown visual puzzles/hidden images, and more. Using the habituation methodology on adults would not allow for an accurate reflection of the subjects' abilities.
5. The design used was a cross-sectional design as it measured different age groups at one time.
6. A longitudinal design would also test changing abilities. The same two-month-old babies would be tested throughout their lifespan. One problem with this design is practice effects where the participants may perform better on the task due to repeated testing. Another problem is selective attrition. Because this is a long study, many subjects may stop participating resulting in a smaller sample that may not accurately reflect the population as a whole.

Development 1- Review Questions

1) C This better resembles learning influencing maturation **2)** A **3)** C **4)** A This is an example of a longitudinal study because a specific group of people need to be studied as they adapt. If we used a cross-sectional design (e.g. immigrants who have already lived in Canada for several years) then we would introduce confounds that would render our results meaningless. For example, these immigrants may have emigrated from Russia due to different cultural events occurring at that time, and may have experienced different social services available to immigrants in Canada at that time.

Development 2 – Courseware Exercises

1. Low quality genes are more influenced by environment than high quality genes. This is seen by the larger increase in gene expression in low quality genes when comparing gene expression in a deprived and enriched environment (i.e., the gap between the two environments is larger for low quality, than for high quality genes). There is also a lot of variability of gene expression, showing that both nature and nurture play a role in this characteristic's expression.
2. The range of reaction principle is key to this experimental design—the environment shapes how the genotype is expressed within its range.
3.

Range of Reaction Principle	Shared	Canalization Principle
-genotype establishes range of responses for each individual -environment shapes within that range for each individual	-genotype establishes range of possible phenotypes	-genotype restricts phenotype for the species -environment has less influence -limited number of outcomes

Development 2 – Review Questions

1) B **2)** A **3)** C The focus of this question surrounds Lucy actively going to libraries and reading. **4)** B **5)** B & D

Development 1 & 2 – Bottleneck Concepts

1. a) Canalization Principle, b) Range of Reaction Principle, c) Canalization Principle, d) Canalization Principle

Evolution 1-Courseware Exercises

1. Selectively breed individuals that have high levels of aggression for several generations. You will end up with a population of individuals with a high degree of aggression. Experimenters can then allow their aggressive population to breed with normal individuals in a particular environment, for example one with a high level of competition. If the resulting generations continue to show a large number of aggressive individuals, aggression may be adaptive in a highly competitive environment. Testing this trait in a different environment may not have the same results.
2. You would use a species that has a very short generation time such as the fruit fly, Drosophila. Because your experiment requires multiple generations to be produced, this short generation time allows the experiment to be completed in a short amount of time.
3. A higher level of aggression may have resulted in defeating more same-sex rivals in competitions over mates, increasing these individual's fitness. Aggression could have also been beneficial when there were less resources as these individuals would have been able to take the resources they needed and survive.
4. Friendliness may have an adaptive origin, especially in species that worked in groups. Groups with individuals that helped each other would result in a group that is more likely to survive and reproduce than groups with individuals that did not.
5. Females: Larger breasts and a smaller body attract males but trying to attain these characteristics may also cause

health problems. Males: A muscular build and having expensive possessions is more attractive but also uses resources that could be put to other use.

Evolution 1- Review Questions

1) B **2)** A **3)** C **4)** C

Evolution 2- Courseware Exercises

1. Increase in inclusive fitness, that is, increase the reproductive success of close genetic kin that will allow the indirect reproduction of one's genes. Prevent inbreeding with close relatives as this decreases fitness.

2.
   a. Neighbours: Those living near you are kin Example: Living in a small town, a woman lives next to her brothers and sisters with her parents living across the road. She helps them out whenever she can. Advantages: Easy to state who kin are. This is a fairly valid assumption for non-migratory species. Disadvantages: Migratory species will have different neighbours every season. Mistakenly assuming neighbours are kin will result in resources being used on individuals who will not increase your fitness.
   b. Association with Mother: Older female figure who reared you from infancy. Example: The woman who raised me and who is taking care of me is my kin. I help her with household chores and child care of my siblings. Advantages: Easy to state who kin is as this person raised you from birth. Strong degree of relatedness (0.5). Disadvantages: May confuse other maternal figures as mother if there are other women who have also been present from infancy.
   c. Co-Residence with Other Children: Individuals near your age you grew up with are kin. Example: The male and female children who live with me, who are near my age and who I've played with my whole life are my kin. Advantages: Easy to state who kin are. Close proximity allows for easy access to resources both for and from siblings. Disadvantages: Large number of children are raised together in school, or in joined families, and may mistakenly assume them to be kin.
   d. Phenotype Matching: Individuals who look similar to you or your kin are kin. Example: At a party, I saw someone who looked like my sister. She was having trouble carrying some chairs and I offered to help out. Later, my mom told me that she was my cousin. Advantages: This is an unconscious phenomenon that is not easily swayed by external factors. Disadvantages: Due to the variability in phenotypes, there are many individuals who look like you who are not related, as well as individuals who don't look like you who are related. May not be accurate.

Evolution 2- Review Questions

1) C **2)** B **3)** D 1 Sister + 3(Cousins) X 1 (100% success) = 0.5 + 3(0.125) = 0.875 (1) = 0.875 > all options **4)** D

Evolution 1 & 2 – Bottleneck Concepts

1) **C** - His sister is related by r=0.5 and so is his daughter, so $rB > C = 0.5(3) = 1.5 > 1$. Saving his two sisters and one daughter has a benefit that is greater than the cost of sacrificing himself. For A and D, the benefit and cost are equal, so unless you are given more information you cannot pick either one of these answers. For B, $rB=0.875$ which is less than 1.

2) Taking care of one's grandchildren is one reason that humans have adapted to live longer lives. As an elder, it is unlikely that you will continue reproducing healthy offspring. Additionally, it is hard to hunt or forage for oneself. These two things combined hinder an elder's ability to survive given that they are no longer contributing to their direct fitness. However, adaptations that assist survival can also evolve if they support one's indirect fitness. Human grandparents add to their indirect fitness by taking care of grandchildren. In our evolutionary history, parents needed to hunt and forage to ensure their offspring's survival. Having to take care of their children hindered their ability to provide for their children effectively. Grandparents helped take care of children, so parents could hunt and forage and ultimately offer better resources to their offspring. By enhancing their indirect fitness, adaptations to live longer have evolved to allow older people to survive past their ability to contribute to their direct fitness. Through indirect fitness, humans live longer than species where a grandparent is not active in child rearing.

Neuroscience 1- Courseware Exercises

1. Resting State, Voltage= -70 mV. Ion Placement: Na^+ is outside the cell, K^+ is inside the cell. State of Channels (open/closed): K^+ leaky channels are open (few K^+ ions leave the cell), all other channels are closed
2. Depolarization (Sodium's Role), Voltage= towards -50 mV. Movement of Ions: Na^+ moves into the cell. Change in Voltage (increase/decrease): Increase. State of Channels (open/closed): Voltage-gated Na^+ channels open
3. Peak, Voltage= towards +40 mV. Movement of Ions: Na^+ rush in until cell reaches peak charge of +40 Mv, then Na^+ stops moving in, and K^+ continues moving out of cell. Change in Voltage (increase/decrease): Increase until peak. State of Channels (open/closed): Voltage-gated Na^+ channels are open until they close when cell reaches +40 mV; leaky K^+ channels are always open.
4. Repolarization (Potassium's Role), Voltage= +40 mV to 0 mV. Movement of Ions: K^+ rushes out of cell. Change in Voltage (increase/decrease): Decrease. State of Channels (open/closed): Voltage-gated K^+ channels open.
5. Hyperpolarization, Voltage= towards -100 mV. Movement of Ions: K^+ moves out of VG K^+ channel until cell reaches -100 mV, then it closes and stops moving out. Change in Voltage (increase/decrease): Decrease. State of Channels (open/closed): Voltage-gated K^+ channels closed
6. Return to Resting Potential, Voltage= towards -70 mV. Movement of Ions: K^+ ions flow into the cell via the K^+ leak channel and 2 K^+ move into the cell, 3 Na^+ move out of the cell following the Na/K pump. Change in Voltage (increase/decrease): Increase. State of Channels (open/closed): K^+ leak channel is open, Na^+/K^+ pump is functioning, and all other channels are closed.
7. Excitatory post synaptic potentials (EPSPs) are occurring. These are not always strong enough to reach -50mV, which would prevent an action potential (AP) from occurring. Multiple EPSPs in time (temporal) or space (spatial) build to trigger an AP.
8. A stronger stimulus would translate into more frequent action potentials. The size of the action potential would not change because they follow an "all-or-none" law that states

that their size (voltage) will not change.

Neuroscience 1- Review Questions

1) B **2)** A **3)** C **4)** B Inaccurate definition. **5)** B

Neuroscience 1 – Bottleneck Concepts

1) **B.** An excitatory post-synaptic potential opens sodium channels allowing sodium to rush into the cell, making it more positive. When a cell becomes more positive than resting potential, it is being depolarized, not repolarized. Remember that repolarization refers to returning towards its resting membrane potential.

2) If sodium could not flow into the cell, depolarization would not happen. The cell would remain at its resting state since positive sodium ions need to rush into the cell to make it more positive and reach the threshold potential to trigger an action potential. As a result of depolarization not happening, repolarization or hyperpolarization would not occur as these processes follow depolarization.

Neuroscience 2- Courseware Exercises

1) **Stimulation and Single Cell Recording:** Electrically stimulate an area of the brain with a microelectrode and notice the change in behaviour. If there is cerebral lateralization, there will be a different response for the left and right hemisphere. *Advantages*: Allows one to record a brain area of choice. *Disadvantages:* Invasive, only gives information about a limited brain region. **Structural Neuroimaging:** This provides an image of brain structure using either CT or MRI scanning. Structural damage to one hemisphere of the brain will give information about brain lateralization. *Advantages:* Large-scale information, not invasive, quick, inexpensive. *Disadvantages:* Low resolution. **Functional Neuroimaging:** This method is used to detect what areas of the brain are active using PET, fMRI and EEG scanning. Cerebral lateralization can be seen if only one hemisphere of the brain is active during a task. *Advantages:* Determines brain region involved in a task or behaviour instead of needing to stimulate random regions. *Disadvantages:* Can be invasive, rough image, cannot conclude that activation is not due to an unrelated variable

2) **Mark:** What information is being tested and where is it processed? Spatial: object identification (right hemisphere), Speech: words (left hemisphere). Will Mark be able to complete this task? No, the information is sent to the left hemisphere, so he can read the word, but he cannot spatially pick up the bird. Is he able to say the word that he saw? Yes because speech is processed in the left hemisphere. **Jane:** What information is being tested and where is it processed? Vision: Object Identification (right hemisphere), Music (right hemisphere), Verbal memory (left hemisphere). Will Jane be able to complete this task? No, the information is sent to the right hemisphere, so she can identify the object, but cannot produce the sound. If she is played a number of different instruments, can she correctly identify the sound of a trumpet? Yes, nonverbal memory is processed in the right hemisphere. **Sue:** What information is being tested and where is it processed? Reading/Speech/Arithmetic (left hemisphere), Spatial (right hemisphere). Will Sue be able to verbally state the answer? Yes, the information is sent to the left hemisphere, so she can read the question and calculate and say the answer.

Will Sue be able to write it down? No, her spatial abilities are processed in the right hemisphere.

Neuroscience 2- Review Questions

1) B **2)** D **3)** C **4)** A **5)** C

Neuroscience 2 – Bottleneck Concepts

1) **Broca's Aphasia.** Individuals with Broca's aphasia often appear frustrated when they try to produce words. Sometimes they can say the words, but their speech is very short and often mumbled. Given that Broca's aphasia is a motor speech production deficit, these individuals will have little problem writing in coherent sentences. If Geoff had Wernicke's aphasia, he would not be able to write coherently. However, Geoff would be able to speak, but the sentences he produced would not make sense, i.e., "home with him cruise for home in moment for dog in me for me". Someone with Wernicke's aphasia would also express frustration, but because no one understands their needs.

2) One must target language production and word-finding when helping someone with Broca's Aphasia. Speech therapy is the ideal method of tackling production deficits. Speech therapy involves facial muscle exercises, word repetition, practicing common conversations all while supplementing these methods with image flashcards and writing exercises. To support word retrieval challenges, speech therapists could ask the client to name items from certain categories, retrieve a word based on a definition, think of the antonyms and synonyms for words and use fill-in-the-blanks to work on grammar and syntax. Recovery from aphasia is a long process that takes years of speech therapy and practice, but it is possible!

Vision- Courseware Exercises

1. 1) Cornea: focuses light (80%). 2) Pupil: allows light into the eyes. 3) Iris: controls pupil size, allowing either more or less light according to the environment. 4) Lens: aids with light focusing, inverts and reverses image, and accommodation (change in lens shape). 5) Vitreous Humour: jelly-like fluid within the eye. 6) Retina: three main layers lining the back of the eye, along with retinal pigment epithelium, which provides nutrition to photoreceptors. Light passes through the first two layers to the 7) photoreceptors: rods and cones, contain photopigments (translate light into a neural signal), activates horizontal cells. 8) Bipolar cells: converges neural signal, activates amacrine cells. 9) Ganglion cells: converge signal, axons converge at optic disc and enter the brain through the optic nerve.

2.

Rods	Cones
125 million; Concentrated in periphery; Poor visual acuity; Very sensitive to light, therefore night vision; No colour	6 million; Concentrated in fovea; Good visual acuity; Low light sensitivity, therefore day vision; Colour

3. Simple eyes: an animal that hunts likely has image forming eyes, and can detect images at far distances (unlike compound eyes). Large eyes: improves light sensitivity

(because the species lives in low light levels). Frontal eye placement (better depth perception because it is a predator).

Vision - Review Questions

1) B **2)** C The iris has more of a role than the lens does in light sensitivity; the darker it is, the more light the iris allows in when it dilates. **3)** C **4)** D **5)** A **6)** B

Vision – Bottleneck Concepts

1) The fovea of the retina is made up entirely of cones. But, these cones have a 1:1 convergence with their related ganglion cells (rather than the 6:1 convergence seen in other cones). One foveal cone feeds information to one ganglion cell. As a result, the visual information presented to that cone is maintained throughout all levels of the brain, which allows for an exceptional amount of information to be processed about its colour, form, movement and more.

2) The foveal cones will only be able to transmit visual information to their ganglion cells in bright environments. Given that only one cone feeds into one ganglion cell, *that* one cone will need a lot of light in order to send an adequate signal to its ganglion cell. This is why we cannot see in the dark with high visual acuity. Rather, it is easier to see in darkness by looking out the periphery of our eye given that the periphery has a high concentration of rods.

Colour Perception- Courseware Exercises

1. **Subtractive Colour Mixing:** Wavelengths are absorbed (subtracted) from white light (containing all wavelengths), resulting in the final (visible) colour, which has been reflected. Red, yellow and blue are considered primary colours as these colours can form all other colours. Their complementary colours are green, purple and orange, respectively. Combined, they form brown. *Example: Overlaying coloured tissue paper.* **Additive Colour Mixing**: Dominant wavelengths are combined (added), the resulting wavelength is the visible colour. Red, green and blue are the primary colours for this type of mixing. Their complementary colours are bluish-green, reddish-purple and yellow. Combined they form white or grey. This type of mixing occurs with light. *Example: Theatres and movies project coloured lights and utilize* additive mixing to create the colour perceived.
2.

Trichromatic Theory	Opponent-Process Theory
Retina contains three different cones (Red, Green, Blue)	Each colour receptor contains a pair of opponent colour processes (two different states)
Each cone responds maximally to a different wavelength	The receptor can be in only one state at a time
Together they produce all the colours	Blue/Yellow, Green/Red, Bright/Dark
Could not explain why yellow was considered a primary colour	Explains afterimages
Could not explain afterimages	Explains why complementary colour mixtures cannot be imagined (What is bluish-yellow?)

3. The theories are complementary and are both necessary to explain colour perception. The trichromatic theory explained how the retina was organized at the photoreceptor level while the opponent-process theory explained how the retina was organized at the ganglion cell level and onwards.

Colour Perception- Review Questions

1) D Insects see in UV, therefore bees see in UV **2)** E Paint pigments via subtractive; visual system via additive **3)** C A green-red ganglion cell has the opposite firing behaviour to a red-green ganglion cell; **4)** E

Colour Perception – Bottleneck Concepts

1) Review the colour wheels presented in the module.

2) **D.** Since additive and subtractive colour mixing have opposite primary and secondary colours, the complementary colours pairs remain the same for the two types of colour mixing.

Form 1 - Courseware Exercises

1. When viewing stimuli that can be grouped by similarity and proximity, which Gestalt principle will dominate? Which principle will be used to group the stimuli?
2. xox oox xxo oxo. Moving the stimuli closer together (manipulating proximity) or including different types of images varying in size, shape and colour (manipulating similarity) will be essential to understanding the interplay between these two Gestalt principles.
3. **Shape Constancy**: Relevant in situations where an object's shape changes when viewed from different angles. **Location Constancy**: When the object appears to be moving, when you are the one who is moving. **Size Constancy**: Objects that change in size as the distance between you and the object increases or decreases. **Brightness Constancy**: Objects that are perceived differently in different lighting. **Colour Constancy:** Objects that change colour due to the environment or internal factors.

Form 1 - Review Questions

1) B **2)** D The features present in Jorge's surroundings guided object recognition (a barn) **3)** B **4)** C

Form 2- Courseware Exercises

1. For example, I am working on this exercise at a table in my residence common room. My friend Jesse is wearing a bright blue shirt and we are trying to work through the answers. However, we are distracted by people entering and leaving the common room. The dorsal "where" stream processes information about how objects are moving and where they are located in the room. The spatial layout of the room and the people coming and leaving would be processed in the dorsal stream. Further, that information will be sent to the parietal cortex for further processing. The ventral "what" stream processes information about what the object is, i.e., its form and colour. Information about Jesse's shirt colour, the shape of the room, and the objects within the room would be processed in the ventral stream. Further, that information will be sent to the temporal lobe for further processing.

2. **Simple:** Responds maximally to a bar of a certain orientation within a specific area of the receptive field. The simple cell is organized in an opponent fashion, a stimulus with an orientation outside of the receptive field will result in the cell firing less than baseline. **Complex:** Responds maximally to a bar of a certain orientation and direction of movement, independent of the location within the receptive field. **Hypercomplex:** Responds maximally to bars of a certain orientation, direction and length. The cell has an inhibitory region within its receptive field which helps perceive length. The "on" and "off" regions, respond maximally to a bar solely in the "on" region, weakly when it is in both regions and below baseline in the "off" region.
3. Jamie will look at Nancy's face because it is more complex than the picture of the sun.
4. As a newborn, Jamie still has poor visual acuity and cannot discern the small squares on Nancy's shirt. He will look at Annie more.
5. Jamie cannot use colour or texture to distinguish objects. He cannot use any perceptual constancies yet.

Form 2- Review Questions

1) B **2)** D **3)** B **4)** C

Form Perception 1 & 2 – Bottleneck Concepts

1) **C.** The features of the big dipper helped Camellia identify the big dipper. This is an example of bottom-up processing. A, B and D are examples of top-down processing. For A, Juan's personal experience with iguanas in Mexico influenced his perceptions. For B, Jose's expectation that he was seeing a rock concert lead him to process the stimuli slower when the guitar-like instrument was not a guitar, but a cello. For D, Jennifer's expectation to find the big dipper by the little dipper helped her process the stimuli more quickly.

2) For example, in my visual scene I see an electronic machine with a screen and a keyboard. I use bottom-up processing to perceive it as a laptop. Using my past preference for Microsoft laptops and the expectation that I most likely purchased another one, I perceive the laptop as a Microsoft laptop, likely an HP.

Audition- Courseware Exercises

1) **1)** Our ears are located on opposite sides of our heads. Sound will be heard at different times. The ear closer to the sound will receive its input before the ear further away. If both ears receive the sound at the same time, the sound is located at an equal distance from our ears. This is measured by the superior olivary complex. **2)** Our ears will perceive an intensity difference; sounds closer to an ear will have a higher intensity sound than they will in the ear that is further away. Sounds that are further away are more detectable using a "sound shadow", which is cast by the head. The superior olivary complex also responds to differences in intensities at different ears. **3)** Pinna ridges diffract sound waves, making changes to the frequency content of sounds. The frequencies can be amplified or attenuated. These pinna cues are unique to each individual. Pinna cues also aid in discerning the elevation of a sound source.

2) **1)** Ear canal: narrows, amplifying sound. **2)** Ossicles: middle ear, the area receiving the signal is 20 times larger than the area transmitting the signal (oval window).

3) The region of the basilar membrane closest to the oval and round windows responds maximally to high frequency sounds, while the region furthest from the oval and round windows responds maximally to low frequency sounds.

Audition- Review Questions

1) C **2)** B **3)** D **4)** C

Audition – Bottleneck Concepts

1) **B.** Topographic maps are common to both tonotopic and retinotopic/topographic organization. A topographic map of frequencies on the basilar membrane are mapped and maintained in the auditory cortex. Additionally, a topographic map of the retina is maintained on the visual cortex. A is wrong because tonotopic organization does not give us any information about the spatial location of sound frequencies. C is wrong because retinotopic organization is the mapping of 2D visual space—3D space requires information about depth to be processed.

2) **B.** The wide end of the basilar membrane, which is near the apex of the cochlea, is more flexible and allows the transmission of a lower frequency of vibration. The narrow end of the basilar membrane, which is near the base of the cochlea, is stiffer which allows the transmission of a higher frequency of vibration. Think of a guitar string's flexibility and stiffness when trying to remember what region of the basilar membrane transmits what frequency of sound. Also recall that frequency and wavelength are inversely related, i.e., low frequency – high/long wavelengths. C is wrong because inner hair cells are primarily responsible for transmitting the auditory signal to the brain, not outer hair cells.

Hunger & Chemical Senses- Courseware Exercises

1. **1)** Low blood glucose and glycogen levels indicate hunger while high levels indicate satiety; involves the liver, muscles, pancreas and blood. **2)** Neuropeptide Y (NPY) in the hypothalamus increases appetite (hunger) and food-seeking behaviours. **3)** Cholecystokinin (CCK) in the small intestine triggers satiety after a meal. It is a short-term satiety signal. **4)** Leptin from adipose tissue indicates satiety by inhibiting NPY. It is a long-term satiety signal. **5)** Endogenous Opioids within the brain contribute to reward-driven feeding.
2. Low blood glucose may have caused a craving for something sweet to temporarily increase these glucose levels. The quick energy boost reinforced sugar seeking behaviours and evolved to include other nutrient seeking behaviours. Satiety may have evolved after individuals realized that the energy spent foraging is being wasted when they are not hungry. Therefore, satiety (halted food seeking) may have evolved to preserve energy, which was beneficial to survival and selected for over time.
3. Those individuals with different mechanisms to control hunger and satiety ate too much or too little and were selected against. Individuals with a maladaptive satiety mechanism may have been too large to run from predators and those with a maladaptive hunger mechanism may not have survived to pass on those genes. In this way, our current mechanisms for hunger and satiety were evolved. There are many mechanisms because some are short-term

solutions (blood glucose and CCK) while others solve the problem of long-term cues (glycogen, leptin). An individual's ability to control their hunger and satiety is essential to their life and multiple mechanisms are used in case one or two of these mechanisms fail, there is a safety net of the other mechanism that will prevent any long-term damage.

Hunger & Chemical Senses- Review Questions

1) D **2)** C **3)** B **4)** D **5)** B **6)** D

Hunger and the Chemical Senses – Bottleneck Concepts

1) Without taste, we would not be able to detect bitter or sour foods and would have difficulty avoiding foods that are poisonous or rancid. Additionally, we may not be able to meet our nutritional requirements if we cannot seek out foods that give us the salt, sugar or amino acids we need. Without smell, our eating experience would be a boring sampling of salty, sweet, umami, bitter and sour foods; this may lead to individuals not eating enough food. Additionally, we would not be able to use our sense of smell to avoid spoilt foods or dangerous situations. Given that smell information is also processed by our amygdala and hippocampus, our ability to avoid situations or foods associated with danger or sickness would be impaired, i.e., swimming in a stinky lake that contains sewage. Both taste and smell are crucial to our ability to experience flavours. We need both taste and smell to experience that yummy strawberry ice cream, but also to avoid that gross expired milk.

2) **D.** The taste pathway follows two main pathways. Through the thalamus, the gustatory cortex processes the five tastes, the orbital cortex combines taste with smell to produce flavour and the primary somatosensory cortex processes the texture of food. The other pathway goes from the taste receptors, to the gustatory nerve, to the brainstem and further to the pons, hypothalamus and amygdala. The hypothalamus is the brain region that processes chemicals associated with hunger and satiety. A is wrong because taste molecules are still processed by taste receptors on the nasal pharynx and therefore follow the taste pathway through the thalamus. B is wrong because the thalamus is a relay to the primary somatosensory cortex which processes the texture of food. Additionally, we cannot sense flavour if taste cannot be transmitted through the thalamus to the gustatory and orbital cortex. C is wrong because the smell pathway does not need to be relayed through the thalamus, it goes directly to the orbital cortex.

Psychological Disorders 1 - Courseware Exercises

2.
1) Doesn't account for the wide range of variance in symptoms that we see within a single disorder.
2) If someone doesn't meet the exact specifications for a disorder, they may feel that they themselves are abnormal.
3) An individual not meeting the criteria for a disorder would most likely not be able to receive health funding.

3.
1) Allows a wider range of mental illness to be diagnosed and treated.
2) Allows for more individualized treatment according to an individual's specific symptoms.
3) Helps avoid situations in which someone cannot receive funding for their treatment because they do not meet the cut off for a particular disorder.

Psychological Disorders 1 - Review Questions

1) A

2) Point prevalence is measured at a specific instance in time. This means that a person who does not display symptoms at that exact moment, but may have displayed symptoms of a particular disorder at some point in the past, would not be included in this point prevalence measure. The annual prevalence of a disorder includes anyone who has the disorder, or has had the disorder, within the past year. The lifetime prevalence of a disorder includes anyone who has the disorder, or has had the disorder, within their lifetime.

3.

Category	Symptomology
Positive Symptoms: odd or excess behaviours	- Disorganized thinking and speech - Delusions - Hallucinations - Disorganized or abnormal motor behaviour (including catatonia)
Negative Symptoms: absence of normal or a reduction in behaviours	- Flat or inappropriate affect - Alogia - Avolition - Anhedonia - Asociality

4. **Causes:** Diathesis-stress hypothesis, genetics, abnormal brain structures, abnormal levels of neurotransmitters, stress and family environment.

Psychological Disorders 1 - Courseware Exercises

1. Biological: An imbalance in neurotransmitters resulting in more anxious behaviour; Environmental: Growing up with parents who continuously worried and criticized behaviour resulted in constant anxiety related to decision making; Behavioural: Whenever the individual exabits anxious behaviour their friends and family provide lots of comfort and support. This builds a contingency between anxiety and loving support which increases the behaviour; Cognitive: Believing that when friends don't return you text immediately they are mad which leads to constant worry and feeling unsupported.

2. Biological: Does not explain why identical twins do not always show the same psychological disorders; Environmental: Does not explain why two individual who grow up with very similar environments show different disorders; Behavioural: Does not account for more sever disorders, like schizophrenia, that would be hard to explain under conditioning alone; Cognitive: Does not account for more sever disorders, like schizophrenia, that would be hard to explain using only maladaptive thoughts.

3. Individual answers will vary.

Psychological Disorders 1 - Courseware Exercises

1. **D**   2. **B**

3. Environmental stress combines with genetic predisposition (diathesis). Individuals who are born with a high diathesis only need to experience a small amount of life stress to develop the disorder. Individuals with low diathesis would need to experience a lot of environmental stress to develop the disorder.

4. Receiving positive feedback (love and support) when exhibiting disordered behaviour can perpetuate the behaviour since a contingency is formed.

Psychological Disorders 1 & 2 – Bottleneck Concepts

1) **C.** The belief that your thoughts are being stolen from you is the delusion of thought withdrawal which is a positive symptom. Ben's lack of interest in food, friends or sex is an example of anhedonia which is a negative symptom. A is incorrect because hallucinations require the individual to perceive sensory stimuli such as sounds or visions that aren't there. B is incorrect because inappropriate affect refers to a disturbed emotional response that does not apply to the context of the situation. D is incorrect because thought withdrawal is a positive symptom and positive symptoms tend to not be constant throughout one's prognosis/life.

2) **D.** All of the symptoms, except that Stephanie can't follow recipes, are in line with a depressive disorder. However, all of the symptoms, including that Stephanie can't follow recipes, are also in line with a schizophrenic disorder. In line with the negative symptom of avolition, Stephanie seems to have trouble initiating and persisting in a goal-directed behaviour such as cooking which requires one to follow a set of steps to a complete task. This symptom is not characteristic of someone with depression, but it is possible that Stephanie is just showing a lack of motivation which is characteristic. Stephanie's psychologist should examine Stephanie further before diagnosing her.

Psychological Treatments – Courseware Exercises

1. A psychiatrist might prescribe medications to help treat the symptoms
2. A clinical psychologist might recommend cognitive behavioural therapy
3.

Medication	Target Activity	Alleviates Symptoms By:
Anti-Psychotics	Decrease dopamine	Reduces the overactive dopamine system that drives psychotic symptoms
Benzodiazepines	Increase GABA	Increases postsynaptic permeability to GABA, inhibiting neuron firing (overactive in anxiety)
Selective Serotonin Reuptake Inhibitors	Increase serotonin	Block serotonin reuptake, increasing serotonin levels (low in depression)

Psychological Treatments – Review Questions

1. D (represents a therapy-receptive person, who might still have maladaptive thought patterns)
2. A (relapse)
3. Psychiatrist = medical approach, pharmacology-based, prescribes medication
Clinical Psychologist = holistic approach, therapy-based, does not prescribe medication
Both = accredited mental health professionals, work on integrated teams
4. A therapist uses a highly standardized procedure to correct maladaptive coping mechanisms (manifested through thoughts and behaviours) that cyclically maintain the patients' disordered symptoms

Psychological Treatments – Bottleneck Concepts

1. **B.** Efficacy studies are often testing treatments for one specific disorder or symptomology. The presence of comorbid disorders would make the data too noisy for an efficacy study. A is incorrect because *statistical* significance is important for efficacy studies; clinical significance is whether the treatment has a noticeable, real-world effect on an individual's life. C is incorrect because a control group is needed to ensure that the manipulation alone had an effect and it was not just an experimenter/participant bias or the placebo effect. D is incorrect because both efficacy and effectiveness studies attempt to explore both the reliability and validity of a treatment

2. **Effectiveness.** 1) Either a psychologist or social worker could provide the treatment. They may have different treatment styles, personalities and other confounds that could influence how each group responded to treatment. 2) Participants were provided treatment within groups. Every group would have a different dynamic and you wouldn't be able to control for the types of contributions that other group members added to the therapy. 3) Participants are not blind to their condition, they know they are receiving treatment and as a result may report an improvement in symptoms simply because they think they should have improved. To make this into an efficacy study, you could utilize an individual therapy methodology, use the same therapist for all participants that is blind to condition, give participants in the cognitive behavioural therapy alone condition a placebo medication, and only look at participants with a sole diagnosis of generalized anxiety disorder (rather than one comorbid with depression). Note: There are many answers that are acceptable for this question.

Glossary of Terms

A

Abnormal Psychology: A branch of psychology studying the unusual patterns of behaviour, emotion and thought that vary between people and cultures. Typically, it is summarized with "the four D's": Deviance, Distress, Dysfunction and Danger. *(Psychological Disorders)*

Accommodation: The process in which the lens of the eye changes shape to focus on objects at varying distances. It becomes flatter when looking at closer objects and rounder when looking at further objects. *(Vision)*

Action Potential: The fundamental unit of communication for neurons. It involves a series of ionic events along the axon: reaching the threshold potential of -50 mV, a rapid increase in membrane potential, a decrease in membrane potential and ending with the refractory period. *(Neuroscience 1)*

Active Correlations: An individual's genotype influences the kinds of environments that person seeks out. This correlation plays a larger role in development as an individual begins to make more of their own decisions. *E.g. a child with natural athletic ability may try out for sports teams and choose to play with friends who also enjoy sports. (Development 2)*

Adaptation: Biological traits or characteristics that help an individual survive and reproduce in its habitat. Each adaptation performs a specific function. *E.g. an owl's wide eyes are an adaptation to allow as much as light as possible into the retina during the night. (Evolution 1)*

Adaptationist Perspective: A label to describe how hypotheses about adaptive functions guide scientists' investigations. *E.g. a scientist who wants to study colour perception in humans may research why humans needed to distinguish specific colours during their evolutionary history. (Evolution 1)*

Additive Colour Mixing: When lights of different wavelengths combine to form a different colour. This is the colour system used by the visual system, where the effects of different wavelengths are added together. *(Colour Perception)*

Adipose: An endocrine organ, this tissue acts as a long-term energy source, stored in virtually every part of the body as fat. It is also an active part of regulatory physiology as it produces leptin. *(Hunger and the Chemical Senses)*

Afterimages: A phenomenon in which the complementary colours of an image are seen after staring at the image, and then viewing a white surface. Afterimages occur when a colour receptor that has been excited for a prolonged period of time while viewing the image goes into the opposite, inhibited state, resulting in the perception of the complementary colour. *(Colour Perception)*

Allele: A single pair of genes, one inherited from each parent. *E.g. an individual may have one allele for straight hair and one allele for curly hair. (Development 2)*

Altruism: A social behaviour in which an actor incurs a cost in order to provide a benefit to a recipient. *E.g. when you give money to your friend for lunch, you are performing an altruistic behaviour by incurring a cost to provide a benefit to your friend. (Evolution 2)*

Amacrine Cells: Similar to the horizontal cells, these cells allow adjacent photoreceptors to combine their information such that 130 million photoreceptors converge on 1 million axons in the optic nerve. *(Vision)*

Amplitude: The height of a wave. For light, amplitude corresponds to the perception of brightness. Larger amplitude corresponds to a brighter colour *(Vision)*. For sound, it corresponds to the perception of loudness. Waves of larger amplitude correspond to louder sound. *(Audition)*

Amygdala: An almond shaped structure located below the surface of the temporal lobe that plays a role in decoding emotions (particularly fear). *(Neuroscience 2)*

Anti-Psychotic Medication: A drug therapy medication used to alleviate symptoms of psychosis. They work to reduce levels of dopamine activity in the brain. *(Psychological Treatments)*

Anvil: Also known as the incus, it is the second of the ossicles found in the middle ear. It projects to the stirrup. *(Audition)*

Axon: A long fibre that projects from the receptive zone of a neuron, through which the electrical signals of an action potential pass. At the end of the axon is the transmission zone, whereby the signal is passed to neighbouring neurons. *(Neuroscience 1)*

B

Babbling Principle: An example of the canalization principle, all infants babble the same speech sounds, regardless of which culture they are born into. Their external environment will later shape this babbling to produce different languages. *E.g. Korean infants will process both /ra/ and /lu/ phonemes but lose this ability as they become adults unless they are exposed to English. (Development 2)*

Basilar Membrane: The flexible membrane that runs the length of the cochlea, vibrating in different regions along its length in response to different frequencies. It contains the hair cells, which transduce sound into the electrical signals perceived by the brain. *(Audition)*

Behavioural Genetics: The study of the evolution of genes that code for behavioural traits, rather than physical traits. *E.g. in experiments with fruit flies, it is possible to determine that aggressive behaviour evolves by selectively breeding aggressive individuals and breeding only to eventually see a change towards more aggressive behaviour in the population. (Evolution 1)*

Behavioural Model: Considering how external factors produce disordered behaviours and emotions. The external factors themselves are not the issue, but rather, our behaviours and emotions in response to them. Conditioned responses play a large role in disordered behaviour. *(Psychological Disorders 2)*

Benzodiazepines: A drug therapy medication used to alleviate symptoms of anxiety. They work to increase levels of GABA activity in the brain. *(Psychological Treatments)*

Biological Model: Also known as the medical or disease model, assumes that a psychological disorder result from malfunction in the brain. It usually points to genetics, atypical neurotransmitter activity, or abnormal brain structures. *(Psychological Disorders 2)*

Bipolar Cells: A layer of cells in the retina that receive information from photoreceptors and then send that information to the ganglion cells. *(Vision)*

Bottom-Up Processing: Object recognition guided by features present in the stimulus itself. *E.g. if you saw a yellow face and hands, white t-shirt, blue jeans and a plump belly, you could use these features to identify the* *object as being Homer Simpson. (Form Perception 1)*

Brightness Constancy: The ability to perceive the brightness of objects as unchanging despite changes in ambient lighting. *E.g. a leaf is viewed in sunlight, in a dark room and under clouds and rain, yet is always perceived as being the same brightness. (Form Perception 1)*

C

Canalization Principle: According to this principle, the genotype restricts the phenotype to a small number of possible developmental outcomes. *E.g. in the example of baby babbling, all infants babble the same sounds, regardless of what culture they are born into. (Development 2)*

Catatonia: A state of motor immobility in which the individual's body is rigid, often associated with mental disorders as schizophrenia. *(Psychological Treatments)*

Cell Division: The process by which a cell reproduces, known as mitosis for autosomal cells and meiosis for sex cells. In mitosis, the resulting daughter cells will have 46 chromosomes. In meiosis, the resulting daughter cells will have 23 chromosomes. *(Development 2)*

Cerebellum: Translating to "little brain", it is a structure in the hindbrain resembling a miniature version of the entire brain. It coordinates motor movement and so damage to this area can result in exaggerated, jerky movements. *(Neuroscience 2)*

Cholecystokinin (CCK): A hormone, produced in the small intestine, which induces satiety (fullness) after eating and serves as a signal to stop eating. *(Hunger and the Chemical Senses)*

Chromosome: A threadlike structure made up of deoxyribonucleic acid (DNA) and consisting of many genes. A single human cell contains 46 chromosomes, 23 from each parent. *(Development 2)*

Clinical Psychologist: A licenced (i.e. has a doctorate) mental health professional that is formally trained in psychological therapies and typically studies mental health and illness from a holistic perspective. *(Psychological Treatments)*

Closure: The Gestalt Principle that refers to our ability to fill in gaps in the contours of a shape, thus perceiving the whole object. *E.g. if a ball is partially occluded by a rock, an individual will still perceive it as a whole ball. (Form Perception 1)*

Cochlea: A coiled, fluid-filled tube in the inner ear containing the basilar membrane. *(Audition)*

Cochlear Nerve: A bundle of axons carrying action potentials from the hair cells of the cochlea toward the brain, through the cochlear nucleus. *(Audition)*

Cochlear Nucleus: A region in the hindbrain that serves as the first stop in the brain for axons from the cochlea. *(Audition)*

Co-Dominance: Two dominant alleles are both fully and equally expressed to produce a phenotype that is an intermediate of the two alleles. *E.g. human blood type proteins A and B are co-dominant alleles. An individual who has one A allele and one B allele expresses the blood type AB rather than one type over the other. (Development 2)*

Coefficient of Relatedness: Referred to as "r", the mathematic term in Hamilton's Rule that represents the probability that an actor and recipient share a gene in question. *E.g. the probability that you and your mother will share any gene in question is 0.5 (r). This is because you inherit half of your genes from your mother and half from your father. (Evolution 2)*

Co-Evolution: The process by which the evolution and adaptation of traits in one species can directly affect the evolution of traits in another species. *E.g. prey may become resistant to a toxin used by its predator. In response, the predator may evolve to produce higher levels of the toxin. (Audition)*

Cognitive-Behavioural Therapy: A type of psychological treatment for mental disorders. It aims to make patients aware of how they think and understand how that contributes to the way they feel. It also teaches patients to apply these thought patterns to more productive behaviours. *(Psychological Treatments)*

Cognitive Model: Suggests that mental disorder result from maladaptive or inappropriate ways of selecting and interpreting information from the environment. *(Psychological Disorders 2)*

Colour Constancy: The ability to perceive objects as being of a constant colour even though the light stimulus reaching the retina changes with different illuminations. *E.g. you will still recognize your white mug if it is under a red light and looks reddish. (Form Perception 1)*

Common Fate: The Gestalt Principle that describes our tendency to group together objects that change in the same way. *E.g. if a flock of crows suddenly change course in the same direction, one would assume that they are part of the same group. (Form Perception 1)*

Competence-Performance Distinction: The fact that an individual may fail a task not because they lack those cognitive abilities, but because they are unable to demonstrate those abilities. *E.g. A preverbal infant may not be able verbalize which of two pictures she prefers, but this does not mean she doesn't have a preference. (Development 1)*

Complementary Colours: In subtractive colour mixing, these are the opposite colours to the primary colours (blue, red and yellow) in the colour wheel. When mixing a primary colour with its complementary colour, the colour brown is formed. *(Colour Perception)*

Complex Cell: A visual cortical cell that responds maximally to a bar of light of a particular length and orientation, regardless of where it is located within the receptive field. *E.g. one visual cell may respond to a 2 cm bar that is rotated 45 degrees. (Form Perception 2)*

Compound Eyes: The type of eye found in arthropods. These are made up of an arrangement of tubular units called ommatidia, each pointing in a slightly different direction to gather light. Signals from each ommatidium combine to form a single image. *(Vision)*

Computed Tomography (CT): A structural neuroimaging technique in which a series of X-ray slices of the brain are taken and pieced together, producing a quick image of the brain. It has poor resolution compared to an MRI but is often used to help diagnose brain injuries. *(Neuroscience 2)*

Cones: A class of photoreceptors, which transmit information about colour at high light intensities. In comparison to rods, they provide better acuity and are much less populous. They are concentrated in the fovea. *(Vision)*

Continuity: The Gestalt Principle that describes our tendency to perceive objects as having a simple, continuous form rather than a combination of disjointed forms. *E.g. an X is perceived as two diagonal lines that cross in the middle rather than a "v" shape on top of an inverted "v". (Form Perception 1)*

Cooperation: According to evolutionary theory, it is the process of an actor working with a recipient to help both themselves and the recipient for personal gain. *E.g. you may help classmates study for an exam so that you can also get a higher grade. (Evolution 2)*

Cornea: The transparent window at the front of the eye allowing light to first pass through and where the focussing of light begins. It is the most external structure of the eye. *(Vision)*

Corpus Callosum: A thick bundle of axons passing through the centre of the brain and allowing for communication between the left and right hemispheres. *(Neuroscience 2)*

Cortex: A part of the forebrain, it is the largest part of the brain. It contains the occipital, temporal, parietal, and frontal lobes and is where most of the actual information processing, behaviours and cognitive functions take place. *(Neuroscience 2)*

Critical Period: A window of time during development in which particular environmental stimulation is necessary to see permanent changes in developmental abilities. After this time, the same environmental stimulation will not have the same developmental benefit. *E.g. a feral child who is raised for the first years of life without exposure to human language will never fully acquire the ability to produce language, even if taught later in life. (Development 2)*

Cross-Sectional Design: A developmental research design in which different age groups are studied at the same point in time to observe age-related differences. *E.g. To study age-related differences in the ability to discriminate between two speech sounds, children between ages 2 and 10 are tested on their ability to discriminate between these two sounds. (Development 1)*

Cross-Sequential Design: A developmental research design that combines both longitudinal and cross-sectional designs. While it combines the strongest features of both designs, it is also the most costly and time consuming. *(Development 1)*

Cumulative Selection: The evolutionary process whereby new adaptations are layered upon old adaptations, gradually increasing the sophistication of a trait. The human eye is an example of cumulative selection. *(Vision)*

Curved "Cup" Eye: The primitive design of the eye that can still be found today in clams. It allows only for basic functions of vision but has an advantage over the light sensitive patch as it allows the organism to sense the direction of the light. *(Vision)*

D

4 D's: A set of criteria used to broadly define abnormal behaviour. These criteria are deviance, distress, dysfunction and danger. These must be used with caution as exhibiting one or more is not necessarily indicative of a psychological disorder. *(Psychological Disorders 1)*

Danger: One of "the 4 D's", it is when an individual presents a danger to themselves or others. *E.g. an individual suffering from drug addiction rehabilitation may become dangerous as a result of the anxiety experienced during withdrawal. (Psychological Disorders 1)*

Darwinian Fitness: The average reproductive success of a genotype relative to alternative genotypes. *E.g. if one genotype leads to brighter colouring in a male bird, relative to another genotype, the bird with the genotype leading to brighter colouring may have a better chance at finding a mate and passing this genotype on to the next generation. (Evolution 1)*

Deuteranopia: A form of red/green colour blindness in which the green cones are missing. *(Colour Perception)*

Development: The changes and continuities that occur within an individual between conception and death. *(Development 1)*

Deviance: One of "the 4 D's", the experience of thoughts, emotions and behaviour that fall far outside of the standards of what others are doing. *E.g. most people save their money for rent, so an individual who spends all of their money on excessive shopping sprees and cannot pay their bills deviates from what may be considered normal. (Psychological Disorders 1)*

Diagnostic and Statistical Manual (DSM): A book categorizing and describing mental disorders using a common set of criteria to 1) apply a diagnostic label of symptoms to patients and 2) to communicate with others via a common language. *(Psychological Disorders 1)*

Differentiation (cellular): The transformation of unspecified cells into specialized cell types that differ in structure and function, usually occurring after migration. *E.g. a particular group of unspecialized cells may become a part of the frontal cortex while another group of unspecialized cells become a part of the Broca's area. (Neuroscience 1)*

Diffusion: The tendency for molecules to distribute themselves evenly through a medium. This is one of the forces controlling the resting potential of a neuron. *E.g. if you put a drop of food colouring in a glass of water, the food colouring will distribute itself evenly throughout the water. (Neuroscience 1)*

Direct Fitness: An individual's genetic contribution to the next generation through personal reproduction. *(Evolution 2)*

Dishabituate: An increase in responsiveness to a stimulus that is somehow different from the habituated stimulus. *E.g. if any infant is repeatedly shown a picture of a red ball, her interest in or response to the picture will decrease. If she is presented a picture of a blue ball and shows increased interest and response, she has dishabituated. (Development 1)*

Distress: One of "the 4 D's", the experience of intense negative feelings due to an individual's own behaviour. *E.g. an individual may feel anxiety as a result of performing poorly on a test. (Psychological Disorders 1)*

Dizygotic Twins: Twins that result from two different sperm and ova and start off as two different zygotes from conception. They are no more genetically similar than any two biological siblings. *(Development 2)*

Dominant Allele: In a heterozygous condition, the dominant allele is expressed in the phenotype over the recessive allele. *E.g. if the allele for brown eyes is dominant over the allele for blue eyes, a heterozygous individual will have brown eyes. (Development 2)*

Dorsal Stream: The "where" pathway in vision, which begins in the occipital lobe and terminates in the parietal lobe. It processes information regarding movement and spatial location of objects. *(Vision, Form Perception 2)*

Dysfunction: One of "the 4 D's", it is the inability to function properly in daily life. *E.g. an individual may have recurring thoughts of a stressful event to the extent that they are unable to focus on work, maintaining a household or building healthy relationships. (Psychological Disorders 1)*

E

Ear Canal: Part of the external ear, it is used to transmit and amplify sounds from the pinna to the eardrum. *(Audition)*

Eardrum: Part of the external ear, it is a thin membrane that vibrates at the frequency of incoming sound waves and forms the back wall of the ear canal. *(Audition)*

Echolocation: The process by which a receiver emits sound pulses and analyzes the returning echo to form a perceptual image of objects in its environment. It is a "visual" technique used by some species of animals, including bats and dolphins. *(Audition)*

EEG: A functional neuroimaging technique in which electrical activity of the brain is recorded through the scalp by wearing a cap of very sensitive electrodes. It provides a very rough image of the brain's overall activity from populations of neurons. *(Neuroscience 2)*

Effectiveness: The ability of a treatment to produce a desired effect in real-world settings. *(Psychological Treatments)*

Efficacy: The ability of a treatment to produce a desired effect in highly controlled settings. *(Psychological Treatments)*

Ego Dystonic: Symptoms of a disorder that are perceived by the individual with the disorder as undesirable. *(Psychological Treatments)*

Ego Systonic: Symptoms of a disorder that are perceived by the individual with the disorder as valued or advantageous. *(Psychological Treatments)*

Electrostatic Force: The repulsion between ions of the same charge. This is one of the forces controlling the resting potential of the neuron. *E.g. sodium ions and potassium ions repel one another because they are both positively charged.* *(Neuroscience 1)*

Endogenous Opioids: Naturally occurring chemical substances that have morphine-like analgesic effects in the body. They contribute to palatability and reward-driven feeding, which may explain the pleasure that results from eating. *(Hunger and the Chemical Senses)*

Environmental Model: Considers the effects of the environmental factors, such as where we live, who we socialize with, and what we consume, on causing psychopathology. *(Psychological Disorders 2)*

Event-related potentials: A method of measuring brain activity evoked by the presentation of stimuli. An electrode cap is placed on an individual's scalp to measure electrical activity across a population of neurons in the brain. *E.g. if you presented an infant with a loud noise, you might expect an ERP in the temporal lobe region, which is an area devoted to sound processing.* *(Development 1)*

Evocative Correlations: In this correlation, traits that an individual has inherited through genes influence how others in their environment behave towards that individual. *E.g. a child who has a naturally happy disposition would cause other people to smile and be happy around that child.* *(Development 2)*

Excitatory Postsynaptic Potential (EPSP): An event in the post-synaptic neuron in which the Na+ channels open, allowing positive ions to flow into the cell, depolarizing it above the -70mV resting potential and bringing it closer to the -50mV threshold to fire an action potential. *(Neuroscience 1)*

Experience-Dependent Growth: The unique way in which the brain develop according to personal experiences. This type of brain growth is specific to each individual. *E.g. a Braille reader will have a specialized area in their brain that responds to specified somatosensory stimulation of the fingertips, which non-Braille readers will lack. (Development 2)*

Experience-Expectant Growth: Brain growth that is dependent on a certain amount of environmental input in order to develop properly. *E.g. the brain relies on a certain, ordinary amount of visual input for the visual cortex to develop properly. (Development 2)*

External Ear: The part of the auditory system that collects sound from the surrounding environment. It is made up of the pinna, ear canal and eardrum. *(Audition)*

External/Internal Barriers: Mental, physical, and/or sociocultural obstacles that prevent an individual from treating their symptoms; external are systemic and environmental obstacles, while internal manifest as the individual's own restrictive beliefs about treatment. *(Psychological Treatments)*

Extrastriate Cortex: Visual processing areas in the occipital lobe that are outside of the primary visual cortex (V1). Processing of more complex visual information occurs here, as well as the beginning of associations and integration with other sensory areas. *(Vision)*

Extreme Behaviourist Point of View: The view that nurture is all-important in development and that development is largely independent of genetics. *E.g. the behaviourist Watson suggested that with proper environmental control and training, any individual could become a doctor, musician or criminal, regardless of their genetics. (Development 2)*

F

Figure-Ground: The Gestalt Principle that describes our ability to determine what aspect of a visual scene is part of the object itself and what is part of the background. *E.g. if a white flower is in field of tall green grass, you would be able to determine that the flower is the object, separate from the grass background. (Form Perception 1)*

Fissure: Very deep fissures found throughout the cortex, which often divide major areas of the cortex. *(Neuroscience 2)*

Forebrain: The most evolutionarily recent and largest part of the human brain, consisting of the cortex and the subcortical structures of the limbic system. *(Neuroscience 2)*

Frequency: The number of waves that pass a fixed place in a given time. A higher frequency corresponds to a smaller wavelength because there is less distance between successive peaks. *(Vision)* With respect to sound, frequency corresponds to pitch, where a larger frequency corresponds to a higher pitch. *(Audition)*

Frontal Lobe: The most anterior part of the cortex, it is the most complex and least understood of the cortical lobes. It is where movements originate (in the motor cortex) and where complex decision-making is performed. *(Neuroscience 2)*

Functional Magnetic Resonance Imaging (fMRI): A functional neuroimaging technique using magnetic fields to measure the relative use of oxygen throughout the brain, creating a functional map of brain activity. *(Neuroscience 2)*

Functional Neuroimaging: A variety of techniques used to learn how brain activity relates to specific cognitive tasks, such as fMRI, PET scans or EEG. *(Neuroscience 2)*

G

Ganglion cells: The layer of cells in the retina that bipolar cells send their information to. They are the front layer of the cells in the retina. Their axons converge on a single point of the eye called the optic disc. *(Vision)*

Generalized Anxiety Disorder: An anxiety disorder characterized by excessive and irrational worry about minor things. An individual with GAD may experience minor life stressors as significant sources of anxiety due to their inability to cope *(Psychological Disorders)*

Genes: Segments of DNA that provide the chemical code for development. *(Development 2)*

Genetic Point of View: The opposite extreme as the behaviourist point of view, it is the view that who a person becomes is largely predetermined by genetics with little to no environmental influence. *E.g. in this view, a child with intelligent, successful parents will necessarily become intelligent and successful. (Development 2)*

Genotype: An individual's roughly 30 to 40, 000 inherited genes. *E.g. Brent has one recessive allele for blue eyes and one dominant allele for brown eyes at the eye colour locus. (Development 2)*

Geons: Simple geometrical forms stored in memory that are used to create millions of recognizable objects, as part of the Geon Theory. *E.g. cones, spheres, cylinders, rectangular prisms are some of the 36 geons. (Form Perception 1)*

Geon Theory: The theory of object recognition that suggests we have 36 different geons stored in memory that make it possible to recognize over 150 million different objects. *E.g. an ice cream cone is made up of a sphere and a cone. (Form Perception 1)*

Gestalt Principles: A set of principles that collectively suggest that the whole is greater than the sum of its parts when it comes to object recognition. *(Form Perception 1)*

Glial Cells: Non-neuronal cells in the nervous system that provide structural support, nourishment and insulation to neurons. *(Neuroscience 1)*

Glomeruli: A set of cells found in the olfactory bulb that receive and encode smell signals from olfactory receptor cells. Some output goes to the olfactory cortex, whereas others go to the hypothalamus and limbic system that deal with basic drives and emotions. *(Hunger and the Chemical Senses)*

Glucose: An important sugar used for energy in the body. It is the primary source of energy for the brain. The level of glucose in the blood directly relates to feelings of hunger as glucose is obtained from food. *(Hunger and the Chemical Senses)*

Glycogen: A short-term store for the energy found in glucose, which can be converted back to glucose at any time. When you exercise, immediate energy is taken from glycogen stores. *(Hunger and the Chemical Senses)*

Gustatory Cortex: The primary taste area in the brain, containing neurons that respond to each of the five basic tastes. From here, taste information is sent to the orbital cortex, where it interacts with smell information from the olfactory cortex to produce the perception of flavour. *(Hunger and the Chemical Senses)*

Gyri: Ridges, or bulge outward, on the cortex. These, along with sulci form folds that provide the additional surface area required for cortical processing. *(Neuroscience 2)*

H

Habituate: A decrease in the responsiveness to a stimulus following its repeated presentation. *E.g. if an infant is presented a picture of a red ball, they will initially show interest. When repeatedly shown the ball, the infant's response will decrease. (Development 1)*

Habituation Procedure: A technique designed to determine whether an infant can detect the difference between two stimuli. *E.g. in determining if an infant can tell the difference between the sounds /ra/ and /la/, a researcher would repeatedly present the /ra/ sound to the infant until they habituate. She will then present the /la/ sound. If the infant's response increases to /la/, it indicates that infant can discriminate between the two. (Development 1)*

Hair Cells: The auditory receptors found in the basilar membrane that convert sound waves into neural impulses that the brain can understand. *(Audition)*

Hamilton's Rule: An equation, which predicts when altruistic behaviour will be performed, defined by the inequality Br>C (benefit to recipient*coefficient of relatedness > cost to altruist). *E.g. according to Hamilton's rule, you would be willing to sacrifice your life for 3 siblings (3*0.5>1) but not for 2 (2*0.5=1) siblings. (Evolution 2)*

Hammer: Also known as the malleus, it is the first of the ossicles found in the middle ear, projecting to the anvil. *(Audition)*

Heterozygous Condition: When two alleles at a locus are different, and the dominant allele is expressed over the recessive allele. *E.g. if the allele for brown eyes is dominant and the allele for blue eyes is recessive, the heterozygous individual will have brown eyes. (Development 2)*

High-amplitude Sucking Method: A technique designed to assess what an infant likes and dislikes using the fact that infants can control their sucking behaviour to influence the presentation of a stimulus. *(Development 1)*

Hindbrain: The brain's evolutionarily oldest region, lying at the base of the brain and consisting of the medulla, pons, reticular formation, and the cerebellum. *(Neuroscience 2)*

Hippocampus: A horseshoe shaped structure in the temporal lobe, it is involved in memory formation and the ability to navigate through the world. *(Neuroscience 2)*

Homozygous Condition: When two alleles at a locus have the same effect on the phenotype. *E.g. an individual who has two recessive alleles for blue eyes will have blue eyes. (Development 2)*

Horizontal Cells: Similar to amacrine cells, these cells allow adjacent photoreceptors to combine their information such that 130 million photoreceptors converge on 1 million axons in the optic nerve. *(Vision)*

Hypercomplex Cell: A visual cortical cell that responds maximally to a bar of light at a particular orientation and begins and ends at specific points within the receptive field. *E.g. a particular hypercomplex cell will respond maximally to a horizontal bar in the "on" region of the receptive field but gives a weak response if it is rotated or falls anywhere in the "off" region. (Form Perception 2)*

Hypothalamus: A part of the limbic system in the forebrain, which regulates the "four F's" (fight, flight, feeding, and reproduction). *(Neuroscience 2)*

I

Inclusive Fitness: Fitness from both direct and indirect sources, including fitness from personal reproduction (such as feeding ability) and the reproduction of close genetic relatives (such as their altruistic behaviour). *(Evolution 2)*

Indirect Fitness: An individual's genetic contribution to the next generation through the reproduction of close genetic relatives. *E.g. a mother may help to raise her daughter's children to ensure that the genes of those children survive and reproduce. (Evolution 2)*

Inhibitory Postsynaptic Potential (IPSP): An event in the post-synaptic neuron in which Cl- channels open, allowing negatively charged chloride ions to flow into the cell, hyperpolarizing it below the -70mV resting potential. This event inhibits the transmission of a signal between neurons. *(Neuroscience 1)*

Inner Ear: The part of the auditory system that contains the neural tissue necessary to transduce sound waves into neural impulses. It is made up of the cochlea, which contains the basilar membrane and hair cells. *(Audition)*

Interactionist Perspective: The view that most developmental changes reflect the interaction of maturation and learning or between genetics and the environment. *E.g. this view would emphasize the fact that both the cognitive capacity to speak and exposure to human language are important for language development. (Development 1)*

Interaural Intensity Differences: A sound localization technique using the difference in intensity caused by the head casting a "sound shadow", which diminishes the sound intensity at the distal ear. *(Audition)*

Interaural Time Differences: A sound localization technique that uses the difference in time it takes for sound waves to reach each ear. Sounds can be localized by differences of sub-milliseconds. *(Audition)*

Iris: The coloured part of the eye. It consists of a band of muscles that receive signals from the brain to dilate and constrict the pupil depending on the amount of light reaching the eye. *(Vision)*

K

Kin Recognition: The ability to recognize the relatedness of other members of a species through aspects such as location or behavioural activity and perform altruistic acts accordingly. *E.g. you know you're related to your younger brother because you've seen your mother care for him from birth. (Evolution 2)*

L

Lateral Geniculate Nucleus (LGN): The part of the thalamus that receives visual information from the optic chiasm and relays it to the primary visual cortex. *(Vision)*

Learning: Acquiring neuronal representations of new information which lead to permanent changes in thoughts and behaviours as a result of experiences. *E.g. an individual is likely to automatically look both ways before crossing the street as she was taught to do so by her parents when she was young. (Development 1)*

Lens: A transparent, flexible structure that does the final focusing of light onto the retina. It may change in shape (accommodate) to focus on objects at different distances, contributing to depth perception. *(Vision)*

Leptin: A hormone produced by adipose tissue and controlled by the OB gene, involved in long-term energy balance and fat mass. High levels of leptin act on the hypothalamus to reduce appetite. *(Hunger and the Chemical Senses)*

Lesion Studies: Studies of brain activity following damage to a particular area, observing a resulting a loss of function. If the occipital lobe is involved with vision an individual may have impaired vision after experiencing a stroke in their occipital lobe *(Neuroscience 2)*

Light Sensitive Patch: An example of what primitive eyes may have started out as. Jellyfish and worms have something like this form of eye today. *(Vision)*

Location Constancy: The ability to perceive objects as being stationary despite constantly moving around on the retina due to movement of our eyes, head and body. *E.g. when walking past a house, its location on the retina will change but it will be perceived as stationary. (Form Perception 1)*

Longitudinal Design: A developmental research design in which the same individuals are studied repeatedly over a subset of their lifespan. *E.g. in studying age-related differences in speech sound discrimination ability, the same group of individuals are studied each year from the age of 2 to 10 years old. (Development 1)*

M

Magnetic Resonance Imaging (MRI): A structural neuroimaging technique using powerful magnetic fields that align the hydrogen atoms in the brain to create an image of the brain. It has good spatial resolution, relative to a CT scan. *(Neuroscience 2)*

Magnocellular Pathway: The pathway from the ganglion cells to the extrastriate cortex that carries movement, depth and brightness information from the magno cells in the periphery of the retina. They have larger receptive fields than parvo cells. *(Form Perception 2)*

Major Depression: A depressive disorder characterized by severe decreased mood, loss of motivation, fluctuations in weight, lack of energy; thoughts of suicide; feelings of emptiness, worthlessness, and guilt. *(Psychological Disorders)*

Mate Choice: A subtype of sexual selection in which the preference of the opposite sex drives selection of a trait. *E.g. peahens (female) prefer peacocks (male) whose tails are symmetrical and have more eyespots. Males with these tails are more likely to be chosen by these females to mate and pass on their genes to the next generation. (Evolution 1)*

Mate Competition: A subtype of sexual selection in which success in combat with opponents of the same sex drives selection of a particular trait. *E.g. male elk have antlers that they use to fight other elk; the strongest males will out-survive their opponents to mate and pass their genes on to the next generation. (Evolution 1)*

Maturation: The growth of neurons by establishing connections with other neurons. This is an important process for a neuron, as those that do not make connections will be pruned away. *(Neuroscience 1)*

Maturation: The biologically timed unfolding of changes within the individual according to that individual's genetic plan. *E.g. if an individual grows up in a healthy environment, he or she is likely to start puberty at a predetermined age based on genetics. (Development 1)*

Medulla: The most caudal part of the hindbrain, located directly above the spinal cord. The medulla is vital for functions such as breathing, digestion, and regulation of heart rate. *(Neuroscience 2)*

Midbrain: Found between the hindbrain and the forebrain, it contains the tectum and tegmentum, both of which are involved in a variety of functions including perception, arousal and motor control. *(Neuroscience 2)*

Middle Ear: The part of the auditory system that begins on with the structures on the inner side of the eardrum. It is made up of the three ossicles that are used to amplify sound. *(Audition)*

Migration: The travelling of neurons from the ventricular zone to their correct location on the surface of the cortex along radial glial cells. *(Neuroscience 1)*

Monozygotic Twins: Genetically identical individuals who originate from the same sperm and ovum and formed one zygote, then split into two separate zygotes later in development *in utero*. *(Development 2)*

N

Natural Selection: Differential survival and reproduction as a result of the heritable differences between organisms. It requires individual differences within a population, differential reproduction between individuals within that population, and heritability of the traits selected for. *(Evolution 1)*

Necker Cube: A visual illusion in which the brain can perceive a two dimensional image of a cube as both popping out or going into a page. *(Form Perception 1)*

Negative Symptoms: Behaviours that decrease in someone with schizophrenia. They generally point to a decrease in the individual's engagement with the outside world. *(Psychological Disorders 1)*

Neurogenesis: The process by which neurons are created in the nervous system. *(Neuroscience 1)*

Neuron: A type of cell found throughout the nervous system, specialized for communication throughout the body. The neuron's unique structure is made up of receptive (dendrites) and transmission (axon and terminal boutons) zones which make it especially good at communication. *(Neuroscience 1)*

Neuropeptide Y (NPY): A hormone in humans and other species. High levels in the hypothalamus leads to increased appetite and food seeking behaviours. Interacts with leptin to regulate weight. *(Hunger and the Chemical Senses)*

Neurotransmitters: A variety of signalling chemicals found in vesicles in the presynaptic neuron. They're released by the presynaptic neuron at a synapse and send signals to the postsynaptic neuron, causing varying effects dependant on type. *E.g. serotonin is believed to be a contributor to the feeling of happiness.* *(Neuroscience 1)*

O

Object Agnosia: A type of visual agnosia in which an individual is unable to identify objects by sight, even though the can see the objects perfectly. This individual will be able to perceive characteristics of that object, but not be able to conclude what the object is by simply viewing it. *(Form Perception 2)*

Occipital Lobe: At the posterior end of the cortex, it is exclusively responsible for visual processing. It contains the primary visual cortex and other visual areas. Damage to it may result in functional blindness. *(Neuroscience 2)*

Olfactory Bulb: Receives information from the olfactory receptor cells which synapses with the glomeruli contained in the olfactory bulb. *(Hunger and the Chemical Senses)*

Olfactory Cilia: Hair-like projections covering the receptor surface of the nasal cavity in the nose that interact with olfactory chemicals. *(Hunger and the Chemical Senses)*

Olfactory Epithelium: The receptor surface of the nasal cavity, in which each receptor cell receives input from between 10 and 20 olfactory cilia. *(Hunger and the Chemical Senses)*

Ommatidia: The tubular units that make up the compound eye of arthropods. These point in slightly different directions to gather light directly in front of them and when multiple units are put together, make up a single image that is perceived by the organism. *(Vision)*

Optic Chiasm: The point at which the optic nerves from the inside half of each eye cross over to the opposite hemisphere. *(Vision)*

Optic Disc: The point on the eye at which the axons of the ganglion cell converge and exit to the optic nerve. It is responsible for the human visual blind spot, as this area contains no photoreceptors. *(Vision)*

Optic Nerve: One of the cranial nerves, it is a bundle of ganglion cell axons that transmit visual information out the back of the eye to the brain. *(Vision)*

Opponent-Process Theory: A theory in colour vision that argues that there are three classes of colour receptors, each made up of a pair of opponent processes. Each receptor is capable of being in the following opponent states, black/white, blue/yellow, and red/green. This theory explains colour vision at the level of ganglion cells. *(Colour Perception)*

Ossicles: A collection of the smallest bones in the body that are found in the middle ear and used to amplify sound. They consist of the hammer, anvil, and stirrup. *(Audition)*

Oval Window: A small opening in the side of the cochlea that, when made to vibrate, causes the fluid inside of the cochlea to become displaced. It is through here that the middle ear connects to the inner ear. *(Audition)*

P

Parietal Lobe: Located anterior to the occipital lobe, the parietal lobe contains the primary somatosensory cortex, where the processing of touch begins. The parietal lobe is also involved in a number of complex visual and spatial functions. *(Neuroscience 2)*

Parvocellular Pathway: The pathway from the ganglion cells to the extrastriate cortex that carries colour, pattern and form information from the parvo cells found throughout the retina. They have smaller receptive fields than magno cells. *(Form Perception 2)*

Passive Correlations: The environment that your parents raise you in is influenced by their own genes, therefore this environment will likely complement your own genes. *E.g. a couple who are both naturally athletic may choose to raise their child in an environment with toys and games that promote hand-eye coordination and reflexes. (Development 2)*

Perceptual Constancy: The ability to perceive an object as unchanging despite the fact that the visual image the object produces is constantly changing. The five constancies are colour, brightness, size, location, and shape constancy. *(Form Perception 1)*

Phenotype: The expression of an individual's genotype in terms of observable characteristics. *E.g. Brent has one dominant allele for brown eyes and one recessive allele for blue eyes (genotype), which is expressed in the phenotype of brown eyes. (Development 2)*

Phenotypic Matching: An evaluation of the relatedness between individuals based on an assessment of phenotypic similarity. *E.g. Lisa DeBruine found that graduate students were more trusting of those who resembled themselves. (Evolution 2)*

Photoreceptors: Cells located on the retina that convert the physical stimulus of light into a neural impulse that is passed to the brain. There are two types of photoreceptors: rods (black and white vision) and cones (colour vision). *(Vision)*

Pinna: Part of the external ear, it is the folded cone on the outside of the head that is used to collect sound waves and direct them into the ear canal. *(Audition)*

Pituitary: Referred to as the master gland of the endocrine system, it has two sub regions. The anterior pituitary receives signals from the brain to release hormones that regulate other endocrine glands such as the thyroid, testes and ovaries. The posterior pituitary is an extension of the hypothalamus and it releases the hormones oxytocin and vasopressin. *(Neuroscience 2)*

Polygenetic Trait: When multiple genes are involved in the expression of a trait. *E.g. traits such as height and weight are determined by the interaction of multiple genes. (Development 2)*

Pons: A small structure in the hindbrain that relays information about movement from the cerebral hemispheres to the cerebellum. It also processes some auditory information and contains nuclei that are a part of the reticular formation. *(Neuroscience 2)*

Positive Symptoms: Behaviours that increase in someone with schizophrenia. These may include disorders of thought, delusions, hallucinations, and disorganized or abnormal motor behaviour. *(Psychological Disorders 1)*

Positron Emission Tomography (PET): A functional neuroimaging technique that uses a radioactive tracer to observe active areas of the brain, creating a functional map of brain activity. It has better temporal resolution but is more invasive than an fMRI. *(Neuroscience 2)*

Postsynaptic Neuron: At a synapse, the neuron to which electrical signals are sent from the presynaptic neuron. *(Neuroscience 1)*

Preference Method: A method of measuring what an infant likes and dislikes. An infant is put into a looking chamber to simultaneously look at two stimuli and the researcher observes whether the infant is directing more attention to one stimulus. *(Development 1)*

Presynaptic Neuron: At a synapse, the neuron from which an electrical signal is sent to a postsynaptic neuron. *(Neuroscience 1)*

Primary Colours: The three colours that can be combined in various proportions to produce every colour in the visual spectrum. They are base colours that cannot be reduced into other colours. *(Colour Perception)*

Primary Visual Cortex: Labeled as area V1 in the occipital cortex, it is the first major visual relay area in the cortex where basic visual information is processed. The receptive fields of many LGN cells combine to form the receptive field of a single V1 cell. *(Vision)*

Priming: An effect in which we respond more quickly and accurately if we expect or have recent experience with a particular stimulus or category. *E.g. in priming experiment, you may be required to name the letter that is presented to you. Being told that the object is a letter results in being faster at naming what that letter is. (Form Perception 1)*

Prosopagnosia: A type of object agnosia in which a person cannot recognize faces, despite being able to recognize regular objects. An individual with this disorder is able to perceive facial features, but will not be able to recognize a person by face. *(Form Perception 2)*

Protanopia: A form of red/green colour blindness in which the red cones are missing. *(Colour Perception)*

Prototype Theory: A theory of object recognition that suggests we store the most typical or ideal member of a category in our memory and compare new objects to this internal average in order to recognize and categorize them. *(Form Perception 1)*

Proximity: The Gestalt Principle that describes our tendency to group elements that are close together in space as belonging together. *E.g. logos often use several shapes that are not attached and we see it as a single image. (Form Perception 1)*

Psychiatrist: Specialized medical doctors who receive extensive training in pharmacological therapies and are qualified to prescribe medication.*(Psychological Treatments)*

Pupil: The round window that appears as a black dot in the middle of the human eye. It is here that light passes through to the lens after it has passed through the cornea. *(Vision)*

Purity: A physical characteristic of light, which affects the perception of the saturation, or richness of colours. A pure light wave is composed of a single wavelength of light, while impure light is a mixture of several wavelengths. *(Vision)*

R

Range of Reaction Principle: An individual genotype establishes a range of possible developmental outcomes to different kinds of life experiences. *E.g. Your final height is determined by a number of environmental factors but the potential range of your height across various environments is determined by genetic factors. (Development 2)*

Rebound Effect: When a colour receptor is excited for a prolonged period of time, that receptor will go into the opposite state when the eye focuses on a neutral colour, causing the brain to perceive the complementary colour. *(Colour Perception)*

Receptive Field: The collection of rods and cones in the retina that, when stimulated, affect the firing of a particular ganglion cell. Certain receptive fields are responsive to different colours, shades, and shapes. *(Vision)*

Receptive Zone: The part of the neuron that consists of the cell body and dendrites. This is where electrical signals are received from other neurons. *(Neuroscience 1)*

Recessive Allele: In a heterozygous condition, the allele that is not expressed in the phenotype. This allele is; however, still heritable. *(Development 2)*

Refractory Period: The period of time following the action potential when the -70mV resting potential is overshot and the neuron slowly returns to -70mV. During this period, the neuron cannot fire another action potential. *(Neuroscience 1)*

Resting Potential: The baseline potential difference between the intracellular and extracellular fluid of a neuron, commonly stated as -70 mV of the inside relative to the outside of the cell. At this voltage, no electrical signals are being sent. *(Neuroscience 1)*

Reticular Formation: An interconnected set of nuclei throughout the hindbrain, it contains the ascending reticular formation (involved in arousal, motivation and circadian rhythms) and the descending reticular formation (involved in posture, equilibrium, and motor movement). *(Neuroscience II)*

Retina: The neural tissue that lines the back of the eye. It consists of photoreceptors where the physical stimulus of light is translated into neural impulses. *(Vision)*

Retinal Pigment Epithelium (RPE): A layer of cells at the very back of the retina to which photoreceptors are connected. The RPE cells provide the photoreceptors with the nutrition required to survive and are the reason for the inside-out arrangement of the eye. *(Vision)*

Rods: The class of photoreceptors that are primarily used for night vision, provide no colour information and have poor visual acuity. They are more populous than cones and are located in the periphery of the retina. *(Vision)*

Round Window: An opening located at the end of the cochlea opposite to the round window, which bulges in and out according to the movement of fluid in the cochlea. *(Audition)*

S

Saturation: A psychological characteristic of light, corresponding to the purity of a light stimulus. Saturated colours are richer than de-saturated colours and de-saturated colours make up the majority of the natural world. *(Vision)*

Schizophrenia: The "splitting of the mind" from reality, it is a mental disorder characterized by a breakdown in thought processes and poor emotional responsiveness. Symptoms include but are not limited to delusions, paranoia and auditory hallucinations. *(Psychological Disorders 1)*

Sclera: A tough structural membrane that covers the portion of the eye not covered by the cornea. The sclera provides the eye with its white appearance. *(Vision)*

Sensitive Period: This term has come to replace the term critical period. It captures the idea that the brain does maintain some residual capacity for change and growth into adulthood and so there is greater flexibility in the timing and type of stimulation that are required for normal development. *(Development 2)*

Sex Chromosome: The 23rd pair of human chromosomes, which determine a person's sex. A female will carry two X chromosomes and a male will carry an X and a Y chromosome. These chromosomes are heritable. *(Development 2)*

Sex-linked Inheritance: The pattern of inheritance that involves genes expressed on the X chromosome. This results in traits more often being expressed in males than in females. *E.g. a recessive gene expressed on the X chromosome causes colour blindness. (Development 2)*

Sexual Selection: The component of natural selection that acts on traits that influence an organism's ability to obtain a mate. *E.g. Peacock tails evolved even though they elevate chances of death because females prefer to mate with peacocks with more elaborate tails. (Evolution 1)*

Shape Constancy: Our ability to perceive objects as being a constant shape despite changes in their shape on our retina. *E.g. when looking at a flat screen TV from the front, it is a rectangle. From the side, it may look like a trapezoid but it is still recognized as being a TV. (Form Perception 1)*

Similarity: The Gestalt Principle that describes our tendency to group together elements that are physically similar. *E.g. when observing a single flamingo among a flock of penguins, one may group the penguins together based on physically similarity. (Form Perception 1)*

Simple Cell: A visual cortical cell that responds maximally to a bar of light of a certain length and orientation in a particular region of the retina. *E.g. one visual cell may respond to a bar of light that is rotated 45 degrees in the centre of a visual field. (Form Perception 2)*

Simple Dominant-Recessive Inheritance: A pattern of inheritance in which the expression of a trait is determined by a single pair of alleles. A heterozygote and a homozygous-dominant individual will express the dominant phenotype, while a homozygous recessive individual will express the recessive phenotype. *(Development 2)*

Simple Eye: The type of eye found in vertebrates and molluscs that contains an eyeball, lens and retina. This type may vary in exact design by species and environment but is the type of eye that we think of when we think of eyes. *(Vision)*

Sine Wave: A mathematical curve describing a smooth repetition or oscillation. Sound waves are made up of individual sine waves that vary in wavelength, frequency and amplitude to produce sounds of different pitch and loudness. *(Audition)*

Single-Cell Recording: During various human functions, extremely precise electrical recordings are made from a single neuron in the nervous system. The human anatomic map related to human function (somatotopic map), discovered by Doctor Penfield, was discovered using single cell recordings. *(Neuroscience 2)*

Size Constancy: Our ability to perceive the size of objects as unchanging despite changes in their size on the retina as distance from the retina varies. *E.g. as a car approaches, its size on the retina increases; however, the car is perceived as being of constant size. (Form Perception 1)*

Somatosensory Cortex: The region in the brain that processes the feeling and texture of food in the mouth and the location of taste on the tongue. *(Hunger and the Chemical Senses)*

Spatial Summation: When multiple EPSPs occur simultaneously from several different presynaptic neurons at the receptive zone of the postsynaptic neuron, causing it to reach the -50mV threshold required to fire an action potential. *(Neuroscience 1)*

Split Brain Syndrome: A condition in which an individual's corpus callosum is severed such that the two hemispheres of the brain cannot communicate with each other. *(Neuroscience 2)*

SSRI: A drug therapy medication used to alleviate symptoms of depression. They work to increase levels of serotonin activity in the brain. *(Psychological Treatments)*

Stabilizing Selection: Selection that acts against any sort of departure from the species-typical adaptive design.

E.g. average neck length in giraffes will remain long over generations because it is adaptive as long as their food is available on the tops of tall trees. (Evolution 1)

Stages of Change: The step-wise process that describes the typical progression of treatment, consisting of Precontemplation, Contemplation, Preparation, Action, Maintenance, and sometimes Relapse. *(Psychological Treatments)*

Stirrup: Also known as the stapes, it is the last of the ossicles found in the middle ear. It projects onto the oval window of the cochlea in the inner ear. *(Audition)*

Structural Neuroimaging: A variety of techniques used to study the large-scale structure of the brain and identify structural abnormalities. *(Neuroscience 2)*

Subtractive Colour Mixing: A form of colour mixing in which coloured pigments selectively absorb (or subtract) some wavelengths and reflect others. This type of colour mixing applies to pigments, dyes or paints. *E.g. a blue object looks blue because all wavelengths are being absorbed by the object except blue, which reflects back to the eyes. (Colour Perception)*

Sulci: The indents, or gaps, between gyri on the cortex. These, along with gyri, give the cortex its ridged structure and provide more surface area for cortical processing. *(Neuroscience 2)*

Synapse: The region consisting of the transmission zone of a presynaptic neuron and receptive zone of a postsynaptic neuron, through which electrical signals may be passed from neuron to neuron. *(Neuroscience 1)*

Synaptic Cleft: The space between two neurons in which neurotransmitters float freely with other molecules. *(Neuroscience 1)*

T

Taste Bud: A raised bump found on the tongue, soft palate and opening of the throat that contains 50 to 150 taste receptor cells. It is the first point at which taste signals start to be converted to electrical nerve signals. *(Hunger and the Chemical Senses)*

Tectum: Part of the dorsal midbrain and including the superior and inferior colliculi, it is involved in perception and action, including eye movements, visual reflexes, and auditory integration. *(Neuroscience 2)*

Tegmentum: The part of the midbrain involved in the regulation and production of movement (partly influenced by the red nucleus), motor planning, learning, and reward seeking (partly influenced by the substantia nigra). *(Neuroscience 2)*

Template Theory: A theory of object recognition that suggests we store many templates in memory and compare new objects to all these templates. *E.g. when seeing a tall metal cylinder with a narrow black cap, it is compared to a very similar object in memory (Form Perception 1)*

Temporal Lobe: Lying at the sides of the brain below the Sylvian fissure, the temporal lobe is involved in visual association, memory and language and contains the primary auditory cortex. *(Neuroscience 2)*

Temporal Summation: When multiple EPSPs occur one after another on the receptive zone of the postsynaptic neuron from the same presynaptic connection, causing a slow climb towards the -50mV threshold required for an action potential to fire. *(Neuroscience 1)*

Thalamus: Part of the forebrain that acts as a "relay station" from the cerebellum, limbic system, and every sensory area (except olfaction) to the cerebral cortex. *(Neuroscience 2)*

Threshold: The -50mV potential difference across the neuronal membrane that must be reached in order for an action potential to fire. *(Neuroscience 1)*

Timbre: Our perception of the complexity and purity of a sound wave, related to the unique properties of a sound. Complexity refers to the fact that sounds we hear are made up of multiple sound waves that vary in frequency. *(Audition)*

Tonotopic Organization: Analogous to the topographical organization of the retina in the visual system, neighbouring frequencies which vibrate on the basilar membrane project to neighbouring areas in the auditory cortex. *(Audition)*

Top-Down Processing: A process of object recognition guided by your own beliefs or expectations. E.g. *people are able to recognize a paragraph of misspelled words when only the first and last letters of each word are correct. They use the context of surrounding words to read.* *(Form Perception 1)*

Topographical Organization: The ordered projection of a sensory surface, found in all sensory systems. In the visual system, two objects that are side by side in the visual field will also be projected side by side in the visual cortex. *(Form Perception 2)*

Topographic Map: Retinal coordinates are topographically mapped onto the visual cortex. Neighbouring locations in the visual field correspond to neighbouring locations in the retina, which project to neighbouring locations in the visual cortex. *(Vision)*

Trichromatic Theory: A theory of colour vision, based on the proposal that the retina contains three different kinds of receptors that are maximally responsive to different wavelengths of light – red, green and blue. This theory explains colour vision at the level of retinal cones. *(Colour Perception)*

Tritanopia: A form of colour blindness in which the blue cones are lacking or defective. It is a very rare form of colour blindness that causes people to see in shades of pink and greenish blues. *(Colour Perception)*

V

Ventral Stream: The "what" visual pathway that starts in the extrastriate cortex and terminates in the temporal lobe. It processes information about object identity (including form and colour). *(Vision, Form Perception 2)*

Visible Spectrum: The portion of the total range of wavelengths of electromagnetic radiation to which humans are visually sensitive, or, what humans can see. The shortest wavelength of the visible spectrum is 360 nanometers (violet) and the longest is 750 nanometers (red) *(Vision)*

Visual Illusion: An ambiguous or incomplete image that is perceived as being something different from what it really is. Such illusions include the Necker Cube, Muller-Lyer illusion, and the Ponzo Illusion. *(Form Perception 1)*

Vitreous Humour: The clear, jelly-like substance comprising the main chamber of the eyeball. Light passes from the lens, through the vitreous humour, to the retina. *(Vision)*

W

Wavelength: A physical characteristic corresponding to the distance between peaks of a wave. It corresponds to the psychological characteristic of colour. On the visible spectrum, the shortest wavelengths appear purple while the longest appear red. *(Vision)*

Conclusion to Psychology: 1XX3 – Foundations of Psychology, Neuroscience & Behaviour

Congratulations on reaching the end of your tour through Introductory Psychology! In Psych 1X03, the overarching theme was the importance of applying the scientific method to understand wide-ranging problems in psychology. This allows you to move beyond common sense and put forth testable hypotheses to refine theories. This theme continued into Psych 1XX3, as you explored the biological basis of human thought and behaviour. Along the way, you have also gained valuable research skills that are not only important in psychology, but in any course of study you plan to pursue.

Although this is the end of your formal tour through Introductory Psychology, I hope it's not the end of your study of psychology. In these courses, I hope you have learned to appreciate that psychology can be applied to your everyday interactions to understand the complex business of human thought and behaviour. Given the very nature of an introductory level survey, there was only limited time available to study any given area. However, if there is a particular area that you are fascinated by, I would encourage you to go on to take some upper level courses in psychology. If just about everything in psychology fascinates you, well, then I would encourage you to pursue an Honours degree in Psychology, Neuroscience & Behaviour or Biology and Psychology. Perhaps you may even be inspired to apply to be a Teaching Assistant for IntroPsych.

Every year, I hear from TAs and students who comment on the improvements we make to the courses each year. Some even say "We never had that in first year!" and that's my point exactly – we are constantly trying to improve every aspect of the course structure and organization. This process extends beyond IntroPsych and into the design of our Honours programs. I am particularly excited about the completely revamped Level 2 Honours Psychology, Neuroscience & Behaviour program. The program features a restructured core and signature courses that will immerse you into the world of a psychologist. Please feel free to drop by and see me to chat about it!

Dr. Joe Kim

Degree Programs

McMaster Undergraduate Degrees offered in the Dept. of Psychology, Neuroscience & Behaviour (PNB)
For students wishing to pursue further study in **P**sychology, **N**euroscience & **B**ehaviour here are some programs for you!

RESEARCH LOVERS: PNB offers research-intensive degrees in **Honours PNB (B.A. or B.Sc.)**
APPLIED APPROACH: Applied Science is offered in **Honours Human Behaviour (B.A.Sc.)**.

All the following programs require **Psych 1XX3** for admission and some also require **Psych 1X03** for admission or completion by the end of year 2.

Honours PNB (B.Sc. or B.A.)
This program prepares students for graduate studies (both clinical and experimental); for professional studies such as medicine and teaching; for research positions in government, university or industry, and for careers in health sciences, community services, education and government. **Within this degree there are two Specializations:**
  (1) **Mental Health** – prepares students for graduate and professional training in Mental Health.
  (2) **Music Cognition** – requires Advanced Rudiments in music to be admitted – brings together science and arts in a unique and innovative way.

PNB B.Sc. and the B.A. programs are identical, with the exception of required courses in Year 1.

Combined Honours Programs offered by PNB and Biology Departments
Honours B.Sc. Biology & PNB: A double major merging leading-edge knowledge from both fields, with an option to do a thesis in Biology or Psychology.
Honours B.Sc. Neuroscience: Interdisciplinary study, comprising all research related to neurons and nervous system. For students interested in a career in neuroscience research.

Combined Honours Programs offered by PNB and Social Sciences or Humanities
Honours B.A. PNB with Another Subject (in Social Sciences or Humanities): Double major merging knowledge in multiple fields: Examples - Hons B.A. Economics & PNB; Hons B.A. PNB & Sociology; Hons B.A. Philosophy & PNB; Hons B.A. Linguistics & PNB etc.)

Honours B.A.Sc. Human Behaviour
Prepares students to enter any work environment that requires understanding the determinants of human behaviour; continue their education in non-research related fields such as law, human resources, journalism, rehabilitation sciences, counselling, advertising, and education; or pursue a range of applied certificate/diploma training.
Within this degree there are two specializations offered jointly by PNB and Mohawk College. Students graduate with an Honours B.A.Sc. degree from McMaster University, and a Graduate Certificate/Diploma from Mohawk College.
Field placements occur during the Spring/Summer sessions
  (1) **Autism & Behavioural Sciences** – leads to opportunities in Behaviour or ABA therapy in community treatment agencies, hospital/clinical settings, private agencies and school boards.
  (2) **Early Childhood Education** – leads to opportunities in full-day kindergarten, child care and early learning agencies, parent-child drop-in programs and professional resource sites.

B.A. Psychology: A 3-year degree requiring Psych 1X03 (or 1F03) for admission. Prepares students for entry-level positions in human services, business, criminal justice, health and recreation, and education.